ALSO IN THE *FOLGER GUIDE* SERIES

The Folger Guide to Teaching *Hamlet*
The Folger Guide to Teaching *Romeo and Juliet*
The Folger Guide to Teaching *Macbeth*
The Folger Guide to Teaching *Othello*

THE FOLGER GUIDE TO TEACHING *A MIDSUMMER NIGHT'S DREAM*

The Folger Guides to Teaching Shakespeare Series
— Volume 4 —

Peggy O'Brien, Ph.D., General Editor

Folger Shakespeare Library
WASHINGTON, DC

Simon & Schuster Paperbacks

NEW YORK   AMSTERDAM/ANTWERP   LONDON   TORONTO   SYDNEY   NEW DELHI

1230 Avenue of the Americas
New York, NY 10020

First Simon & Schuster trade paperback edition March 2025

SIMON & SCHUSTER and colophon are registered trademarks
of Simon & Schuster LLC

For information about special discounts for bulk purchases,
please contact Simon & Schuster Special Sales at 1-866-506-1949
or business@simonandschuster.com.

The Simon & Schuster Speakers Bureau can bring authors
to your live event. For more information or to book an event, contact the
Simon & Schuster Speakers Bureau at 1-866-248-3049
or visit our website at www.simonspeakers.com.

Manufactured in the United States of America

1   3   5   7   9   10   8   6   4   2

Library of Congress Cataloging-in-Publication Data is available upon request.

ISBN 978-1-9821-0566-2
ISBN 978-1-6680-1761-6 (ebook)

THE FOLGER SHAKESPEARE LIBRARY

The Folger Shakespeare Library makes Shakespeare's stories and the world in which he lived accessible. Anchored by the world's largest Shakespeare collection, the Folger is a place where curiosity and creativity are embraced and conversation is always encouraged. Visitors to the Folger can choose how they want to experience the arts and humanities, from interactive exhibitions to captivating performances, and from pathbreaking research to transformative educational programming.

The Folger seeks to be a catalyst for:

Discovery. The Folger's collection is meant to be used, and it is made accessible in the Folger's Reading Room to anyone who is researching Shakespeare or the early modern world. The Folger collection has flourished since founders Henry and Emily Folger made their first rare book purchase in 1889, and today contains more than 300,000 objects. The Folger Institute facilitates scholarly and artistic collections-based research, providing research opportunities, lectures, conversations, and other programs to an international community of scholars.

Curiosity. The Folger designs learning opportunities for inquisitive minds at every stage of life, from tours to virtual and in-person workshops. Teachers working with the Folger are trained in the Folger Method, a way of teaching complex texts like Shakespeare that enables students to own and enjoy the process of close-reading, interrogating texts, discovering language with peers, and contributing to the ongoing human conversation about words and ideas.

Participation. The Folger evolves with each member and visitor interaction. Our exhibition halls, learning lab, gardens, theater, and historic spaces are open to be explored and to provide entry points for connecting with Shakespeare and the Folger's collection, as well as forming new pathways to experiencing and understanding the arts.

Creativity. The Folger invites everyone to tell their story and experience the stories of and inspired by Shakespeare. Folger Theatre, Music, and Poetry are programmed in conversation with Folger audiences, exploring our collective past, present, and future. Shakespeare's imagination resonates across centuries, and his works are a wellspring for the creativity that imbues the Folger's stage and all its programmatic offerings.

The Folger welcomes everyone—from communities throughout Washington, DC, to communities across the globe—to connect in their own way. Learn more at folger.edu.

IMAGE CREDITS

If you are a teacher,
you are doing the world's most important work.
This book is for you.

CONTENTS

THE FOLGER GUIDE TO TEACHING *A MIDSUMMER NIGHT'S DREAM*

PART ONE

Shakespeare for a Changing World

Why Shakespeare?

Michael Witmore

You have more in common with the person seated next to you on a bus, a sporting event, or a concert than you will ever have with William Shakespeare. The England he grew up in nearly 400 years ago had some of the features of our world today, but modern developments such as industry, mass communication, global networks, and democracy did not exist. His country was ruled by a monarch, and his days were divided into hours by church bells rather than a watch or a phone. The religion practiced around him was chosen by the state, as were the colors he could wear when he went out in public.

When Shakespeare thought of our planet, there were no satellites to show him a green and blue ball. The Northern European island where he grew up was, by our standards, racially homogeneous, although we do know that there were Africans, Asians, Native Americans, Muslims, Jews, and others living in London in the early 1600s—and that Shakespeare likely saw or knew about them. The very idea that people of different backgrounds could live in a democracy would probably have struck him as absurd. What could an English playwright living centuries ago possibly say about our changed and changing world? Would he understand the conflicts that dominate our politics, the "isms" that shape reception of his work? What would he make of debates about freedom, the fairness of our economies, or the fragility of our planet?

The conversation about Shakespeare over the last 250 years has created other obstacles and distance. Starting around that time, artists and promoters put Shakespeare on a pedestal so high that he became almost divine. One such promoter was an English actor named David Garrick, who erected a classical temple to Shakespeare in 1756 and filled it with "relics" from Shakespeare's life. Garrick praised Shakespeare as "the God of our idolatry," and in his temple included a throne-like chair made of wood from a tree that Shakespeare may have planted. Today, that chair sits in a nook at the Folger Shakespeare Library. The chair's existence reminds us that the impulse to put Shakespeare in a temple has been at times overwhelming. But temples can exclude as well as elevate, which is why the Folger Shakespeare Library—itself a monument to Shakespeare built in 1932—needs to celebrate a writer whose audience is contemporary, diverse, and growing.

While Shakespeare was and is truly an amazing writer, the "worship" of his talent becomes problematic as soon as it is expected. If Shakespeare's stories and poetry continue to be enjoyed and passed along, it should be because we see their value, not because we have been told that they are great. Today, if someone tells you that Shakespeare's appeal is "universal," you might take away the idea that his works represent the experience of everyone, or that someone can only be fully human if they appreciate and enjoy his work. Can that possibly be true? How can one appreciate or enjoy the things in his work that are offensive and degrading—for example, the racism and sexism that come so easily to several of his characters? What about such plays as *The Merchant of Venice, Othello,* or *The Taming of the Shrew,* where the outcomes suggest that certain kinds of characters—a Jew, an African, a woman—deserve to suffer?

When we talk about Shakespeare, we have to confront these facts and appreciate the blind spots in his plays, blind spots that are still real and reach beyond his specific culture. In acknowledging such facts, we are actually in a better position to appreciate Shakespeare's incredible talent as a writer and creator of stories. Yes, he wrote from a dated perspective of a Northern European man who was a frequent flatterer of kings and queens. Within those limits, he is nevertheless able to dazzle with his poetry and offer insights into human motivations. We are not *required* to appreciate the language or dramatic arcs of his characters, but we can appreciate both with the help of talented teachers or moving performances. Memorable phrases such as Hamlet's "To be or not to be" are worth understanding because they capture a situation perfectly—the moment when someone asks, "Why go on?" By pausing on this question, we learn something at a distance, without having to suffer through everything that prompts Hamlet to say these famous words.

Had Shakespeare's plays not been published and reanimated in performance over the last few centuries, these stories would no longer be remembered. Yet the tales of Lady Macbeth or Richard III still populate the stories we tell today. They survive in the phrases that such characters use and the archetypal situations in which these characters appear—"out, out damned spot" or "my kingdom for a horse!" Marvel characters and professional politicians regularly channel Shakespeare. When a supervillain turns to the camera to brag about their evil deeds, we are hearing echoes of King Richard III. When the media criticizes a leader for being power-hungry, some version of Lady Macbeth is often implied, especially if that leader is a woman.

While they are from another time, Shakespeare's characters and situations remain exciting because they view life from a perspective that is both familiar and distant. The better able we are to recognize the experiences described in Shakespeare's plays in our lives, the broader our vocabulary becomes for understanding ourselves. We see and hear more when the plays dramatize important questions, such as:

- What does a child owe a parent and what does a parent owe their child? Why must children sometimes teach their parents to grow up? *King Lear, Hamlet,* and *Henry IV, Part 1* all ask some version of these questions.

- Are we born ready to love or is the capacity to love another something that is learned? Shakespeare's comedies—*Twelfth Night, As You Like It, Much Ado About Nothing*—are filled with characters whose entire stories are about learning to accept and give love.

- How does one deal with an awful memory or the knowledge of a brutal crime? Hamlet is burdened with both, just as many are today who are haunted by trauma.

These questions get at situations that anyone might experience at some point in their life. If you are a teenager whose mad crush is turning into love, you will have to go out on that balcony, just like Juliet. Will you be confident or afraid? If a "friend" who knows you well is feeding you lies, you will be challenged to resist them—as Othello is when faced with Iago. Will you be able to think for yourself? These questions come up in any life, and the answers are not predetermined. A goal in any humanities classroom is to improve the questions we ask ourselves by engaging our specific experiences, something very different from looking for "timeless truths" in the past.

Do not believe that you must master Shakespeare in order to appreciate literature, language, or the human condition. Do, however, be confident that the time you and your students spend with these plays will result in insight, new skills, and pleasure. Shakespeare was a deeply creative person in a deeply polarized world, one where religious and economic conflicts regularly led to violence. He used that creativity to illustrate the many ways human beings need to be saved from themselves, even if they sometimes resist what they need most. He also understood that stories can change minds even when the facts cannot. If there was ever a time to appreciate these insights, it is now.

The Folger Teaching Guides are the product of decades of experience and conversation with talented educators and students. The Folger continues to offer teachers the best and most effective techniques for cultivating students' abilities in the classroom, starting with Shakespeare but opening out on the great range of writers and experiences your students can explore. We invite you to visit the Folger in person in Washington, DC, where our exhibitions, performances, and programs put into practice the methods and insights you will find here. And we extend our gratitude to you for doing the most important work in the world, which deserves the dedicated support we are providing in these guides.

Good Books, Great Books, Monumental Texts—Shakespeare, Relevance, and New Audiences: GenZ and Beyond

Jocelyn A. Chadwick

"People can find small parts of themselves in each character and learn what it may be like to let the hidden parts of themselves out. Regardless of personal background, everyone can relate to the humanity and vulnerability that is revealed in Shakespeare's works." (Student, 2023)

" 'To me, there is no such thing as black or yellow Shakespeare,' Mr. Earle Hyman, a celebrated African-American actor said. 'There is good Shakespeare or bad Shakespeare. It's simply a matter of good training and opportunity.' " ("Papp Starts a Shakespeare Repertory Troupe Made Up Entirely of Black and Hispanic Actors," *New York Times*, January 21, 1979)

"The question for us now is to be or not to be. Oh no, this Shakespearean question. For 13 days this question could have been asked but now I can give you a definitive answer. It's definitely yes, to be." (President Volodymyr Zelenskyy's speech to the UK Parliament, March 8, 2022)

"I, at least, do not intend to live without Aeschylus or William Shakespeare, or James, or Twain, or Hawthorne, or Melville, etc., etc., etc." (Toni Morrison, "Unspeakable Things Unspoken: The Afro-American Presence in Literature," *The Source of Self-Regard*, 2019)

How have William Shakespeare's brilliant and probing plays about the human condition come to an *either/or* to some contemporary audiences? The preceding quotes reveal appreciation, understanding, and metaphorical applications along with definitions of the playwright's depth and breadth. And yet, a misunderstanding *and* sometimes *conscious cancellation* of the man, his work, and his impact have undergone substantial *misunderstanding and misinterpretation.*

For as long as any of us can or will remember, William Shakespeare has continued to be with us and our students. True, this is a bold and assertive declarative statement; however, in the 21st century, is it and will it continue to be accurate and still *valid*?

Playwright Robert Greene, a contemporary of William Shakespeare, did not think much of Shakespeare's work or his talent:

> There is an upstart Crow, beautified with our feathers that with his Tygers hart wrapt in a Players hyde, supposes he is as well able to bombast out a blank verse as the best of you: and being an absolute Johannes factotum is in his owne conceit the onely Shake-scene in a country. (Robert Greene, *Greene's Groats-Worth of Wit,* 1592)

Clearly, Greene was jealous of Shakespeare's popularity and talent.

Interestingly, what Greene objects to parallels some 21st-century perspectives that at this writing recommend removal of Shakespeare's plays and poetry from curricula throughout the country—*just because.* For Greene, the objection was Shakespeare's talent, his appeal to his contemporary audience, his rising popularity, and cross-cultural exposure—not only angering Greene but also resulting in his undeniable jealousy.

Today, however, the primary argument is that Shakespeare's texts are old and dated; he is white and male—all of which from this perspective identify him, his time, and his work as disconnected from the realities of 21st-century students: antiquated, anachronistic, even racially tinged. These arguments persist, even though without doubt, Shakespeare's London was metropolitan, multicultural, and influenced by the city's international trade—imports as well as exports.

And further, to be clear, as Toni Morrison and so many other scholars, writers, *and* readers have asserted, the *durability* of a text lies with its present *and* future audiences. I should add here that Morrison was engaging with, and "talking back to," Shakespeare's play *Othello* when she wrote her play *Desdemona* in 2011.

At this writing, there are a number of contemporary catalysts pointing out the necessity of rethinking, reflection, and consubstantiation of such texts that have long been a part of the canon. We are experiencing not only that resurgence but also a book-banning tsunami in schools and public libraries. The result of such movements and actions indeed causes us to rethink; they have also compelled educators at all levels, parents, librarians, writers, and GenZ students to speak up and out.

To illustrate concretely students' responses, this essay necessarily includes the perspectives and voices from some high school students (grades 9–12), who attend Commonwealth Governors School (CGS) in Virginia. I asked a number of them what they thought about Shakespeare, and they told me. Their statements are in *their own words;* I did no editing. In addition, the students within the CGS system represent the panoply of inclusion and diversity.

> It's the big ideas that make Shakespeare relevant to myself and other students. Everyone loves, and everyone feels pain, so while we each might experience these feelings at different points in our lives, in different degrees, and for different reasons than others, I think Shakespeare's work is enough out of our times so that all students can connect to his themes and imagine themselves in the positions of his characters. (Student, May 2023)

And . . .

> I feel his general influence; I feel like he created a lot of literary words, and
> musicians like Taylor Swift draw from the works of earlier people, and
> Shakespeare continues to be relevant. (Student, 2023)

Interestingly, students *tapestry* what they read and experience in Shakespeare's works into their contemporary world, concomitantly, reflecting Umberto Eco's assertion about the import, impact, and protean qualities of a text's life: students create their own meaning and connections—building onto and extending Shakespeare's words, expression, characters, and challenges, ultimately scaffolding into their present realities, experiences, and challenges.

With all of these developments and conversations in mind, this Folger series of teaching guides provides that crossroad and intersection of analysis and rethinking. The central question that joins both those who see at present limited or no redeemable value in Shakespeare and those who view these texts as windows of the past, present, and, yes, the future is *"Do William Shakespeare's plays resonate, connect, and speak to 21st-century readers of all ages, and especially to our new generations of students?"*

Let us consider Eco's assertion: each time playwrights, directors, and artists reinterpret, every text undergoes a disruption, thereby reflecting new audiences. To *re-see* a character or setting when producing Shakespeare's plays is with each iteration a kind of disruption—a disruption designed to bring Shakespeare's 16th-century texts to audiences from multiple perspectives and epochs. The term *disruption* here takes on a more modern definition, a more protean and productive definition: Every time a reader enters a text—one of Shakespeare's plays, to be specific—that reader can meld, align, interweave experiences, memories, thoughts, aspirations, and fears, and yes, as the first student quote alludes, empower the reader to *identify* with characters, and moments and consequences. This reading and/or viewing is indeed a positive kind of disruption—*not to harm or destroy;* on the contrary, a positive disruption that expands and interrelates both reader and viewer with Shakespeare and each play. Past *and* present intersect for each generation of readers. In this positive disruption texts remain relevant, alive, and *speak verisimilitude.*

Similarly, we ask 21st-century students studying Shakespeare to bring their *whole selves* to the work, and to come up with their own interpretations. Allowing and privileging 21st-century students to compare and contrast and then examine, inquire, and express their own perspectives and voices remains the primary goal of English Language Arts: independent thinking, a developed voice, and the ability to think and discern critically for oneself. Both the primary text and adaptations are reflections *and* extended lenses:

The man i' th' moon's too slow—till new-born chins
Be rough and razorable; she that from whom
We all were sea-swallowed, though some cast again,
And by that destiny to perform an act
Whereof what's past is prologue, what to come
In your and my discharge (The Tempest 2.1, 285–89).

Just as the past continuously informs and reminds the present, the present—each new generation—brings new eyes, new thoughts, new perspectives. Of course, each generation sees itself as unique and completely different; however, the echoes of the past are and will always be ever-present.

In so many *unexpected* ways, the 21st-century Shakespeare audience in school—students, teachers, and others—share far more with William Shakespeare and his time than we may initially recognize and acknowledge. From his infancy to his death, Shakespeare and his world closely paralleled and reflects ours: upheavals and substantial shifts culturally, sociopolitically, scientifically, and religiously, as well as the always-evolving human condition. Each of the plays represented in this series—*Hamlet, Macbeth, Othello, Romeo and Juliet,* and *A Midsummer Night's Dream*—illustrates just how much William Shakespeare not only observed and lived with and among tragedy, comedy, cultural diversity, challenges, and new explorations, but also, from childhood, honed his perspective of both past and present and—as Toni Morrison expresses—*rememoried* it in his plays and poems. Tragedy and Comedy is rooted in the antiquities of Greek, Roman, and Greco-Roman literature and history. William Shakespeare uniquely crafts these genres to reflect and inform his own time; more importantly, the plays he left us foreshadow past and future connections for audiences to come—audiences who would encounter cross-cultures, ethnicities, genders, geography, even time itself.

More than at any other time in our collective history experienced through literature, the past's ability to inform, advise, and even "cushion" challenges our students' experiences today. It will continue to do so into the foreseeable future and will continue to support and inform, and yes, even protect them. Protecting, meaning that what we and our students can read and experience from the safe distance literature provides, allows, even encourages, readers to process, reflect, and think about how we respond, engage, inquire, and learn.

> The play . . . *Macbeth* . . . is about pride; there are lots of common human themes. He's the basis for a lot of literature like *Hamlet* is just the *Lion King*; it is just *Hamlet,* but it's lions. (Student, May 2023)

One fascinating trait of GenZ readers I find so important is *the how* of their processing and relating canonical texts to other contemporary texts and other genres around them: TV, movies, songs, even advertisements. What I so admire and respect about *students' processing* is their critical thinking and their ability to create new and different comprehension pathways that relate to their own here and now. In this new instructional paradigm, we *all* are exploring, discovering, and learning together, with William Shakespeare as our reading nucleus.

Although many writers and playwrights preceded William Shakespeare, his scope and depth far exceeded that of his predecessors and even his peers. His constant depiction and examinations of the human condition writ large and illustrated from a myriad of perspectives, times, cultures, and worlds set Shakespeare decidedly apart. The result of his depth and scope not only previewed the immediate future following his death, but more profoundly, his thematic threads, characters, settings, and cross-cultural inclusions continue to illustrate *us to us.*

The pivotal and critical point here is GenZ's continued reading and experiencing of William Shakespeare's plays. As they experience this playwright, they take bits and pieces of what they have read and experienced directly into other texts they read and experience in classes and daily living. In fact, in the "tidbits" they experience initially through Shakespeare, students will connect and interpret *and make their own meaning and connections,* even *outside* of textual reading. Malcolm X, in fact, provides us with an example of how that works:

> I read once, passingly, about a man named Shakespeare. I only read about him passingly, but I remember one thing he wrote that kind of moved me. He put it in the mouth of Hamlet, I think, it was, who said, "To be or not to be." He was in doubt about something—whether it was nobler in the mind of man to suffer the slings and arrows of outrageous fortune—moderation—or to take up arms against a sea of troubles and by opposing end them. And I go for that. If you take up arms, you'll end it, but if you sit around and wait for the one who's in power to make up his mind that he should end it, you'll be waiting a long time. And in my opinion the young generation of whites, blacks, browns, whatever else there is, you're living at a time of extremism, a time of revolution, and now there has to be a change and a better world has to be built, and the only way it's going to be built—is with extreme methods. And I, for one, will join with anyone—I don't care what color you are—as long as you want to change this miserable condition that exists on this earth. (Oxford Union Queen and Country Debate, Oxford University, December 3, 1964)

Like Malcolm X, GenZ students turn toward the wind, staring directly and earnestly into their present and future, determined to exert their voices and perspectives. Their exposure to past and present literature, sciences, histories, and humanities allows, even empowers, this unique generation to say, "I choose my destiny." And the myriad texts to which we expose them informs, challenges, and compels them to always push back and move toward a truth and empowerment *they* seek. Some of us who are older may very well find such empowerment disconcerting—not of the "old ways." But then, just what is a comprehensive education for lifelong literacy supposed to do, if not expose, awaken, engage, even challenge and open new, prescient doors of inquiry, exploration, and discovery? This is the broad scope of not just education for education's sake but of reading and experiencing for oneself *devoid of outside agendas—whatever they may be or from wherever they may emanate.*

A student put this succinctly:

> Elements of his writing are still relevant in today's films and books, like his strong emotional themes, tropes, and character archetypes. Shakespeare's works are quoted often by common people [everyday people] and even by more influential individuals, including civil rights leader Martin Luther King Jr., who was known to quote Shakespeare often. I believe the beautiful and unique work by William Shakespeare is still greatly relevant and appreciated now and will go on to remain relevant for centuries more. (Student, May 2023)

The plays comprising this series represent curricula inclusion around the country and also represent the angst some parents, activists, and politicians, even some fearful teachers, have about our continuing to include Shakespeare's works. That said, there are many, many teachers who continue to teach William Shakespeare's plays, not only allowing students from all walks of life to experience the man, his time, and the sheer scope of his thematic and powerful reach, but also privileging the voices and perspectives GenZ brings to the texts:

> We can see in Shakespeare our contemporary and sometimes frightening range of humanity today—I am specifically thinking of our current political turmoil—is not unique, and that just like the evil monarchs such as Richard III appear in Shakespeare's plays, they are always counterbalanced by bright rays of hope: in *Romeo and Juliet*, the union between the Montagues and Capulets at play's end restoring peace and civility . . . It is impossible for me to watch any performance or read any Shakespeare play—especially the tragedies—without leaving the theatre buoyed up by hope and respect for humankind, a deeper appreciation of the uses of the English language, and a feeling that I have been on a cathartic journey that leaves my students and me enriched, strengthened, and hopeful. (Winona Siegmund, Teacher, CGS)

> I'm going to be honest, I'm not very knowledgeable on the subject of Shakespeare . . . I never really went out of my way to understand and retain it. All I know is that I can't escape him. No matter how hard I try, and trust me, I try, he will always be somewhere, running through the media with his "art thous" and biting of thumbs. Perhaps people see themselves in the plays of Shakespeare. Maybe Shakespeare is a dramatization of the hardships we experience every day . . . Shakespeare has stained my life. One of those annoying stains that you can't get out. A bright, colorful stain that's easy to notice. But who cares? It was an ugly shirt anyway; might as well add some color. (Student, May 2023)

> Taylor Swift's "Love Story." I LOVE the STORY of *Romeo and Juliet*. See what I did there? But in all honesty, there are so many Shakespeare inspired works (*Rotten Tomatoes, West Side Story, Twelfth Grade Night*, etc.) that I liked and remained relevant to me, and prove that Shakespeare will always be relevant. The first Shakespeare play I read was *Macbeth* when I was twelve and going to school in Azerbaijan. And even as a preteen studying in a foreign country, I loved the story and found it morbid, funny, and wise all at the same time. My Azerbaijani classmates liked it, too. Due to this unique experience, I think that anyone can enjoy and identify with Shakespeare's works, no matter their age or country of origin. (Student, May 2023)

The five plays in this Folger series represent the universal and social depth and breadth of all Shakespeare's poetry and plays—verisimilitude, relevance, *our* human condition—all writ large in the 21st century and beyond. Through characters, locations, time periods, challenges, and *difference,* William Shakespeare takes us all into real-life moments and decisions and actions—even into our *not yet known or experienced*—to illustrate the human thread joining and holding us all as one.

> Despite being several hundred years old, Shakespeare's works have yet to become antiquated. There are several reasons for this long-lasting relevance—namely the enduring themes. Shakespeare's themes on humanity, morality, loss, and love remain relatable for people across all walks of life. (Student, May 2023)

In sum, a colleague asked me quite recently, "Jocelyn, why do you think students just don't want to read?" To add to this query, at this writing, I have tracked an increasing, and to be honest, disturbing sentiment expressed on social media: some teachers positing, essentially, the same perspective. My response to both is the same: our students—elementary through graduate school—*do* read and write every day. They will also read what we assign in our classes. However, this generation of students first thinks or asks outright—*Why?* What do I *get* if I invest the time and effort? Most assuredly direct inquiries with which many veteran teachers *and* professors are unfamiliar—perhaps even resentful. But let's be honest. Our students of a now-patinated past most likely felt the same way. Remember the plethora of *CliffsNotes* and *Monarch Notes*? I know I threw my share of students' copies in the trash—wanting them to read for themselves.

Just like adults, our students, especially today, have a right to ask us *Why?* What *do* they *get* if they invest their time in reading assigned texts? Umberto Eco brilliantly answers why our students *must* continue reading and experiencing texts—for this series, William Shakespeare's plays—and learning through performance:

> Now a text, once it is written, no longer has anyone behind it; it has, on the contrary, when it survives, and for as long as it survives, thousands of interpreters ahead of it. Their reading of it generates other texts, which can be paraphrase, commentary, carefree exploitation, translation into other signs, words, images, even into music. ("Waiting for the Millennium," *FMR* No. 2, July 1981, 66)

To illustrate Eco's assertion, I will leave it to one student and two people with whom all teachers and many students are familiar:

> Shakespeare's work is relevant because his legacy allows people from all walks of life to understand that they can make a difference. Although people from all walks of life may not always relate to his works, the impact that he made on modern literature and theater is undeniable. The lasting dreams that his works have provided for young people lay the groundwork for our future. Shakespeare's living works are proof that one small man with one small pen can change the future of everything around him. (Student, May 2023)

I met and fell in love with Shakespeare . . . It was a state with which I felt myself most familiar. I pacified myself about his whiteness by saying after all he had been dead so long it couldn't matter to anyone anymore. (Maya Angelou on her childhood introduction to and love of Shakespeare in *I Know Why the Caged Bird Sings*, 1969)

and, as Malcolm X proclaimed:

I go for that. (Oxford Union Queen and Country Debate, Oxford University, December 3, 1964)

Why This Book?

Peggy O'Brien

First, let's start with YOU: If you are a schoolteacher, know that you are the most precious resource in the world. In every school, town, city, state, country, civilization, solar system, or universe, there is none more valuable than you. It is hard, hard work and yet . . . you are doing the most important work on earth. Period.

At the Folger Shakespeare Library, we know this well and deeply, and that's why you are a clear focus of our work. If you teach Shakespeare and other complex literature—and particularly if you are a middle or high school teacher—it is our mission, passion, and honor to serve you. Therefore . . . welcome to *The Folger Guides to Teaching Shakespeare* and our five volumes on teaching *Hamlet, Macbeth, Othello, Romeo and Juliet,* and *A Midsummer Night's Dream.*

Here's why this book: our overall purpose. We know that many of you find yourselves teaching plays that you don't know well, or that you've taught so often that they are beginning to bore you to death. (You talk to us, and we listen.) So, these books give you fresh information and hopefully meaningful new ideas about the plays you teach most frequently, along with a very specific way to teach them to *all* students—highfliers, slow readers, the gamut. We see the Shakespeare content and the teaching methodology as one whole.

We often get these questions from y'all. You may recognize some or all of them:

- How on earth do I even begin to think about teaching a Shakespeare play? No one has really ever taught me how to teach Shakespeare and my own experience with Shakespeare as a high school student was . . . not great.

- How can Shakespeare possibly make sense in this day and age? In this changing world? Old dead white guy?

- Shakespeare can't possibly be engaging to *all* my students, right? I mean, it's true that really only the brightest kids will "get" Shakespeare, right?

- SO . . . what's the Folger Method and how does it fit into all of this?

- I have to teach the "10th-grade Shakespeare play"—whatever it is—and I haven't read it since high school, or maybe I have never read it.

- I'm a schoolteacher and don't have extra time to spend studying up before I teach this stuff.

- Doesn't using those watered-down, "modernized" Shakespeare texts make it easier? Aren't they the most obvious way to go?

- Can learning and teaching Shakespeare really be a great experience for my kids and for me too?

Our *Folger Guides to Teaching Shakespeare* are hopefully an answer to these questions too.

Here's why this book: the Folger Method. At the Folger, not only are we home to the largest Shakespeare collection in the world but we have developed, over the last four decades or so, a way of teaching Shakespeare and other complex texts that is effective for *all* students. We're talking well-developed content and methodology from the same source, and in your case, *in the same book.* Imagine!

The Folger Method is language-based, student-centered, interactive, and rigorous, and provides all students with ways into the language and therefore into the plays. Our focus is words, because the words are where Shakespeare started, and where scholars, actors, directors, and editors start. Shakespeare's language turns out to be not a barrier but *the way in.* The lessons in this book are sequenced carefully, scaffolding your students' path. They will find themselves close-reading, figuring out and understanding language, characters, and the questions that the play is asking. All of this when they may have started out with "Why doesn't he write in English?" It's pretty delicious. If you want to know more about the Folger Method right this minute, go to the chapter that starts on page 39.

A few things I want you to know right off the bat:

- Because the Folger Method involves lots of classroom work that is interactive and exciting (and even joyful), sometimes teachers are tempted to pull a few lessons out of this book and use them to spruce up whatever they usually do. Oh resist, please. Take the whole path and see what your students learn and what you learn.

- There is no "right" interpretation of any play (or work of literature, for that matter). In working with the Folger Method principles and essentials, your students come up with their own sense of what's going on in *A Midsummer Night's Dream..* Their own interpretation. Not yours, or the interpretation of famous literary critics, but their own. And then they bring it to life. Exciting! That's what we're after, because the skills that they'll develop in doing this—close-reading, analysis, collaboration, research—they will use forever.

- The Folger Method may call on you to teach differently than you have before. Be brave! You are not the explainer or the translator or the connector between your students and Shakespeare. You're the architect who sets up the ways in which Shakespeare and your students discover each other . . . and we'll show you very explicitly how to do that.

Here's why this book: parts of the whole. Each of these guides is organized in the same way:

- **Part One is the big picture:** Folger director Michael Witmore and Jocelyn Chadwick both take on the "Why Shakespeare?" question from very different angles. And Jocelyn brings students into the conversation too. Delicious!

- **Part Two is YOU and *A Midsummer Night's Dream*.** Through a set of short takes and one delicious long take, you'll get a stronger sense of the play. The shorts are some speedy and pretty painless ways to learn both the basics and a few surprises about both *A Midsummer Night's Dream* and Shakespeare.

  The long take is "Teaching the *Dream*, Bitter and Sweet," an essay written for you by Gail Kern Paster, an accomplished and celebrated Shakespeare scholar, and former director of the Folger Library. We know that you have no "extra" time ever, but we also know that schoolteachers find connecting with new scholarship to be enlivening and compelling. New ways to look at old plays—new ways most often sparked by the changing world in which we live—continue to open up many new ways to look at Shakespeare. What you take away from Paster's essay may show up in your teaching soon, or maybe at some point, or maybe never—and all of those are good. You may agree with or grasp her perspective on *A Midsummer Night's Dream*, or you may not; she will get you thinking, though—as she gets us thinking all the time—and that's what we're about.

- **Part Three is you, *A Midsummer Night's Dream*, your students, and what happens in your classroom.**

  - The Folger Method is laid out clearly—and bonus: with the kind of energy that it produces in classrooms—so that you can get a sense of the foundational principles and practices before you all get into those lessons, and your own classroom starts buzzing.

  - A five-week *A Midsummer Night's Dream* unit, day-by-day lessons for your classes, with accompanying resources and/or handouts for each. We know that the people who are the smartest and most talented and creative about the "how" of teaching are those who are working in middle and high school classrooms every day. So, working schoolteachers created all of the "What Happens in Your Classroom" section of this book. They do what you do every day. While these writers were writing, testing, and revising for you and your classroom, they were teaching their own middle and high school kids in their own. And I am not mentioning their family obligations or even whispering the word "pandemic." At the Folger, we are in awe of them, and for many of the same reasons, are in awe of all of you.

  - Two essays full of practical advice about two groups of students whom teachers ask us about often. The first details and demonstrates the affinity that English Learners and Shakespeare and *A Midsummer Night's Dream* have for one another. The second focuses on the deep connections that can flourish between students with intellectual and emotional disabilities and Shakespeare and *A Midsummer Night's Dream*. No barriers to Shakespeare anywhere here.

  - The last essay is packed with information and examples on pairing texts—how we make sure that students are exposed to the broad sweep of literature while at the same time are busy taking Shakespeare right off that pedestal and into conversations with authors of other centuries, races, genders, ethnicities, and cultures. This is where magic starts to happen!

And now . . . YOU! Get busy! And as Bottom says, "No more words! Away!" Get into this play! A joyful and energized journey of mutual discovery is at hand—for you and your students. Get it all going in Theseus' court, in the forest, in class! And tell us how it goes. As always, we want to know *everything*.

PART TWO

Getting Up to Speed, or Reviving Your Spirit, with *A Midsummer Night's Dream*

Ten Amazing Things You May Not Know About Shakespeare

Catherine Loomis and Michael LoMonico

The basics: Shakespeare was a playwright, poet, and actor who grew up in the market town of Stratford-upon-Avon, England, spent his professional life in London, and returned to Stratford a wealthy landowner. He was born in 1564—the same year Galileo was born and Michelangelo died. Shakespeare died in 1616, and Cervantes did too.

1. In the summer of 1564, an outbreak of bubonic plague killed one out of every seven people in Stratford, but the newborn William Shakespeare survived.

2. In Shakespeare's family, the women were made of sterner stuff: Shakespeare's mother, his sister Joan, his wife, Anne Hathaway, their daughters, and granddaughter all outlived their husbands. And Joan lived longer than all four of her brothers. The sad exception is Shakespeare's younger sister, Anne. She died when she was seven and Shakespeare was fifteen.

3. Shakespeare appears in public records up until 1585, when he was a 21-year-old father of three, and then again in 1592, when he turns up in London as a playwright. During those lost years, he may have been a schoolmaster or tutor, and one legend has him fleeing to London to escape prosecution for deer poaching. No one has any idea really, but maybe there is a theatrical possibility: An acting company called the Queen's Men was on tour in the summer of 1587, and, since one of their actors had been killed in a duel in Oxford, the town just down the road, the company arrived in Stratford minus an actor. At age 23, did Shakespeare leave his family and join them on tour?

4. Shakespeare wrote globally: in addition to all over Britain, his plays take you to Italy, Greece, Egypt, Turkey, Spain, France, Austria, Cyprus, Denmark and, in the case of *The Tempest*, pretty close to what was to become America.

5. Shakespeare died of a killer hangover. The Reverend John Ward, a Stratford vicar, wrote about Shakespeare's death on April 23, 1616, this way: "Shakespeare, [Michael] Drayton, and Ben Jonson had a merry meeting, and it seems drank too hard, for Shakespeare died of a fever there contracted."

6. On Shakespeare's gravestone in Stratford's Holy Trinity Church is a fierce curse on anyone who "moves my bones." In 2016, archeologists used ground-penetrating radar to examine the grave, and . . . Shakespeare's skull is missing.

7. Frederick Douglass escaped slavery and as a free man became a celebrated orator, statesman, and leader of the American abolitionist movement—and he was a student and lover of Shakespeare. Visitors to Cedar Hill, his home in DC's Anacostia neighborhood, can see Douglass's volumes of Shakespeare's complete works still on his library shelves and a framed print of Othello and Desdemona on the parlor wall. In addition to studying and often referencing Shakespeare in his speeches, Douglass was an active member of his local Anacostia community theater group, the Uniontown Shakespeare Club.

8. Shakespeare is the most frequently produced playwright in the U.S. Despite this, *American Theatre* magazine has never crowned him America's "Most Produced Playwright," an honor bestowed annually based on data from nearly 400 theaters. He always wins by such a large margin—usually there are about five times more Shakespeare productions than plays by the second-place finisher—that the magazine decided to just set him aside so that other playwrights could have a chance to win.

9. While Nelson Mandela was incarcerated on South Africa's Robben Island, one of the other political prisoners retained a copy of Shakespeare's complete works, and secretly circulated it through the group. At his request, many of the other prisoners—including Mandela—signed their names next to their favorite passages.

> *Cowards die many times before their deaths;*
> *The valiant only taste of death but once.*
> *Of all the wonders that I yet have heard,*
> *It seems to me most strange that men should fear,*
> *Seeing that death, a necessary end,*
> *Will come when it will come.*

These lines from *Julius Caesar* were marked "N. R. Mandela, December 16, 1977." Nelson Mandela was released from prison in 1990.

10. The Folger Shakespeare Library is in Washington, DC, and houses the largest Shakespeare collection in the world, just a block from the U.S. Capitol. We are Shakespeare's home in America! We are abuzz with visitors and audience members from our own DC neighborhoods, from across the country and around the world: teachers and students, researchers and scholars, lovers of the performing arts, all kinds of learners, and the curious of all ages and stages. Find us online at folger.edu/teach—and do come visit our beautiful new spaces. Be a part of our lively and accessible exhibitions and programs, explore rare books and other artifacts, join a teaching workshop, and enjoy the magic of theatre, poetry, and music. We're waiting for you, your classes, and your families!

Ten Amazing Things You May Not Know About *A Midsummer Night's Dream*

Catherine Loomis and Michael LoMonico

1. As U.S. teachers, we sometimes tend to think of *A Midsummer Night's Dream* as a "middle school play," but *Midsummer* (for short) is studied by students at all levels and is one of the most frequently performed Shakespeare plays. Many theaters and festivals often like to perform it in the summer! *Midsummer* is Shakespeare's second shortest play—the whole thing is only 2,233 lines long, a little more than half as long as *Hamlet* (4,167 lines). Only *The Comedy of Errors* is shorter, coming in at 1,898 lines.

2. Shakespeare probably wrote *A Midsummer Night's Dream* sometime between 1594 and 1596, and he might have been working on two other plays at the same time—*Romeo and Juliet* and *Richard II.*

3. Shakespeare was inspired by earlier literature and wove it into his work to create new and dramatic plays. *A Midsummer Night's Dream* is full of characters from mythology. The English translation of Plutarch's *Lives of the Noble Grecians and Romans* (1579) was a source for *Midsummer* and other of Shakespeare's plays too. It contains sections titled "Life of Theseus" and "Life of Demetrius" and "Life of Lysander," although in the case of the two lovers, he borrowed their names and nothing else about them. In places, *Midsummer* echoes Chaucer's "The Knight's Tale," written around 1384–1385, as well as Ovid's narrative poem the *Metamorphoses,* written sometime in 8 CE. We think that Shakespeare probably read the *Metamorphoses* in school; reference to it pops up in other plays as well. From the *Metamorphoses,* Shakespeare enhanced to our delight the now-famous story of Pyramus and Thisbe.

4. Scholars estimate that *A Midsummer Night's Dream* was first performed in the mid-1590s. It appeared in print, first in 1600 (entitled, because spelling and grammar were not yet codified, *A Midsommer nights dreame*) and later in the 1623 First Folio. Theater reviews were not frequent and public as they are now, but Samuel Pepys, an avid London theatergoer, wrote about *Midsummer* in his diary in 1662, "I found the play to be the most insipid ridiculous play that ever I saw in my life." However, he also included that it featured "some good dancing and some handsome women, which was all my pleasure."

5. Beginning in 1840 and for about 70 years, it became customary for the roles of Oberon and Puck to be played by women. In many productions of the play from then until now, the same actor plays both Theseus and Oberon, and other actors double up as well: one plays both Hippolyta and Titania, and another both Puck and Philostrate, or maybe Puck, Philostrate, and Egeus.

6. Though a short play, *A Midsummer Night's Dream* has had enormous impact in worlds far beyond the theater stage. Just at the time of this writing, the number of films and film adaptations of *Midsummer* is too long to list here. In the world of science, British astronomer William Herschel discovered two new moons of Uranus in 1787. In 1852, his son John Herschel named them Oberon and Titania. Another Uranian moon, discovered in 1985 by the *Voyager 2* spacecraft, has been named Puck.

7. *A Midsummer Night's Dream* has inspired—and continues to inspire—other adaptations and works of art. By 1692, Henry Purcell had already written the music for a semi-opera called *The Fairy-Queen,* an adaptation of the play. In 1842, at age seventeen, Felix Mendelssohn wrote a musical overture for the play, and many years later, composed more music for it, including his famous wedding march. In 1967, based on the play and Mendelssohn's music, George Balanchine created his *A Midsummer Night's Dream* ballet, which continues to be performed by ballet companies around the world.

8. Walt Disney Studios made *A Midsummer Night's Dream* into an animated short in 1999. It featured Mickey Mouse as Lysander, Minnie Mouse as Hermia, Donald Duck as Demetrius, and Daisy Duck as Helena, with Scrooge McDuck as Egeus and Goofy as Puck.

9. The Pyramus and Thisbe play that the tradesmen rehearse and perform for the newlyweds has had a life of its own as well. Poet Luis de Góngora wrote a Spanish version, *Fábula de Píramo y Tisbe,* in 1618, and French poet Théophile de Viau, *Les amours tragiques de Pyrame et Thisbée,* in 1621. The Beatles performed a hilarious version of it on a 1964 television special with Paul McCartney as Pyramus, John Lennon as his lover Thisbe, George Harrison as Moonshine, and Ringo Starr as Lion. A 2012 episode of *The Simpsons* was based on the Pyramus and Thisbe story.

10. *A Midsummer Night's Dream* thrives here at the Folger Shakespeare Library in many, many ways! On our shelves and in our vault, we have 296 stand-alone copies of *Midsummer,* including one that the author of *Alice in Wonderland,* Charles Lutwidge Dodgson (his pen name was Lewis Carroll), gave to the book's illustrator as a Christmas present in 1869. You can find *Midsummer* here in twenty-nine different languages: Catalan, Chinese, Croatian, Czech, Danish, Dutch, English, Esperanto, Estonian, French, German, Greek, Hebrew, Hungarian, Italian, Japanese, Latvian, Norwegian, Persian, Polish, Portuguese, Romanian, Russian, Spanish, Swedish, Thai, Turkish, Ukrainian, and Western Frisian. *A Midsummer Night's Dream* has always been a favorite of artists; the Folger collection contains more images of *Midsummer* than of any other play. Eight productions of *A Midsummer Night's Dream* have been performed at the Folger, all on our Elizabethan stage except one spectacular production staged during the summer of 2022 when our building was closed for construction. In partnership with the National

Building Museum in Washington, DC, we built a working playhouse inside the museum's massive and wonderful Great Hall and performed *A Midsummer Night's Dream* all summer long to large and enthusiastic audiences of all ages. At our student festivals, thus far we have been treated to probably 500 versions of the Pyramus and Thisbe play scene, and we're ready for 500 more! We teach thousands of teachers annually how to teach *Midsummer* and many other plays. Find us online (folger.edu) and come visit us in person. We look forward to greeting you warmly as new and old friends!

What Happens in This Play Anyway?

A Plot Summary of *A Midsummer Night's Dream*

In *A Midsummer Night's Dream*, residents of Athens mix with fairies from a local forest, with comic results. In the city, Theseus, Duke of Athens, is to marry Hippolyta, queen of the Amazons. Bottom the weaver and his friends rehearse in the woods a play they hope to stage for the wedding celebrations.

Four young Athenians are in a romantic tangle. Lysander and Demetrius love Hermia; she loves Lysander and her friend Helena loves Demetrius. Hermia's father, Egeus, commands Hermia to marry Demetrius, and Theseus supports the father's right. All four young Athenians end up in the woods, where Robin Goodfellow, who serves the fairy king Oberon, puts flower juice on the eyes of Lysander, and then Demetrius, unintentionally causing both to love Helena. Oberon, who is quarreling with his wife, Titania, uses the flower juice on her eyes. She falls in love with Bottom, who now, thanks to Robin Goodfellow, wears an ass's head.

As the lovers sleep, Robin Goodfellow restores Lysander's love for Hermia, so that now each young woman is matched with the man she loves. Oberon disenchants Titania and removes Bottom's ass's head. The two young couples join the royal couple in getting married, and Bottom rejoins his friends to perform the play.

What Happens in This Play Anyway?

A PLAY MAP OF *A MIDSUMMER NIGHT'S DREAM*

Mya Gosling and Peggy O'Brien

A MIDSUMMER NIGHT'S DREAM

What happens when **one** crabby father...	...**two** quarrelling fairies...	...**four** lost and confused lovers...	...and **six** earnest (but terrible) amateur actors...	...all get tangled up in a web of friendship and magic one night?

Who's Who

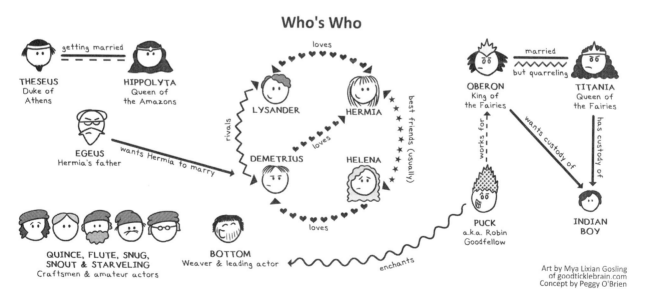

Art by Mya Lixian Gosling
of goodticklebrain.com
Concept by Peggy O'Brien

Teaching the *Dream*, Bitter and Sweet

Gail Kern Paster

A Midsummer Night's Dream is often the Shakespeare play first taught to students because it is thought to be a lighthearted confection, a romantic comedy about fairies, lovers, and amateur actors who lose themselves temporarily in the woods overnight. A closer look at the play's language and action, however, reveals a significant amount of cruelty, violence, bullying, and even hints of sexual perversion that threaten to derail any joyful response to its lyricism, physical comedy, and the multiple weddings at its conclusion. As we will see in this essay, the challenge and the delight in thinking about *A Midsummer Night's Dream* is to find its comic beauty precisely in the harmonious union of opposites—between high and low, dark and light, violent and tender, painful and pleasurable, serious and trivial, realistic and fanciful. All these qualities Shakespeare renders symbolically in the iconic central image of fairy queen Titania enfolding the ass-headed Bottom the weaver in her arms.

Every generation of teachers and students finds its own way into Shakespeare's plays. His greatest gift to us may be that each play offers a story-world highly particularized in time, place, characters, and actions, inviting us to lose and find ourselves within its rich environs. For students, the setting and characters of *A Midsummer Night's Dream* may be obscure. How can teachers help them find pathways into the heart of this 400-year-old play, set in ancient Athens, filled with unfamiliar legendary figures (Theseus and Hippolyta); fairy royalty (Titania and Oberon) quarrelling over custody of a foster child whom we never see; four lovers who bully and insult each other as they chase around the woods; and unsophisticated working men whose livelihoods as bellows-mender, tinker, and joiner our students can know little about and whose intentions to act in a tragedy seem absurd—if not irrelevant? How, in short, should we think about—and teach—*A Midsummer Night's Dream* in the 21st century?

The task for the teacher—in this as in so many other complex texts—is to find the big ideas in the telling details. The most obvious connection may be a generational link to the young lovers Hermia, Helena, Lysander, and Demetrius, allowing students to track their romantic misunderstandings and their deep disconnect from the world of their elders. But students also care a lot about issues such as the environment, gender equality, and social justice. Is there a pathway into *A Midsummer Night's Dream* through those concerns, too? I believe the answer is yes, as long as we make sure not to look at the action and language of *A Midsummer Night's Dream* through a protective lens denying the play's cruelty—Oberon's desire to humiliate his wife by making her foolishly fall in love and the abusive, even racist language with which the lovers taunt each other as they fall suddenly in and out of love. We need to emphasize the woods as a powerful and fickle environment; remember the human and animal suffering caused by the fairies' quarrel; think about the Indian boy as the absent center of a gender struggle; and figure out the thematic relevance of bumbling amateur theatricals to the rest of the play.

A Midsummer Night's Dream is rightly understood as a celebration of imagination, theater, and the power of love, even in odd pairings such as Titania and Bottom. The play climaxes with three weddings and Oberon's nighttime blessing on the lovers' marital happiness. But it is important to recognize that the play begins "in another key" (1.1.19), delivering a stark picture of female subjection to the power of warriors, rulers, and fathers. Theseus weds Hippolyta, Queen of the Amazons, after (and presumably because) he has defeated her in battle. "I wooed thee with my sword / And won thy love doing thee injuries" (1.1.17–18), he tells her in a paradoxical statement that raises questions about Hippolyta's consent to her marriage and her onstage demeanor. Many Elizabethans would have read about the self-governing society of warrior women in Greek mythology in Plutarch's "Life of Theseus." They might have believed that a society of warrior women existed in the New World because Spanish conquistadors reported fighting battles where indigenous women fought alongside men. (This is why the region was named Amazonia!)

In Theseus's brief mention of his victory, Shakespeare quickly moves past Hippolyta's status as POW fiancée. (Productions rarely highlight it.) But in the play's opening predicament, the threat to another marriageable woman is presented in significant detail. A formal complaint is brought to Theseus by Egeus, whose daughter Hermia has refused to marry the father's choice, Demetrius. A son or daughter's rebellion is a familiar opening gambit in comedy (and sometimes in tragedy, if we think about *Romeo and Juliet*, composed close in time to *A Midsummer Night's Dream*, or *Othello*). But Hermia is faced with dire consequences for disobedience—a choice between cloistered life in a convent as "a barren sister" (1.1.74) or state execution. (No wonder her lover Lysander proposes that they leave Athens instead.)

It is important to take the father's appeal to law seriously rather than as a conventional device for moving the play's action from Athens to the fairy-haunted woods. Doing so has the advantage of linking Hermia's plight to that of young women in traditional societies today who may face jail, corporal punishment, or death at the hands of their families or governments for refusing to accept their parents' choice in an arranged marriage. Theseus takes a tough line on paternal power, telling Hermia, "To you your father should be as a god" (1.1.48). He says he is unable to "extenuate" (1.1.122) the law of Athens. Hermia's stubborn choice of Lysander, then, asserts her right as an individual to self-determination and subjective preference: "I would my father looked but with my eyes" (1.1.58). Significantly, this threat against Hermia echoes the terms of Hippolyta's defeat and anticipates the quarrel of Oberon and Titania. So, it is telling—perhaps even Shakespeare's buried stage direction to the actress—that Theseus asks Hippolyta about her mood as they exit the stage, "What cheer, my love?" (1.1.124). No less astonishing, Lysander asks Hermia, "Why is your cheek so pale?" (1.1.130). These questions may be the first sign that we should pay attention not only to gender difference and the alignment of state power with fathers, but to a certain obtuseness in these men about how the women they love might react to societal constraints in freely choosing whom to love and how to live. It is as if these men do not acknowledge the power differential so decidedly in their favor.

For all four lovers, the play's opening underscores their motivation to leave an environment full of roadblocks to happiness. Lysander and Hermia cannot marry there; Demetrius cannot compel Hermia's affection; and Helena is hopelessly in love with Demetrius, who tells her brutally, "I am sick when I do look on thee" (2.1.219). As the domain of nature rather than law, the woods seem to promise an alternative environment of liberty and sexual freedom. Like many of us today, the lovers consider the natural world a pleasurable environment for outdoor recreation. Lysander tells Hermia to meet him "Where I did meet thee once with Helena / To do observance to a morn of May" (1.1.168–69). (Elizabethans would have recognized this as a reference to their own free-wheeling May Day.) Hermia identifies the place where she and Helena "Upon faint primrose beds were wont to lie" (1.1.220). But the play invites us to ask hard questions about Demetrius and Helena, as they follow Lysander and Hermia out of the city. Why does Helena alert Demetrius to the escape and betray her friend Hermia in doing so? Why does Demetrius persist in following a woman who wants nothing to do with him? And, perhaps most disturbingly, why does Helena declare her subjection to Demetrius in language that seems so extravagantly masochistic? "Use me but as your spaniel: spurn me, strike me," she tells him. "Neglect me, lose me; only give me leave / (Unworthy as I am) to follow you" (2.1.212–214). How should we explain Helena's drive toward abjection? Is such emotional pain, for her, the only way to feel anything? (Students may know about this on their own.) Does our difficulty in answering these questions about their behavior prepare us for the lovers' transformation during their night in the forest and their cruelty to one another?

Because, instead of freedom, the woods produce powerlessness of another sort as all four lovers quickly lose their way in the dark. And this happens even before Oberon and Puck intervene in their affairs and create even more confusion. At first, Puck's mistake in putting love juice first on Lysander and then on Demetrius seems to change the power dynamic among the lovers. The two women exchange places in the love triangles, as the men spurn Hermia and court Helena. Lysander and Hermia begin to know what unreciprocated love feels like, and Helena is surprised to hear the language of adoration directed at her: "O Helen, goddess, nymph, perfect, divine! / To what, my love, shall I compare thine eyne?" (3.2.140–41). But Lysander and Demetrius remain romantic rivals, and the change in their affections brings them no closer to achieving the object of their desire. Helena, true to form, understands the men's sudden declarations of love for her as mockery, and accuses the bewildered Hermia of joining with them "to fashion this false sport in spite of me" (3.2.199). Hermia responds not by accusing Lysander of infidelity, but Helena: "You thief of love! What, have you come by night / And stol'n my love's heart from him?" (3.2.297–98).

In Athens, the roadblocks to satisfaction in love came from outside. But, in the woods, romantic unhappiness seems to proceed from within—for the men, from a change in whom they love; for the women, a change in who loves them. The women themselves say they have not changed at all: "Hate me? Wherefore? . . . I am as fair now as I was erewhile," Hermia tells Lysander (3.2.284–87). Helena can only hear words of love as derision: "I see you all are bent / To set against me for your merriment . . . Can you not hate me, as I know you do, / But you must join in souls to mock me too?" (3.2.148–53). The derision, she thinks, has spread from Demetrius to the other two.

Our reaction to the male lovers' state of illusion may be ambivalent—painful, amused, disappointed, surprised. We understand the fairy-haunted woods as an environment creating confusion and powerlessness, not as an arena of personal choice and sexual freedom. And the modern Western idea of romantic love as the highest expression of personal choice comes under severe scrutiny: Lysander and Demetrius believe they are now discovering the truth of their affections, whereas we know instead that they are acting under the influence of a psychotropic herb. More disturbing, however, is that the men experience their changes of heart less as something changed within themselves than as change in the attractiveness of the women. From the very beginning the lovers' language has tended toward extremes, as if the absence of love reveals the presence of hatred, as if there is no middle or neutral ground, no place for simple indifference. Demetrius tells Helena he hates her (2.1.218); Hermia tells Demetrius she hates his presence (3.2.82); Helena says she knows the other three hate her (3.2.152); Lysander tells Hermia, "the hate I bear thee made me leave thee so" (3.2.195). Such hatred takes an even darker turn when language becomes racialized, as when Lysander describes Hermia as an "Ethiop" (3.2.265) and "tawny Tartar" (3.2.274), or when the physical difference in height between petite Hermia and tall Helena (a difference probably reflecting height difference in Shakespeare's two teenage boy actors) becomes another means for abuse. Hermia taunts Helena as a "painted maypole" (3.2.311) even as she internalizes her own shame as being "so dwarfish and so low" (3.2.310). Lysander soon picks up the thread: "Get you gone, you dwarf, / You minimus of hind'ring knotgrass made" (3.2.346–47). Rather than seeing Shakespeare or even the characters themselves as the source of this racial abuse and physical bigotry, it is more productive to think of it as the collective voice of a culture that—like ours—imposes arbitrary values and preferences upon neutral physical facts such as height, skin color, and bodily norms. Shakespeare knows the social power of such language and uses it to highlight the extremes in language and feeling to which the lovers so quickly have turned. In the confusion of the love chase, all four lovers reveal their inner bully. It is as if they think that using such violence is to assert their own individuality and choice in circumstances where—as we are in a position to know—genuine individuality and freedom of choice have been taken away by Oberon's love potion. We know that love in the forest is an illusion created within its confines and—thanks to Oberon—by means of its natural resources.

But subtract—for a moment—Oberon's love potion as an external justification for the men's behavior and look at the behavior itself. Critics often find Lysander and Demetrius virtually indistinguishable. But in fact, Lysander is always the first to identify his object of affection—first Hermia, then Helena—and Demetrius follows suit, as if mimicking Lysander's desire is a goal not known even to himself. The men's fickle behavior resembles what critic René Girard has called "mimetic desire" and what Eve Kosofsky Sedgwick labeled "male homosocial desire." These terms name romantic rivalry between men caused by one man's desire to replicate another man's choice, to stand in that man's place, and to form a bond with him through choosing the same love object. Mimetic desire would explain Demetrius's behavior toward Lysander, since his affections mimic Lysander's at every step. In these romantic triangles, the woman is less an object in herself than the means to a relationship between men. Thus, the "cure" for this hopelessly entangled love knot can come only when Robin anoints Lysander's eyes with an antidote that returns him to loving Hermia, and leaves the love potion on the eyes of Demetrius. Even back in Athens at the very end of the play, Demetrius remains under the potion's influence—and thus in love with Helena. And, with the love potion now on the eyes of only one of the men, there is a difference between them in perception and consciousness that breaks the endless cycle of mimetic desire and allows the two men to love different women.

It should be clear that how we judge the behavior of the male lovers is a function of how we interpret the meaning of the fairies. There are several different ways to think about them. We may see Oberon's love juice as merely an imaginary excuse for the lovers' cruelty to one another or we may see it as an outside agent activating a capacity, always potential within them, for extremes of cruelty and betrayal. We know the power of psychotropic drugs; we know that such drugs are available to those who know how to administer the different properties of plants to human subjects. But since the fairies' abilities are consistently described in meteorological terms, it is also possible to interpret these spirits as anthropomorphized forces of a natural world presided over by that symbol of change—the moon. The word *moon* appears far more times in *A Midsummer Night's Dream* (23) than in any other Shakespeare play. The Elizabethans associated the moon with changeability, flux, control over weather and water in the environment, and control over the mental states of human beings. For a human to wander about at night was deemed risky for mental and physical health, not so much because the Elizabethans believed in fairies (which most of them did not), but because of bad vapors in the night air that could penetrate and alter both body and mind. Titania reminds Oberon that the moon is not happy with their quarrel over the custody of the Indian boy, causing a natural disaster for humans, animals, agriculture, and the whole natural world:

> The human mortals want their winter here,
> No night is now with hymn and carol blessed.
> Therefore the moon, the governess of floods,
> Pale in her anger, washes all the air,
> That rheumatic diseases do abound.
> And thorough this distemperature we see
> The seasons alter. (2.1.104–110)

What Titania describes is a significant loss of control for "human mortals," based on human expectations for seasonal weather, good harvests, and a productive environment. What she describes is not the human effect on environment, but an environmental effect on human life and culture. Elizabethans in the mid-1590s, living in an agricultural society, would have heard in her words an accurate description of recent harvest years bad enough to cause social unrest and significant food insecurity. Titania and Oberon know their role in this natural disaster, but he is far more indifferent than she to the "progeny of evils" their quarrel has caused. "Do you amend it, then," he tells her coldly. "It lies in you. / Why should Titania cross her Oberon?" (2.1.118, 121–22). He is seeking custody of her godchild, son of Titania's dead votaress: "for her sake do I rear up her boy, / And for her sake I will not part with him" (2.1.141–42).

Even if the Elizabethans did not really believe in fairies, they certainly believed in the existence of spirits and the ability of such spirits to use natural forces on the human body. Thus, it is only logical in such a world that the lovers would describe their feelings in meteorological terms. Lysander describes love as "brief as the lightning in the collied night" (1.1.147). Demetrius, waking up from his night in the forest, experiences his old love for Hermia now "melted as the snow" (4.1.173) and remembers the overnight events "like far-off mountains turnèd into clouds" (4.1.195). Given the widespread human distress caused by this quarrel over the boy, we may understand the lovers' cruel language and behavior as a result of the predictable fear and helplessness engendered by their night lost in a dangerous, spirit-filled forest. More than anything, their experience feels like a dream. "Are you sure / That we are awake?" Demetrius asks the others. "It seems to me / That yet we sleep, we dream" (4.1.201–3). And their belief in this dream allows for the amnesia essential for forgetting and forgiving what they have said and done to each other.

But there is no reason to attach a single meaning to the fairies any more than to any other element of this complicated play. In addition to seeing them as natural forces, we should also wish to see the fairies in literary terms—as larger-than-life creations of myth and folklore blessed with immortality, allegorical significance, and an array of superhuman powers such as invisibility, flight, and transformation. Elizabethans would certainly have recognized Titania as an allegorical figure for their own queen, Elizabeth I. At a moment in cultural history when women were deemed the inferior sex, the rule of a female monarch was paradoxical—the image of a world turned upside down. Titania's quarrel with Oberon over the Indian boy is a reflection of that paradox in matters of child-rearing, since Oberon wishes to take the boy away from Titania's female household and bring him up properly in a male-only environment. Since Titania insists on raising the boy as a tribute to the boy's dead mother, Oberon's anger toward her may be misogynist mockery of misplaced female loyalties and usurpation of power belonging properly to fathers. By anointing Titania's eyes with love juice and making her fall in love with "some vile thing" (2.2.40), Oberon intends to humiliate Titania by making her thrall to a ridiculous passion—passion of the kind Shakespeare would have read in Roman poet Ovid's *Metamorphoses*. And, from Oberon's point of view, the asinine behavior of Titania's ridiculous love object works as a fitting rebuke to what he regards as Titania's misplaced maternal hold upon the Indian boy.

But, however ridiculous ass-headed Bottom may be, Shakespeare endows him with such a multitude of rich meanings that he and Titania become the play's central representatives of the wonder, inexplicability, and variety of love. Even as he accepts her devotion and the ministrations of her fairy servants, Bottom never believes he deserves her love: "Methinks, mistress, you should have little / reason for that. And yet, to say the truth, reason / and love keep little company together nowadays" (3.1.144–46). At first, Titania intends to improve Bottom, telling him, "I will purge thy mortal grossness so / That thou shalt like an airy spirit go" (3.1.162–63). But her efforts prove so unavailing that Bottom—in the lap of unaccustomed luxury—instead regresses into an infantile state, asking the fairies to scratch his head, fetch him honey, and sing him to sleep. The blissed-out prisoner of his physical appetites, Bottom is a version of the demanding child whom only his mother could love, the child whom Freud called His Majesty, the Baby. Whether Bottom and Titania actually have sex in their off-stage interval between Acts 3 and 4 (as was clearly implied in Peter Brook's famous production in the late 1960s) is an interpretive choice in any production. If they do, then, we ought to recognize that Oberon, ironically, has brought about his own cuckolding—a self-punishment he would doubtless prefer to ignore.

For us in the classroom or in the audience, it is far easier to identify with the human Bottom than with the immortal Titania, and there is good reason to think that Shakespeare intended this to be so. For Elizabethans, to see Bottom the weaver welcomed into the bower of the fairy queen was to see a satirical version of the court favorite whom the monarch inexplicably showers with undeserved attention and privileges. Bottom would represent a cultural fantasy, available to them all, of magical access to power and dominion. But, the significance of this fantasy can be almost as great for us as it was for Shakespeare's contemporaries. In the sublime tableau of the fairy queen doting upon the ass-headed weaver and enfolding him in her arms, Shakespeare brilliantly unites a whole set of cultural oppositions—low/high; mortal/immortal; subject/queen; worker/ruler; child/parent; animal/human. It is just because this enchanting image carries such enormous cultural significance, just because it is an image of the spirit of comedy itself, that Titania's love for Bottom—for the Bottom in all of us, in effect—is not the humiliation intended by Oberon but instead a joyous celebration of the power of illusion over reality and of the childlike fantasy of unmerited adoration from on high. Even so, let us not forget that Oberon only removes the love juice from Titania's eyes once he has gained custody of the Indian boy: "Now I have the boy, I will undo /This hateful imperfection of her eyes" (4.1.63–64). And it is only with Oberon's victory that the natural world may return to its former cycles of seasons and harvests.

Bottom, restored to his proper human form, can only experience his night in the forest as the lovers do. It was a dream from which he is loath to awaken and a memory whose transcendent power he can barely articulate: "I have had a dream past the wit of man to say / what dream it was . . . Methought I was and / methought I had— but man is a patched fool if / he will offer to say what methought I had" (4.1.215–20). Experiencing a creative urge to record this memory for posterity, he decides to turn it into art by getting Peter Quince to "write a ballad of this dream" (4.1.224–25). This impulse serves to link Bottom's time with the fairy queen to the twinned themes of art and the imagination and thus to the amateur theatricals that have brought Bottom and his companions to the forest in the first place. The working men—called "mechanicals" in critical tradition—have decided to enter a competition to perform at the wedding of Theseus and Hippolyta and earn valuable patronage thereby. Shakespeare keeps the plot line of the mechanicals' efforts to perform *Pyramus and Thisbe* completely separate from other events in the forest: the lovers never encounter the mechanicals and know nothing about Bottom's transformation. It is as if the two groups inhabit different spheres within the same universe, and none of them—save Bottom—sees the fairies. What unites them is not dramatic but thematic: the role of the imagination in the experience of love and in the creation of art.

For the Elizabethans, the imagination was a separate faculty, even sometimes a separate place in the brain, often associated with fancy or fantasy. As we have seen, Oberon's manipulation of the faculties of perception in Lysander and Demetrius highlights the role of the subjective imagination in the process of falling in and out of love. But Shakespeare's introduction of the mechanicals' amateur theatricals serves to put the role of imagination in artistic creation at the forefront of our attention too. In their efforts to stage *Pyramus and Thisbe,* the mechanicals replicate the entire process of putting on a play—from casting roles to considering scenery and other effects, distributing parts, gathering to rehearse, thinking about audience response, and finally performing before an audience. Their hilarious difficulties at every stage is Shakespeare's affectionate celebration of his own company's virtuosity and professionalism as well as his sly challenge to his skilled fellow actors to act badly well—or well badly, or some version thereof. The problem is not only that the mechanicals are not used to doing the work of the creative imagination for themselves, but also that they lack faith in the imaginative capacity of their onlookers to distinguish between reality and theatrical illusion. They worry that ladies will be frightened by Snug in character as a lion and by the presence of real swords onstage. Confused about how to "bring in a wall" (3.1.64), they decide to cast Snout as the fateful wall that divides the lovers, and they hope for real moonshine to perform at their postnuptial performance. It's Bottom's rehearsal performance as a scenery-chewing Pyramus that seems to prompt Robin to single him out for the punishment of a monstrous transformation.

In the event, the amateur actors fail to win over their onstage audience, who respond mostly with ridicule even as they watch both Pyramus and Thisbe (like Romeo and Juliet, whose play Shakespeare wrote just before or just after the first staging of *A Midsummer Night's Dream*) stab themselves in mistaken despair over their beloved's death. Having watched the intellectual and creative struggles of these amateur actors, we may be more sympathetic than the Athenian audience even as we find the clumsy language and melodramatic performance of *Pyramus and Thisbe* genuinely hilarious, if at moments overlong. But we are probably inclined to be even more sympathetic to their earnest, if awkward attempt at playmaking because of Theseus's outright dismissal of the imagination as he listens skeptically to the lovers' account of their night in the forest:

> More strange than true, I never may believe
> These antique fables, nor these fairy toys.
> Lovers and madmen have such seething brains,
> Such shaping fantasies, that apprehend
> More than cool reason ever comprehends.
> The lunatic, the lover, and the poet
> Are of imagination all compact. (5.1.2–8)

In the contest between reason and imagination that Theseus famously sketches out here, reason cannot begin to account for the poetic truths about the imagination that we have witnessed in the forest because, unlike imagination, reason has no way to account for its own limitations. Imagination is not afraid of its own limitations, thanks to the work of poets giving "a local habitation and a name" to "the form of things unknown" (5.1.18, 16). Revealed in this speech—it is fair to say—is that Theseus neither knows who he is (a fictional hero of exploits in antique fables) nor where he is (at the end of a play by William Shakespeare). Hippolyta is wiser, reminding Theseus that, with "their minds transfigured so together" (5.1.25), the lovers cannot simply have been dreaming. The only correct response to their story, therefore, is wonder at "something of great constancy, / But howsoever, strange and admirable" (5.1.27–28).

At the end of the play, it is important to remember that the love juice has been removed only from the eyes of Lysander. Demetrius must remain in a permanent state of ignorance and illusion, and we know why: to demonstrate the necessity of imagination in matters of love, to save Hermia's life, to provide for Helena's happiness, to permit two marriages to take place, and to right the social order of Athens. Theseus decides, in the end, to "overbear" Hermia's father (5.1.186)—though the point is significantly mooted by the fact that Demetrius no longer wants to marry Hermia anyway and the harsh law remains ordinarily in force. Even with these caveats, it is only fitting that the last words of this play belong not to Theseus, the skeptical voice of reason, but to the fairies as representatives of imagination and the spirit world. Oberon casts a blessing on the three marriages that have taken place, mandating that "all the couples three / Ever true in loving be" and wishing that no harm come to their children: "And the blots of Nature's hand / Shall not in their issue stand" (5.1.424–26). And finally, Robin addresses us:

> If we shadows have offended,
> Think but this and all is mended:
> That you have but slumbered here
> While these visions did appear. (5.1.440–44)

We, in the afterglow of this bittersweet comedy, know that the greatest gift of *A Midsummer Night's Dream* is to affirm the necessary work of imagination and illusion not only in our loves but also in our lives. And if we can convince our students of this truth—the truth of poetry—they will have it forever.

PART THREE

A Midsummer Night's Dream in Your Classroom with Your Students

The Folger Method:
You Will Never Teach Literature
the Same Way Again

Corinne Viglietta and Peggy O'Brien

Imagine a classroom where every student is so immersed in reading that they don't want to stop. A place that is buzzing with the energy of student-driven learning. Where students shout, whisper, and play with lines from Shakespeare and other authors. Where small groups discuss, with textual evidence and passion, which parts of a text are the most compelling and how to perform them effectively. Where all students bring their identities and customs, their whole selves, to fresh performances of juicy scenes. Where every student experiences firsthand that literary language is *their* language, demanding to be interpreted and reinterpreted, questioned, and yes, even resisted sometimes. Where students are doing the lion's share of the work, and the teacher, who has thoughtfully set up this zone of discovery, is observing from the side. Where joy and rigor work hand in hand. Where everyone is engaged in something that feels important and adventurous. Where every student realizes they can do hard things on their own.

This is a real place. This is *your* classroom as you try the lessons in this book. Yes, *you.*

Will it be perfect all the time? Heck no. Will it be messy, especially at first? Almost certainly. Will you have to take risks? Yes.

Does this way of teaching really work? You bet.

Don't take our word for it, though. For four decades, the Folger has been working with teachers on what has become known as the Folger Method, and here's a small sample of what teachers—mostly middle and high school teachers—have had to say:

- *"With the Folger Method, my students are reading more deeply than they ever have before. They are breaking down language and really understanding it."*

- *"I was unsure of myself and my ability to tackle Shakespeare, but this has been empowering."*

- *"Students complain when it's time to leave. I have gleefully stepped back so they can create scenes, shout words and lines, and cut speeches. They volunteer to read aloud even when reading aloud is hard for them. We dive in and focus on the words. It's working."*

- *"Over the course of this Folger unit, I've seen amazing things in my special education students. This one student has had an entire transformation—like, fellow teachers are asking me what happened. Before, he always had great pronunciation and sounded fluent, but he could never really understand what it was he was saying. And then all of a sudden in the middle of this play, something clicked. I think it's because he has all these strategies for understanding the words on the page now."*

- *"The Folger Method didn't just transform how I teach Shakespeare—it's changed how I teach everything."*

Great, but what *is* the Folger Method, exactly?

It is a transformative way of approaching complex texts. (And not just Shakespeare, but any complex text.) Consisting of both principles and practices, it provides a framework for everything that goes into great teaching: designing, planning, assessing, reflecting, revising, communicating, guiding, growing, listening, laughing, learning—all of it.

Behind it all is a precise, tried-and-true philosophy that we've broken down into 8 parts.

8 Foundational Principles

The more you practice this way of teaching, the more you'll see these **8 foundational principles** in action, and the clearer it all becomes. Watching your students move through the lessons in this book will give you (and them) a profound, almost visceral, understanding of these principles. They will become part of the fabric of your classroom. Teaching this way—even if it's completely new to you—will feel intuitive in no time.

1. Shakespeare's language is not a barrier but a portal. The language is what enables students to discover amazing things in the texts, the world, and themselves.

2. All students and teachers deserve the real thing—whether it's Shakespeare's original language, primary source materials, new information that expands our understanding of history, or honest conversations about tough issues that the plays present.

3. Give up Shakespeare worship. If your Shakespeare lives on a pedestal, take him down and move him to a space where he can talk to everyday people and great writers like Toni Morrison and Julia Alvarez, Frederick Douglass and Joy Harjo, F. Scott Fitzgerald and Azar Nafisi, Amy Tan and George Moses Horton, Jane Austen and Pablo Neruda, James Baldwin and Homer.

4. Throw out themes, tidy explanations, and the idea of a single right interpretation. Resist the urge to wrap up a text with a neat bow, or, as Billy Collins puts it, to tie it to a chair and "torture a confession out of it." With ambiguity comes possibility. Alongside your students, embrace the questions. How liberating!

5. The teacher is not the explainer but rather the architect. Set up the interactions through which your students and Shakespeare discover each other. This might be hard to hear (it was for Corinne at first!), but the helpful teacher is not the one who explains what the text means or who "translates" Shakespeare's words for students. The truly helpful teacher is the one who crafts opportunities for students to be successful at figuring things out for themselves. It's about getting out of the way so students can do things on their own.

6. Set students on fire with excitement about literature. When reading brings mysteries, delights, and surprises, students are motivated to read closely and cite evidence. And they gain confidence in their ability to tackle the next challenge.

7. Amplify the voice of every single student. Shakespeare has something to say to everybody, and everybody has something to say back to Shakespeare. Student voices, both literal and figurative, create the most vibrant and inclusive learning communities. The future of the humanities—and our world—depends on the insights and contributions of *all* students.

As tempting as it may be to impose our own interpretation of the text on students, or to ask students to imitate the brilliant arguments of seasoned scholars, we beg you to resist that urge. Students need to dive into a play and shape and reshape their own interpretations in order to become independent thinkers. Teaching literature is about the sparks that fly when readers of an infinite variety of perspectives engage directly and personally with the text.

8. The Folger Method is a radical engine for equity. Every student can learn this way, and every teacher can teach this way. The goal is to help all students read closely, interrogate actively, and make meaning from texts.

Now let's put these ideas into practice.

The Arc of Learning

The first step to applying these principles in class is understanding the journey, what we call **the arc of learning**, that your students will experience.

The activities in this book are not isolated, interchangeable exercises. They are a complete set of practices that work together to bring the 8 principles to life. Sequencing, scaffolding, pacing, differentiating—it's all here.

And because each of your students is unique, each journey will be unique too. If you teach AP or IB classes, this book will help each of your students navigate their own path and reach rigorous course outcomes, starting right where scholars, editors, directors, and actors start—with the words. If you teach students who have the ability and desire to dive deep—and we mean *deep,* luxuriating in the mysteries and puzzles of complex literature—the Folger Method will enable them to do just that. Alongside these students you probably also have students who need some extra support before diving deep, and these lessons are just as much for them (more on differentiation later). By its very design, this way of teaching is flexible and roomy enough to challenge and support every single learner. Use this book to meet *all* students where they are, give them space to stretch, and be amazed at what they do.

What happens over the course of a Folger unit often astonishes teachers, administrators, families, and students themselves. Remember that spirited classroom from the first paragraph? Pass by and hear students shouting Hermia's and Helena's lines in a cacophony. *(What in the world?)* Poke your head in and watch them mark up their scripts with notes on which words ought to be stressed or cut out entirely, which tone to use when. *(Hmmm . . . this is interesting.)* Walk into the classroom, take a seat, and observe different student performances of the same scene—and a robust whole-class discussion about the textual evidence and knowledge that led to each group's interpretive decisions. Listen to students question and teach one another. *(Whoa! Every single student just totally owned Shakespeare.)*

What at the start might appear simply as a "fun" way to meet Shakespeare's words reveals itself to be a wild and daring, deep and demanding, meaty and memorable learning experience. Behind this magic is a very deliberate design.

From day one, your students will engage directly with the language of the text(s). That's right: There's no "I do, we do, you do" teacher modeling here. Students are always doing, doing, doing. Beginning with single words and lines, your students will learn to read closely and critically and eventually tackle longer pieces of text such as speeches, scenes, text sets, and whole texts. (Real talk: Yes, scaffolding learning by increasing the length and complexity of the language means doing some prep work. It's part of being the architect. Good news: This book has already selected and chunked most of the text for you!) Like other teachers using this method, you will likely notice that pre-reading *is* reading, just in small bites. You'll also notice your students using and reusing strategies. Sometimes you'll revisit a strategy from Week One later in the unit, with a new piece of text or an added layer of complexity. For example, Choral Reading and Cutting a Scene are favorite classroom routines that teachers use multiple times not just in a Shakespeare unit but throughout the school year. Over time, as you progress through the lessons, you will observe your students doing literacy tasks that are increasingly demanding and sophisticated, and you'll all have gained a method to help you tackle any complex text.

The process of speaking lines, interrogating and editing text, negotiating meaning, deciding how language should be embodied and performed, and owning literature—and doing it all without much teacher explanation—is what matters most. Simply put, the process is more important than the product. Don't fret if the final product is not perfect (what human endeavor is "perfect," anyway?). Did the students collaborate to analyze language and create something new? Do they know what they're saying? Have they made Shakespeare's language their own? So what if a group's performance has some awkward pauses or someone mispronounces a word? If your students have been reading actively, asking and answering good questions, and reaching their own evidence-based conclusions, it's all good. The real work happens along the arc, not at the end.

9 Essential Practices

This is the moment in our live workshops when teachers typically tell us how simultaneously *excited* and *nervous* they are about trying the Folger Method.

Excited because the Principles, the Arc, the whole philosophy of turning the learning over to the students, speaks to their own deeply held conviction that all students can do much more than is often asked of them. As one high school English teacher put it, "These Principles express something I know deep down and want to act on."

Nervous because this Folger thing is really different from how most of us were taught in school. Exactly how does a teacher "act on" the 8 Foundational Principles? What happens in class? What does the teacher do and not do? What does the student do and learn? What do teachers and students have to "unlearn" or let go of in order to try this approach?

The answers to these questions lie in the nine core practices of the Folger Method—the 9 Essentials. Within the lessons that follow this chapter, you will find step-by-step instructions for these Essentials right when you need them. For now, we will provide you with a brief overview of each one.

1. Tone and Stress boosts students' confidence in speaking text aloud and explores how a text's meanings are revealed through vocal expression. Students experience firsthand how variations in tone of voice and word stress influence a listener's understanding of subtext. They see and hear that there's no single right way to interpret a text. Longtime teacher and Teaching Shakespeare Institute faculty member Mike Lo-Monico spent a lot of time and expertise developing this!

2. Tossing Words and Lines puts text into students' hands and mouths and gets them up on their feet reading, speaking, and analyzing the language together. Bonus: Students are able to make inferences about the text based on the words they encounter.

3. Two-line Scenes get all students up on their feet, creating and performing two-person mini-scenes. They discover how making collaborative decisions to enact text is exciting and reveals new understandings. They also realize they can encounter a text "cold" and make meaning from it all on their own—dispelling the myth that Shakespeare's language is too dense to understand.

4. Twenty-minute Plays involve the whole class in performing lines of text that becomes an express tour through the play. Early on, students learn and own the story and the language of the play and are motivated to keep reading. Folger Director of Education Peggy O'Brien originated this Essential and has perfected the art of finding the most fun-to-say lines in a play!

5. Choral Reading asks all students to read and reread a text aloud together. By changing what the "chorus" does in each rereading, this exercise gives students multiple opportunities to refine their understanding of the text. Students discover how the simple acts of speaking and rereading strengthen comprehension and analysis—all without any teacher explanation. In the chorus, there's an anonymity that's freeing, especially for English Learners and shy readers. Choral Reading is immersive, low-stakes, and really, really powerful.

6. 3D Lit enables a class or group of students to work together, figuring out (a) what is going on in a scene they have never before read with no explanation and very little help from you, and (b) how to informally act it out, making decisions as they go. This process enables them to refine their understanding as they transform the text from the page to a 3D "stage" in class. Michael Tolaydo, an actor, director, and faculty member of the Teaching Shakespeare Institute, created this groundbreaking Essential.

7. Cutting a Scene gets students close-reading with a purpose by challenging groups to eliminate half the lines from a piece of text while retaining its meaning. Since editors, scholars, directors, actors, and students have been cutting Shakespeare *forever*, yours are in good company. In fulfilling their mission as editors, students will naturally have to examine what the text says and implies, how the scene works, who's who, how language functions, and what's at stake. The fun part? Listening to your students debating which lines should stay or go and what the scene's "meaning" is anyway.

8. Promptbooks engage students in a process of text-based decision-making and collaborative annotation that reflects how they would stage a text. Many teachers and students call promptbooks "annotating with a real purpose." As with other Essentials, promptbooks are useful for students grappling with an unfamiliar text.

9. Group Scenes enable students to put all the pieces together. Students collaborate to select, cut, rehearse, memorize, and perform a scene for their classmates. Sometimes group scenes consist entirely of the original language of the text; other times they might include mashups or adaptations that incorporate home languages, pop culture, and/or the wide world of literature. Students make their own Shakespeares, demonstrating how they have used textual evidence and background knowledge not only to understand but also reinvent complex dramatic language.

A Note on Differentiation

You know better than anyone else that inside every single one of your students is a whole lot of talent and a whole lot of room to improve. Therefore, when we talk about "differentiation," we are not talking about "struggling readers" or "remediation." We are talking about the rich diversity of what everyone brings to—and takes from—the learning. And everyone—*everyone*—has a great deal to bring and take!

So, are we talking about students in your AP or IB classes? Neurodiverse students? Students with IEPs? Nontraditional students? English Learners? So-called "high-fliers"? Yes. All of the above. In other words, differentiation is about hearing, seeing, challenging, supporting, and inspiring each unique learner.

When teachers experience the Folger Method for themselves, they often point out how differentiation is woven right into the Essentials. Because this mode of teaching relies so heavily on student voice, it is inherently personalized.

Beyond this general fact, though, there are several specific ways in which the Folger Method accounts for the variety of learners in your classroom. Allow us to zoom in on just two of them.

Example #1: The Essential called "Two-line Scenes" provides opportunities for students of all reading abilities to be successful. Each student works with a partner to make a "mini-play" from just two lines of Shakespeare. If, in one pair, Student A knows just two words in their assigned line, they can base their performance on those two words, or they can collaborate with their scene partner, Student B, to work out the meaning of the rest of their line. And if Student B knows not only the literal but also the figurative meaning of both lines, they can share their understanding with Student A and work together to take on the additional challenge of expressing subtext with their voices and bodies. Differentiation is happening on two fronts here: first, through the "wiggle room" that allows each student to bring their own knowledge and creativity to the final product (sometimes called "variable outcomes" by learning experts); second, through peer collaboration. Throughout this book, you will see that students are supporting and stretching each other, and developing their own independent thinking skills, thanks to all kinds of grouping configurations.

Example #2: Since much of the Folger Method relies on selecting and chunking text for our students, there is a ready-made structure for matching students with passages that meet them where they are and stretch them to the next level. In this book you will find that a relentless focus on language is one of the best tools you have for differentiating learning. In other words, don't change the task, water anything down, or make it overly complicated—just chunk the text into appropriately challenging parts. (If you teach English Learners and multilingual students—who are used to attending very carefully to language, its sound, its sense, its nuance—all this will strike you as familiar. For more on the unique power of the Folger Method with English Learners, turn to Dr. Christina Porter's excellent essay in this book.)

7 Touchstone Questions

As you jump into this book and these lessons, try using the following "Touchstone Questions" as your guide to reflecting on your own teaching. Think of them as a kind of checklist for student-driven, language-focused learning. Like everything else in this book, they are grounded in the 8 Foundational Principles.

If you can answer "yes" to each Touchstone Question, there must be some serious sparks flying in your classroom!

1. Did I, the teacher, get out of the way and let students own their learning?

2. Is the language of the text(s) front and center?

3. Are the words of the text in ALL students' mouths?

4. Are students collaborating to develop their own interpretations?

5. Are students daring to grapple with complex language and issues in the text?

6. Has every voice been included and honored?

7. Am I always giving students the real thing, whether it's Shakespeare's language, or primary sources, or supporting tough conversations as prompted by the text?

You've Got This

The Folger Method is proof of what's possible when we as teachers step back and let students own their learning. When we teachers realize we don't need to have all the answers. When students are invited to question and grapple. When they approach language with curiosity and care. When they tackle the real thing. When everyone tries new challenges, takes big risks, and supports one another along the way. When all students realize they can do hard things on their own.

You have everything you need to make this happen. We believe in you and can't wait to hear how it goes.

A Midsummer Night's Dream Day-by-Day: The Five-Week Unit Plan

TEACHER-TO-TEACHER THOUGHTS AND THE GAME
PLAN FOR THIS *A MIDSUMMER NIGHT'S DREAM*

Jessica Cakrasenjaya Zeiss and Vidula Plante

Teacher-to-Teacher Thoughts

We're both eager to get busy with you on *A Midsummer Night's Dream*! Over the course of 5 weeks, your students will be close-reading, collaborating, talking, listening, and making Shakespeare's language, characters, and this play their own. They'll be putting together their own interpretations of *A Midsummer Night's Dream*. Not your interpretation or that of any scholar, but their own, achieved by the close work and analysis that you will set up for them. Does this sound improbable? For all of your students? It's not. They'll be out of their seats. Your classroom will be loud sometimes, loud with passionate discussions, collaboration, scene work, and excitement. During the first 4 weeks, you and they will discover the play via the Folger Method and the Folger Essentials, which connect students directly with the language and everything that comes after that. Students dive into the discovery and active learning that you and the Essentials set up for them. You'll see that students will do their own heavy lifting. And your students will be more engaged and more invested because they'll be in it, making their own decisions based on what they are reading and observing, on who they are, and on what they have learned and believe. This makes for great learning for them, and we learn a lot too!

Week 5 consists of their final projects, which are their final assessments. They are on their own—using all they have learned in the first 4 weeks as they work in groups to select, annotate, cut, cast, and perform a scene from *Midsummer*. They work all week on this . . . and on the last day, your classroom or hallway or multipurpose room or empty gym is transformed into a *Midsummer* festival like no other.

A Midsummer Night's Dream . . . what about this play? Fairies. People in love. Bumbling actors. Mix-ups and misunderstandings. What could be funnier? Yet it's more intriguing and more compelling than it seems at first. As students get under the surface, they see that nothing is exactly as it seems. The actors can't get out of their own way, the lovers are angry with each other, and the fairies are fighting. Lots of power struggles. And is love really that complex?

Wait, isn't *Midsummer* supposed to be a comedy? What about that fairy in love with an ass? Yes, that's funny, but Titania's infatuation is due to Oberon's plot to win their argument. And what are they arguing over? An Indian boy and who he belongs to. He's an important force in this play, and yet . . . he does not have one line in this play. Why doesn't he get a voice?

What about those workmen trying to put on a play? Also funny, but bumbling though they are, they show a love for their craft and dedication—even though nobody will take them seriously, they are serious! And they are determined to put on a play regardless of the obstacles.

What about those lovers? One minute there's a love triangle, in the next minute it collapses. Okay, that's funny, too. But at the end of the play, one of the lovers remains under the influence of the magical potion. Does this play have a happy ending after all? Who actually gets what they want at the end of the play?

A Midsummer Night's Dream is a play with great language, humor, and so many other aspects to dig into. Students will absolutely get into those—stories, characters, and the deeper questions. They will stop waiting for the "right" answer from you, because they will learn pretty quickly that there is no one right answer, that we have to look to the language for clues. And they will collaborate on how to dig in and find the answer. They'll be working for their own understanding.

Our *A Midsummer Night's Dream* lessons invite a deeper look into the big ideas of agency, voice, and power. Confronting these ideas in Shakespeare helps students consider how they are present in their own worlds. Putting Shakespeare in conversation with other authors helps to develop their thinking in this way. In working with and owning Shakespeare's language, and at the same time connecting him with other authors, doors and windows start to open up for students. Then the fun really starts, for them *and you too*.

Working on this part of *The Folger Guide to Teaching A Midsummer Night's Dream* has caused us to think a lot about our own experiences as students. Fast-forward to our teacher-selves: Jess is a public high school (grades 9–12) teacher in Iowa and Vidula is a public middle school (6–8) teacher in Massachusetts. Though we are a generation apart and miles apart, each of us had the same experience as students. We both distinctly remember sitting at our desks in high school and reading a Shakespeare play out loud. We'd read . . . and then the teacher would tell us what the lines meant and what happened in the play. When we started out as teachers, our students sat at their desks and read the text out loud. Then we would tell our kids what the lines meant and what happened in the play. It was dreary. We knew it didn't work for us as students, so why did we carry those experiences forward to our students? Because we didn't imagine there was any other way.

Here comes the Folger. The Folger Method works for both middle and high school students. And college students. It works for all students. It improves their ability to read closely, to cite evidence from the text, and to approach complex texts (not just Shakespeare!) with confidence. It gives students the power of agency. It freed us from the misconception that we had to explain everything to our students, that they couldn't understand any of this by themselves.

Every teacher can teach this way. You don't need all the background information about Shakespeare's life. Please skip it; they can get that on the internet. Instead, we jump right in with getting Shakespeare's words into every student's mouth. In your classroom, it can be anxiety-provoking to take a risk in teaching this way—to do something different from how you learned or what your peers are doing. Go for it, though! You will see that it's totally worth it. Don't worry if students don't "get" it immediately. Students will collaborate, perform, and "get" multiple interpretations instead of a single correct answer. And while you stay out of the way and let their learning process proceed, you are the one who set up all the connections and caused it to happen!

Some kids—and adults too—believe Shakespeare is inaccessible and only for "smart" people. This is nonsense. All students and teachers deserve the real thing—Shakespeare's language, the complexities that characters bring—and can grapple with the real thing. The real thing is not inaccessible. You're here because you want something different or something more for ALL of your students, and yourself too. In your teaching not only of Shakespeare but of all complex texts. We—and the Folger Shakespeare Library—are pleased to hand you this version of something more, and the support to make it happen in your classroom!

The Game Plan for *A Midsummer Night's Dream*

We know you're busy. Even so, take a few minutes and go through the chapter on the Folger Method (page 39) again. It's a quick read and it will give you the principles and the framework that are the foundations of the Folger Method.

You'll notice that we haven't addressed homework. This work can be done without homework or you can have your students read the scenes the night before to prepare for the next class. You could also give a homework assignment after a day's activity to have kids further reflect on what happened in class. You know your students and your school's expectations best.

The lessons come ready with all the instructions and handouts/materials that you need. The day-by-day chart outlines each lesson. They are carefully sequenced so that they bring all students into the text—then expand their horizons as they dive into the play, making observations about the text, characters, and what's going on in the play. While you're making your way through the play together, their confidence and independence will build as you go. When Week 5 rolls around, they will be ready and geared up to take on their final projects/final assessment!

DAY-BY-DAY

Week/Act	Questions guiding exploration of the play	Lessons
Week One	What?! Shakespeare *isn't* hard to understand? What's going on in this play anyway? How will we go about reading and understanding *A Midsummer Night's Dream*?	**1.** The First Taste of *A Midsummer Night's Dream*: All Language and Action! **2.** Your Students Produce Their Own *Midsummer*! **3.** Shakespeare in the Larger World: Essential Context **4.** *Midsummer* Act 1, Scene 1 on Its Feet – Part 1 **5.** *Midsummer* Act 1, Scene 1 on Its Feet – Part 2
Week Two	Who wants what? Where are the conflicts and what causes them? Does anyone get what they want? What is beauty, and who defines it?	**6.** Helena's Decision: A Deeper Dive into 1.1 **7.** Oberon and Titania's Conflict: A Deep Dive into 2.1 **8.** Hermia and Helena: Friends? Frenemies? **9.** Getting the Lovers Off the Page: Promptbooks! **10.** Exploring Ideas of Beauty: Tagore's "Krishnakoli" Talks Back to Shakespeare *A Midsummer Night's Dream*, 3.2
Week Three	Who has the power in *A Midsummer Night's Dream*? How do we know? What do writers from other centuries and cultures have to say about power? What do magic and power have to do with each other?	**11.** Where Is the Indian Boy?: Voice and/or the Lack of It in *Midsummer* **12.** The Mechanicals' Path: Getting Them into the Action **13.** Power and Representation Across the Sweep of Literature: Chimamanda Adichie and Shakespeare **14.** Students Put Adichie and Shakespeare in Conversation **15.** "Fetch Me That Flower": The Story of That Special Flower, in Relay!

Week Four	Things begin to come together . . . or do they? What is clearer? What still seems messy? What could happen in Act 5 to make it all come out right?	**16.** Beginning to Weave It All Together – Part 1, Digging In **17.** Beginning to Weave It All Together – Part 2, Acting Out **18.** Exploring 4.1 in Two Different Ways – Perspective #1 **19.** Exploring 4.1 in Two Different Ways – Perspective #2 **20.** Refresher on the Power of Movement: The Dumb-Show
Week Five	YOUR Shakespeare!	**21.** Your Final Projects! **22.** Your Final Project: Making *A Midsummer Night's Dream* Your Own **23.** The Final Project: Your Own *A Midsummer Night's Dream,* Performed!

WEEK ONE: LESSON 1

The First Taste of *A Midsummer Night's Dream*: All Language and Action!

Here's What We're Doing Today and Why

Today we begin *A Midsummer Night's Dream,* and we'll start with the basics. We're going to get the words right into the kids' mouths and let them play. Let's be honest: texts read by anyone in a robot-like way takes away the excitement, fun, and meaning of those words! With these Folger Essentials, students can see how changing and playing with the tone and stress of words can make different meanings. This is an essential step that the kids will build on throughout these five weeks as they go from word, to line, to scene, to the whole play.

In the second part of the lesson, they will collaborate with a partner and make up their own scenes with juicy lines from all over *A Midsummer Night's Dream.* This will let them have a little taste of what is in the play, and the fun of fooling around with these lines. An important part of Two-line Scenes is limiting both the time and the amount of text—this makes the task doable and moves students right to decision-making on their own. The lines can go in any order. You'll be impressed with how your kids make meaning of the text as they build their confidence. And you, the teacher, are appropriately out of the way!

We'll end class with a Reflection Round. We use these a lot at the Folger—they are the magic that pulls everything together at the end of class. And they are a chance for all students to share what they have learned that day in class and for them—and you—to hear from one another. Even the quiet ones. While students speak individually, the experience is collective and gives the class a deeper understanding of what they have just done, allowing students to process their own learning.

What Will I Need?

- The letter "O" written out on the board
- The line "I didn't say he killed our king" written out on the board
- Lines from *A Midsummer Night's Dream* – **RESOURCE #1.1**

How Should I Prepare?

- Set up your room so that there's space for students to stand up and walk around during the lesson and stand in a big circle for the reflection round at the end of the lesson.
- Write "O" and the line "I didn't say he killed our king" written out big enough for all to see.
- Be ready to divide your class into 7 groups.
- 1 copy of **RESOURCE #1.1** – cut into 30 separate strips, one line per strip

Agenda (~ 45-minute class period)

- ❏ Part One: Introduce Tone and Stress (15 minutes)
- ❏ Part Two: Using lines from *A Midsummer Night's Dream* to make a Two-line Scene (20 minutes)
- ❏ Part Three: Wrap-up using Reflection Rounds (10 minutes)

Here's What Students Hear (From You) and (Then What They'll) Do

Part One: We're going to start off by paying attention to something called TONE.

1. Let's review/discuss the idea of tone for a bit:

   a. Sometimes what people say is different from how they feel. Can anyone give us an example of that? When what someone *said* seems different from what they *mean*?

   b. Have you HEARD a friend say "I'm fine," but you know they're not really fine?

   c. Say "I'm fine" with a happy tone. Now say "I'm fine" with an angry tone.

   d. How can you tell that they're not really fine through their voice?

2. So now, let's think about tone:

   a. We're going to start with a very complex and complicated word—the letter O. Shakespeare uses it all the time! You see this big "O" on the board. Let's all say "O" together. I'll count you down: 3-2-1 "O!" Let's do it again! 3-2-1 "O!"

   b. We know feelings behind a word affect our tone of voice. I'm going to read out an emotion, and while I count us down 3-2-1, you think about how you would say O with that emotion behind it. We'll try each emotion a couple of times.

      i. **Angry.** 3-2-1. "O!" Okay!

      ii. **Confused.** 3-2-1. "O!"

      iii. **Surprised.** 3-2-1. "O!"

      iv. **Excited.** 3-2-1. "O!" You got it.

   c. Thoughts on what you just did?

   d. The sound of the feeling behind the word tells us what's going on underneath the words—and the underneath part is called the subtext. Keep this in mind when we're reading aloud today.

3. We've got TONE, and now let's experiment a little with STRESS:

   a. **Stress** is when the speaker puts emphasis on a specific word in a line to create a specific meaning.

   b. Let's all together read this line that's on the board: **I didn't say he killed our king.**

c. Now we're all going to teach each other what stress does to this sentence. I'm going to divide you up quickly into 7 groups. Each group is going to read the whole sentence, but each group will stress a separate word. I'll call out the group and point out the word that you will stress.

Group 1: **I** didn't say he killed our king.

Group 2: I **DIDN'T** say he killed our king.

Group 3: I didn't **SAY** he killed our king.

Group 4: I didn't say **HE** killed our king.

Group 5: I didn't say he **KILLED** our king.

Group 6: I didn't say he killed **OUR** king.

Group 7: I didn't say he killed our **KING**.

d. Quickly, let's go through your lines again and after your group says your line, share what you think the line might mean. What is the meaning you hear when the speakers put stress on that word?

e. Okay! We talked about tone—the feeling or attitude behind the words—and now we've added stress, the emphasis on a specific word to create meaning. These two things help us create more meaning than just the words on the page.

Part Two

1. Now we're going to use what we know about tone and stress and fool around with some lines from *A Midsummer Night's Dream*. (*Hand out strips of paper with lines.*)

2. Everybody, let's all move around the room. Read your line aloud to yourself and try out different tones: try angry . . . confused . . . surprised . . . Don't worry if there are words that are new to you, or that you don't understand. We'll get to all that later. [**TEACHER NOTE:** Let the students play with the language without talking about meaning or pronunciation. Neither of those are important now. If they ask you how to pronounce something, tell them that we had no idea how people pronounced words when Shakespeare was writing plays, so they should take a shot at pronouncing it themselves.]

   Keep walking around the room and try out stressing different words in your line. How does that change the meaning of the line?

3. Now FREEZE! The person you're standing closest to will be your partner. You and your partner will have 5 minutes to practice making a mini-scene using just your two lines. Add some action to spice up your scene. Then we are all going to share. [**TEACHER NOTE:** It's important to limit their time here. Don't offer scene suggestions, but give lots of encouragement. This is you giving all the students direct access to the text without you as the explainer.]

4. Let's share these great scenes. We'll make a big circle. On your turn, you and your partner step forward into the circle and share your scene. When you're

done, the next duo will take their turn. We'll have wild applause, and we'll all celebrate one another.

5. You've done a great job—all of you acting Shakespeare!

6. Let's stay in this circle to do some predicting. What do you think the lines might tell you about the play? How do you know? What do you think will happen in this play? [**TEACHER NOTE:** Don't correct, but do encourage students to connect their prediction to specific words and lines.]

7. Excellent job, everyone!

Part Three: Now we're all going to reflect a bit on all that you have just done—on your first day of our Shakespeare work!

[**TEACHER NOTE:** Remember:

- This is a time for every voice to be heard.

- Expect students to share, but let them pass if they choose to, especially in the early days of the unit.

- *YOU* participate in this process, too! It's important for students to see that you're experiencing and reflecting on today's lesson as part of the class.]

1. I'll start us off with the beginning of a sentence, and we'll go around the circle and each of us—including me—will finish the sentence. When it's your turn, keep it to just one sentence. And we'll let each of us speak without interrupting, responding, or giving feedback to what they said. And that includes me too!

2. We'll do 3 rounds today. The first is **"I noticed that . . ."** Who will start? (*A student volunteers. After the student speaks, the next person in the circle takes a turn.*)

3. Now that everybody has done that round, the second is **"I was surprised that . . ."**

4. Last one: **"I learned that . . ."**

5. Thanks, everybody! You've made a great start!

Here's What Just Happened in Class

- Students saw firsthand how Shakespeare's language is not as difficult as they may have initially thought. And how fun and exciting it can actually be!

- Students explored how the tone of speaking something can impact meaning.

- Students explored how stressing individual words can impact meaning.

- Students made predictions based on textual evidence from *A Midsummer Night's Dream*.

- Students used Shakespeare's language to create their own stories without you (the teacher) explaining anything.

- Students reflected on their own learning—and shared these reflections—through the reflection round.

RESOURCE #1.1

Lines from *A Midsummer Night's Dream*

1. As she is mine, I may dispose of her.

2. The more I hate, the more he follows me.

3. The more I love, the more he hateth me.

4. Let me play the lion too!

5. I love thee not, therefore pursue me not.

6. Hence, get thee gone, and follow me no more.

7. For I am sick when I do look on thee.

8. And I am sick when I look not on you.

9. O monstrous! O strange! We are haunted.

10. Thou art as wise as thou art beautiful.

11. You juggler, you cankerblossom, You thief of love!

12. How answer you that?

13. I have a device to make all well.

14. Pray, master, fly, masters! Help!

15. O Bottom, thou art changed! What do I see on thee?

16. What do you see? You see an ass-head of your own, do you?

17. This is to make an ass of me, to fright me, if they could.

18. On the first view to say, to swear, I love thee.

19. And I do love thee.

20. O, why rebuke you him that loves you so?

21. For thou, I fear, hast given me cause to curse.

22. Nor is he dead, for aught that I can tell.

23. O dainty duck! O dear!

24. Can you not hate me, as I know you do.

25. The hate I bear thee made me leave thee so?

26. Should I hurt her, strike her, kill her dead?

27. Although I hate her, I'll not harm her so.

28. I do hate thee and love Helena.

29. Come, my queen, take hands with me.

30. Methought I was enamored of an ass.

Your Students Produce Their Own *Midsummer*!

Here's What We're Doing and Why

Yesterday, for starters, it was students bringing their own meaning to Shakespeare's words by adding tone, stress, and action. We're still asking them to do that, but now we're adding another layer by showing them how their lines tell the story of the play. In this Folger Essential, students themselves create a 20-Minute version of *Midsummer.* This empowers them to create their own express tour of the story while you get out of the way! It involves the whole class close-reading, collaborating, and performing—and at the same time, they're learning the story—a very handy window into the whole play.

If you are worried that knowing the whole story will ruin the play for your students, let us help you with that: most of the time, people who went to see a Shakespeare play in his time knew the story before they got there—because Shakespeare based his plays on many familiar stories. Your students work with "juicy" lines from throughout the play and you organize the order of their performance with your narration. It also sets the stage for the collaboration that is so essential to creating the culture that they will benefit from all the way through this unit. The collaborative achievement at the end of the lesson is electric, and it's always fun when students remember these lines as they come across them later in the play.

What Will I Need?

- Student lines – **RESOURCE #1.2A**
- Teacher narrative – **RESOURCE #1.2B**

How Should I Prepare?

- Set up your classroom for students to work in small groups and make space for students to make a circle for the performances and reflection round.
- Copy of the student lines and cut them out – **RESOURCE #1.2A**
- Copy of the teacher narrative – **RESOURCE #1.2B**
- Be ready to put your students in groups of 2 or 3.

Agenda (~ 45-minute class period)

- ❏ Part One: Review & Set-up (5 minutes)
- ❏ Part Two: Groups Practice (10 minutes)
- ❏ Part Three: Performance (20 minutes)
- ❏ Part Four: Reflection Round (10 minutes)

Here's What Students Hear (From You) and (Then What They'll) Do

Part One: Review & Set-up

1. Today you are going to put on your own production of *A Midsummer Night's Dream!* We're going to start by getting into small groups. Let's call them acting companies.

2. I'm going to give each group a few lines.

[**TEACHER NOTE:** There are 28 lines in all; divide them up as evenly as you can. It's great if each group can have 2 to 3 lines to perform.]

3. You're going to rehearse your lines quickly! Then we'll all collaborate on a production of *A Midsummer Night's Dream*. When you perform them, your group will all say the lines together and add some action to the lines.

4. Don't worry about the numbers on your line sheets. I'll explain them later. And don't worry at all that you don't know the story of the play . . . because you will before class is over!

5. Here's some advice about how to practice/rehearse your lines:
   - Work with one line at a time.
   - Read it out loud together as a group.
   - Make decisions about the line: How will you say it? And what physical action will you add? There is no right way to act out any of these lines. You all decide!
   - Practice it together (with tone, stress, and movement) a few times.

Part Two: Acting Companies Rehearse

You have 10 minutes to rehearse your lines!

[**TEACHER NOTE:** Step back so students work directly with each other and the text. Encourage the group to make their decisions based on the lines they have, and not on the larger plot of the play if they happen to know it already.]

Part Three: Performance

1. Okay, performance time! When you are not performing, you are the attentive audience!

2. I'm going to read the story of the play (**RESOURCE #1.2B**). Next to each line on your paper is a number. When I call your number, your group will run into this open area as fast as you all can to perform your line. We'll have wild applause after each performance. Then, I will continue to read, call the next number, and so on. Take a moment right now to put your lines in order by number.

[**TEACHER NOTE:** This activity is high energy, so having students run up to the "stage" and go back to the "audience" helps to keep the activity moving.]

3. Welcome to our very special production of *A Midsummer Night's Dream!* I'll read

the story, and when I call out a number, it's your turn to perform. And let's have applause by all for all!

4. Fantastic performance! Everyone stand up! Actors, take a bow. And, applause! Now let's head to the reflection round.

Part Four: Now we'll reflect for a few minutes on what you all just did!

1. Remember from yesterday . . . I'll start us off with the beginning of a sentence, and we'll go around the circle and each of us—including me—will finish the sentence. When it's your turn, keep it to one sentence. And we'll let each of us speak without interrupting, responding, or giving feedback to what they said. And that includes me too!

2. We'll do two rounds today. Let's start with "**I noticed that . . .**" Who will start? And then we'll just continue on around the group.

3. Now that everybody has done that round, let's go to "**I was surprised that . . .**"

4. Great job, everybody!

Here's What Just Happened in Class

- Students created their own production of *A Midsummer Night's Dream.*

- Students learned the story of the play and lots of key lines too.

- Students own a piece of Shakespeare's language, by collaborating to perform it.

- Students worked together to speedily create a group performance of the text that becomes part of the class understanding.

- Students (and YOU) created a supportive environment that celebrates student choices and decisions.

RESOURCE #1.2A

20-Minute *Midsummer* Lines

1. THE COURSE OF TRUE LOVE NEVER DID RUN SMOOTH!

2. LORD, WHAT FOOLS THESE MORTALS BE!

3. I WOOED THEE WITH MY SWORD . . . BUT NOW I WILL WED THEE . . . WITH POMP, WITH TRIUMPH, AND WITH REVELING!

4. FULL OF VEXATION COME I, WITH COMPLAINT AGAINST MY CHILD!

5. AS SHE IS MINE, I MAY DISPOSE OF HER, WHICH SHALL BE EITHER TO [DEMETRIUS] . . . OR TO HER DEATH!

6. I SWEAR TO THEE BY CUPID'S STRONGEST BOW

7. THE MORE I LOVE, THE MORE HE HATETH ME!

8. I AM YOUR SPANIEL!

9. IS ALL OUR COMPANY HERE?

10. WHAT IS PYRAMUS—A LOVER OR A TYRANT?

11. WE WILL MEET AND THERE WE WILL REHEARSE MOST OBSCENELY AND COURAGEOUSLY!

12. AM NOT I THY LORD?

13. I WILL NOT PART WITH HIM!

14. I AM THAT MERRY WANDERER OF THE NIGHT!

15. I LOVE THEE NOT! THEREFORE PURSUE ME NOT!

16. GODDESS, NYMPH, PERFECT, DIVINE!

17. VILE THING, LET LOOSE!

18. I YIELD YOU UP MY HEART

19. YOU JUGGLER! YOU CANKERBLOSSOM! YOU THIEF OF LOVE!

20. I AM NOT YET SO LOW BUT THAT MY NAILS CAN REACH UNTO THINE EYES

21. WILL NOT THE LADIES BE AFEARED OF THE LION?

22. YOU CAN NEVER BRING IN A WALL!

23. O MONSTROUS! O STRANGE! WE ARE HAUNTED!

24. I WILL WIND THEE IN MY ARMS

25. METHOUGHT I WAS ENAMORED OF AN ASS!

26. MY LOVE, MY LIFE, MY SOUL, FAIR HELENA!

27. THUS I DIE . . . NOW AM I DEAD. NOW AM I FLED . . . NOW DIE, DIE, DIE, DIE, DIE!

28. SWEET FRIENDS, TO BED!

20-Minute *A Midsummer Night's Dream*

Once upon a time in Athens . . . in the court, in the forest, and in fairyland . . . there is A LOT going on [**1. THE COURSE OF TRUE LOVE NEVER DID RUN SMOOTH!**]. In *A MIDSUMMER NIGHT'S DREAM*, there's . . . happiness/unhappiness, love/anger, confusion, fear, and even an angry parent . . . just like real life, right? Oh, and there's also revenge, mischief, and magic [**2. LORD, WHAT FOOLS THESE MORTALS BE!**].

Theseus, the Duke of Athens, is about to get married to Hippolyta, the Amazon Queen [**3. I WOOED THEE WITH MY SWORD . . . BUT NOW I WILL WED THEE . . . WITH POMP, WITH TRIUMPH, AND WITH REVELING!**].

Also in Athens, Egeus is furious with his daughter, Hermia [**4. FULL OF VEXATION COME I, WITH COMPLAINT AGAINST MY CHILD!**]. He wants his daughter to marry Demetrius, but she's in love with some other guy named Lysander. Egeus tells the Duke [**5. AS SHE IS MINE, I MAY DISPOSE OF HER, WHICH SHALL BE EITHER TO [DEMETRIUS] . . . OR TO HER DEATH!**]. Hermia has four days to decide her fate.

So here's the "tea" (or situation):

- Hermia loves Lysander and Lysander loves Hermia [**6. I SWEAR TO THEE BY CUPID'S STRONGEST BOW**]

- Hermia's BFF Helena loves Demetrius, but . . . Demetrius loves Hermia [**7. THE MORE I LOVE, THE MORE HE HATETH ME!**].

- And NOBODY loves Helena [**8. I AM YOUR SPANIEL!**].

Meanwhile, a group of workmen are preparing to perform a play about doomed love for the Duke and Hippolyta's wedding. And they begin to practice [**9. IS ALL OUR COMPANY HERE?**]. They have the whole discussion about who plays whom [**10. WHAT IS PYRAMUS—A LOVER OR A TYRANT?**] and they schedule their next rehearsal [**11. WE WILL MEET AND THERE WE WILL REHEARSE MOST OBSCENELY AND COURAGEOUSLY!**].

There's a lot going on in the play, and we're just getting started!

In the fairy kingdom, Oberon and Titania, king and queen of the fairies, are arguing over a darling orphaned Indian boy. Each wants to take care of him. Titania won't bend to Oberon's will, and it makes him so angry, he says [**12. AM NOT I THY LORD?**]. And she says [**13. I WILL NOT PART WITH HIM!**]. Oberon's not happy.

In the forest, we meet Puck (a.k.a. Robin Goodfellow), who is kind of Oberon's minion [**14. I AM THAT MERRY WANDERER OF THE NIGHT!**]. When the lovers escape to the forest to straighten things out, Puck starts working the fairy magic. But mistakes are made. Things get all mixed up [**15. I LOVE THEE NOT! THEREFORE PURSUE ME NOT!**] and [**16. GODDESS, NYMPH, PERFECT, DIVINE!**] and [**17. VILE THING, LET LOOSE!**] and [**18. I YIELD YOU UP MY HEART**]. There's also a pretty epic fight [**19. YOU JUGGLER! YOU CANKERBLOSSOM! YOU THIEF OF LOVE!**] and [**20. I AM NOT YET SO LOW BUT THAT MY NAILS CAN REACH UNTO THINE EYES**]. It's all a big mess!

And through all of this . . . those workmen keep rehearsing that play! They worry about all kinds of things [**21. WILL NOT THE LADIES BE AFEARED OF THE LION?**] and the set [**22. YOU CAN NEVER BRING IN A WALL!**].

Puck also helps with Oberon's revenge on Titania: he turns one of the workmen-actors into a kind of ass (a donkey kind of ass), causing the workmen to say [**23. O MONSTROUS! O STRANGE! WE ARE HAUNTED!**]. But the Fairy Queen falls in love with the ass. She says [**24. I WILL WIND THEE IN MY ARMS**].

All the happy stuff comes right at the end:

- Titania and Oberon make up [**25. METHOUGHT I WAS ENAMORED OF AN ASS!**].

- The lovers are happily arranged [**26. MY LOVE, MY LIFE, MY SOUL, FAIR HELENA!**] and there's a triple wedding! Finally, Hermia's father can relax.

Then it's time for the play by the workmen! In the play, there's a fabulous death [**27. THUS I DIE . . . NOW AM I DEAD. NOW AM I FLED . . . NOW DIE, DIE, DIE, DIE, DIE!**]. And everyone obeys Theseus's last command [**28. SWEET FRIENDS, TO BED!**]. Those couples loved the play, and we have all loved putting on *this* play—a very special, once-in-a-lifetime *A MIDSUMMER NIGHT'S DREAM!*

Shakespeare in the Larger World: Essential Context

Here's What We're Doing and Why

The universe of Shakespeare is bigger, more diverse, and more interesting than your students may realize. This lesson is all about giving everyone a glimpse into some of the most expansive, exciting, and surprising aspects of studying Shakespeare, his words, and his world. It zooms out beyond *A Midsummer Night's Dream* for a moment!

By the end of this lesson, students will have examined their own ideas about Shakespeare's world. They will have enlarged their sense of history by studying 5 primary source documents spanning the 1600s to the 1900s, and thinking about 6 mind-blowing facts. They will have reflected on the wide world of Shakespeare and their place in it.

What Will I Need?

- Portrait of Abd el-Ouahed ben Messaoud ben Mohammed Anoun, Moroccan Ambassador to Queen Elizabeth I, ca. 1600 – **RESOURCE #1.3A**

- John Smith's Map of Virginia and the Chesapeake, a 1631 copy of the 1612 original – **RESOURCE #1.3B**

- Portraits by Wenceslaus Hollar, 1645 – **RESOURCE #1.3C**

- Ira Aldridge's First Appearance at Covent Garden as Othello, 1833 – **RESOURCE #1.3D**

- *Romeo y Julieta*, "Prologo," Pablo Neruda, written in 1964, published in 2001 – **RESOURCE #1.3E**

- 6 Mind-blowing Facts about Shakespeare and History – **RESOURCE #1.3F**

- Large paper, markers, and/or Post-it Notes for the gallery walk that we're calling "Document Speed Dating"

How Should I Prepare?

- Set up your classroom for "Document Speed Dating": Post the documents at various stations around the room, and make sure that (1) the images are big and clear enough for everyone to see details and (2) there's enough space around each document for students to respond in writing. You can use whiteboards, butcher paper, or Post-it Notes—just make sure that there's room for everyone to "talk back" to each image.

- Organize your students into 5 groups, each one starting at a different station.

Agenda (~ 45-minute class period)

- ❏ Part One: Prior Knowledge Free Write (7 minutes)

- ❏ Part Two: Document Speed Dating Instructions & Exercise (24 minutes)

❏ Part Three: The List (6 minutes)

❏ Part Four: Reflection Round (8 minutes)

Here's What Students Hear (From You) and (Then What They'll) Do

Part One: Prior Knowledge Free Write

1. **Write:** Jot down your thoughts on any of the following questions. When you imagine the world of Shakespeare, what do you see? What images come to your mind? Who are the people? What do they look and sound like? What are the places and objects? What's the vibe?

2. **Talk:** Turn to a classmate and discuss what each of you wrote.

3. **Share:** As a class, we'll share the images and ideas that arose in the paired conversations.

[**TEACHER NOTE:** Record student responses on the board in a broad way—no need to be exhaustive here. The point is to capture things like "people in ruffs and crowns" or "outdoor theaters" or "white Europeans" or "candlelight and quills" or "street fighting" or "plague" or "boring" or "lively" or "smelly clothes" or "harp music"—whatever comes to your students' minds. Welcome all responses without editorializing.]

Part Two: Document Speed Dating

1. Now you are going to meet actual historical documents from the world of Shakespeare. Your job is to look very closely at what you see and write down your observations right alongside the document. Keeping in mind your earlier impressions of Shakespeare's world, what in each image jumps out at you? What do you wonder about? [**TEACHER NOTE:** You can keep the "What in the image jumps out at you?" prompt posted for students to see throughout this exercise.]

2. Get into your groups and begin at your assigned station. Each group should be at a different station.

3. You will have roughly 3 minutes at each station. As a group, move to the next station when you hear "Next!" Continue until every group has studied and written observations about all 5 documents.

4. Now that everyone has gone on a "speed date" with each document, return to your seat and find a partner. With this partner, discuss the main things that jumped out at you from these documents. Did anything surprise you? Did you learn anything new about the world of Shakespeare? We'll share more as a whole class in a few moments.

Part Three: The List

Let's look at the list of "6 Mind-blowing Facts about Shakespeare and History"—**RESOURCE #1.3F**. Let's have 6 volunteers to read each fact aloud. We'll save discussion for the reflection round below.

Part Four: Reflection Round

1. Now it's time for each of you to share your reflections on today's learning. We'll do 2 rounds. Remember, just one sentence and not more at this point. We want to hear from EVERY voice!

2. First, finish the sentence, "Something that changed my original mental picture of Shakespeare's world was . . ."

3. Second, finish the sentence, "I am still wondering . . ."

Here's What Just Happened in Class

- Students have identified and interrogated their prior knowledge—and assumptions—of Shakespeare's world.

- Students have examined 5 different primary source documents spanning 4 centuries in order to enlarge their understanding of Shakespeare and history. They have seen for themselves that Shakespeare's Britain was multicultural and very much connected to the Americas.

- Students know important and surprising facts about the wide world of Shakespeare.

RESOURCE #1.3A

Abd el-Ouahed ben Messaoud ben Mohammed Anoun,
Ambassador from Morocco to the court of Queen Elizabeth I,
beginning in 1600

RESOURCE #1.3B

John Smith's Map of Virginia and the Chesapeake, a 1631 copy of the 1612 original

RESOURCE #1.3C

Portraits by Wenceslaus Hollar, made in and around 1645

RESOURCE #1.3D

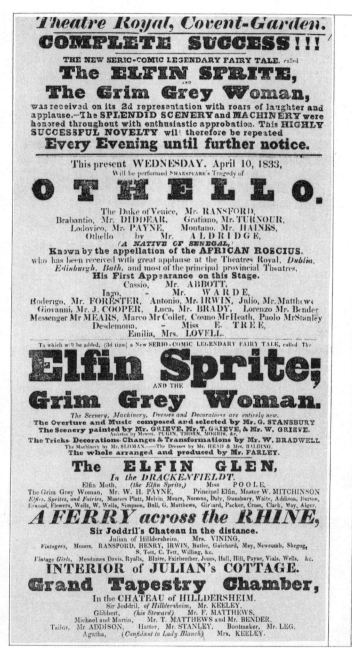

Ira Aldridge's First Appearance at Covent Garden as Othello

RESOURCE #1.3E

PRÓLOGO

ENTRA EL CORO

CORO
En la bella Verona esto sucede:
dos casas ambas en nobleza iguales
con odio antiguo hacen discordia nueva.
La sangre tiñe sus civiles manos.

Dos horas durará en nuestro escenario esta historia: escuchadla con paciencia, suplirá nuestro esfuerzo lo que falte.

Romeo y Julieta, "Prologo," Pablo Neruda,
written 1964, published 2001

6 Mind-blowing Facts about Shakespeare and History

1. There were many people of different ethnicities and religions in Shakespeare's Britain. An important facet of this history: Africans participated in life at many social levels. Many were baptized—Protestant parishes retain the records. Black citizens included merchants, silk weavers, seamstresses, shoemakers, a circumnavigator who sailed with Sir Francis Drake, and a royal musician.

2. During her coronation festivities in 1600, Queen Elizabeth I entertained a large delegation of Muslim African officials, including Moroccan Ambassador Abd el-Ouahed ben Messaoud ben Mohammed Anoun. He returned to court often and served as her advisor. Some think that Shakespeare might have seen him and African diplomats at court and drawn inspiration from them.

3. William Shakespeare was writing plays as English settlers colonized Jamestown, Virginia, in 1607. He is even thought to have based his play *The Tempest* on accounts of the wreck of a ship called the *Sea Venture*, which was on its way to Jamestown.

4. Ira Aldridge was the first Black man and African American actor to play the role of Othello at a professional theater: the Theatre Royal, Covent Garden, London, in 1833. Born in New York City, Aldridge performed Shakespeare all over Europe because as a Black man, he could not have done so in America. He was perhaps the first American star of the international Shakespeare stage. More than 100 years later in 1943, Paul Robeson was only the second Black actor to play Othello in the United States—on Broadway.

5. It was not until 1660 that the first woman actor performed Shakespeare onstage. Until then, men and boys had played all the parts. After this point, though, women took on not just female characters but also male characters. (Hang on for more on Sarah Bernhardt!)

6. Shakespeare's works have been adapted and performed around the globe for centuries, and they have been translated into over 100 languages.

WEEK ONE: LESSON 4

Midsummer Act 1, Scene 1 on Its Feet—Part 1

Here's What We're Doing and Why

At this point, your students have been practicing and gaining confidence with words and lines from *A Midsummer Night's Dream* and learning a bit about the larger Shakespeare universe. Next, you provide the process that they will use to work through the text on their own—without much preparation and without any explanation from you, they will be reading closely and interactively. The Folger Essentials of Choral Reading and 3D Lit will get you there. Students work collaboratively to make meaning of the text, and in tomorrow's lesson, they will use textual evidence to put the scene "on its feet" in an informal performance in which everybody has a role.

As you're skimming through today's agenda, you'll see that your students will read this scene FOUR TIMES. *(Four times!?)* Take a deep breath and trust the process here. They need these multiple readings—all your students—and you'll soon see why. Go for it. This routine of varied readings puts the students at the center of the learning and allows teachers to remove ourselves as the "fountain of knowledge." Important: Continue to resist the urge to correct the pronunciation of words (we don't know how they were pronounced in 1600), or to explain a nifty metaphor that you love, or to provide definitions of words. Your students will find their way together if you give them the time and space to do so. Follow the steps specifically, please. You'll see that all of this has students making their own discoveries and observations, and doing their own learning—and feeling great about it.

We've cut Act 1, scene 1 so that it's a manageable length to work with over two class periods. The free and online Folger Shakespeare (folger.edu/shakespeares-works) is a great resource for us and you too.

Agenda (~ 45-minute class period)

- ❏ Part One: Set-up (5 minutes)
- ❏ Part Two: First Choral Reading (5 minutes)
- ❏ Part Three: Second Reading (10 minutes)
- ❏ Part Four: Third Reading: character to character (10 minutes)
- ❏ Part Five: Fourth Reading: Identifying and defining new words and/or references (10 minutes)
- ❏ Part Six: Closure (5 minutes)

What Will I Need?

- Copies of the scene for the reading (one for each student) – **RESOURCE #1.4**
- Students will need a writing utensil.

How Should I Prepare?

- Set up your classroom in a large circle of students with space in the middle.

Here's What Students Hear (From You) and (Then What They'll) Do

Part One: Set-up

We're going to work with an edited version of Act 1, scene 1 from *A Midsummer Night's Dream*. We're going to work with this script today and tomorrow, so put your name on it and hang on to it. (**RESOURCE #1.4**). We're not going to talk a lot about it up front; we're just going to dive right in.

Part Two: First Reading

1. We're going to read this together in several different ways. These are called Choral Readings—we all read the text aloud together, like a chorus. Let's read this loud, fast, and try to stay together.

[**TEACHER NOTE:** Don't let the energy lag; keep it moving. Don't correct pronunciation. Don't discuss the text. Don't define any words. Students also might be hesitant to read it aloud, but they'll get there.]

Go for it.

2. Thoughts on what that reading felt like? Let's try it again!

Part Three: Second Reading

1. Now we're going to read it again in a different way. Each person will read to an end punctuation mark—when you get to a period, semicolon, exclamation point, dash, or question mark, stop. And then the next person starts where you left off. Read right through a comma, but stop at those end punctuation marks. We'll start at one point in the circle and go around the circle reading the whole scene this way.

2. Take a look at your script. See where those first few end punctuation marks are? Right. Let's go.

[**TEACHER NOTE:** Let students take as much time as they need to make their way through. If they struggle with certain words, that's part of the process. Don't correct or help them, and try to keep students from correcting one another.]

3. Now that you've read this a couple of different ways, let's see what's going on here. I'm going to ask you a few questions about what you might be able to tell is happening here, in this scene.

From what we've done so far and just from this piece of text:

   a. *Who are these people? And how do you know from the text?* [**TEACHER NOTE:** Wait for student response as long as you need to. And they must be able to point to the text to justify their answer. Examples: "Well, somebody's getting married" followed by what's in the text. "There's a father that seems pretty angry" followed by where the text clued them in to that.]

    b. *What is going on here? How do you know that from the text?*

    c. *Where are they? Can you tell? How do you know that from the text?*

[**TEACHER NOTE:** Take 10 to 15 minutes with this, and give them time to think, mull things over, agree or disagree with colleagues. It's all about them discovering, and starting to learn how to do this for themselves. Please do not insert yourself here, even though it may be hard!]

    4. Now check your own understanding for a minute. You can hold up *a closed fist*—that means "Zero, I have NO idea what I just read" OR you can hold up *all five fingers wagging*—that means "I understand every single word of what's going on in this scene" OR you can hold up any number of fingers in between. Let's see your hands and where your understanding might be. There is no right answer here because we're at the beginning of a learning process. Let's see those hands—all good!

[**TEACHER NOTE:** Anything is all good here. Students may give a rating of 0 or 1: that's okay!]

Part Four: Third Reading, Character-to-character reading

    1. Okay, great job—and now we're going to read this again! In another way! In this round, we'll change readers each time the character who is speaking changes. So instead of stopping at an end punctuation, like last time, you will read to the end of whatever that character has to say. And then the next reader/character takes over. We'll keep reading around the circle until everyone has had a chance to read this way.

    2. Fantastic! Okay, now that you've read character-to-character:

        a. *What else have you noticed about these folks? Anything else you want to point out? Share your observations and of course, tell us how you know this from the text.*

        b. *How do they feel about each other? How do you know that from the text?*

        c. *Who seems to have the most power? How do you know that from the text? And who may have the least power? Where does the text tell us that?*

Part Five: Fourth Reading, Discovering new words and/or references

    1. Let's read this scene again in the same way we did last time—character to character. And this time, as we read, mark on your scripts words or ideas that you don't fully understand and that you want to know more about.

Alright, another great reading! What words or ideas have you marked, and together let's see if we can figure out and decide the meaning of those words or ideas. [**TEACHER NOTE:** Students need to own the text, so let them infer meaning together and, if they need to, but only if they need to, they can look up definitions that they want to know. You are setting up and working with them through the tools of discovery. Keep stepping back and let their discoveries proceed.]

Part Six: Taking Stock

Let's see where we're ending up in terms of our understanding. Like we did at the beginning, check your understanding again. You can hold up *a closed fist*—that means "Zero, I have NO idea what I just read" OR you can hold up *all 5 fingers wagging*— that means "I understand every single word of what's going on in this scene" OR you can hold up any number of fingers between 0 and 5. Let's see your hands and where your understanding might be. Again, no right answer here because we're in the midst of learning. Let's see those hands—all good! Do you remember how you rated your understanding after your first reading? Are you making a little progress? And if you aren't, don't be discouraged. You're doing great work here!

[**TEACHER NOTE:** Students may give a rating of 2 or 3, and that's okay! It's super exciting to see students recognize their own improvement in understanding. And did you, as the teacher, act as a connector rather than an explainer today? Yes! You were the connector and the kids are doing ALL the work. Brava/o!]

Here's What Just Happened in Class

- Students used a variety of close-reading strategies to approach a difficult text.

- Students cited textual evidence to support their claims.

- Students evaluated their own learning throughout the process.

- Students gained confidence with using Shakespeare's language.

A Midsummer Night's Dream: 1.1, edited

Enter Theseus and Hippolyta.

THESEUS

Hippolyta, I wooed thee with my sword
And won thy love doing thee injuries,
But I will wed thee with triumph and with reveling.
                         Enter Egeus, Hermia, Lysander, and Demetrius.

EGEUS

Happy be Theseus, our renownèd duke!

THESEUS

Thanks, good Egeus. What's the news with thee?

EGEUS

Full of vexation come I, with complaint
Against my child, my daughter Hermia.—
Stand forth, Demetrius.—My noble lord,
This man hath my consent to marry her.—
Stand forth, Lysander.—And, my gracious duke,
This man hath bewitched the bosom of my child.
I beg the ancient privilege of Athens:
As she is mine, I may dispose of her,
Which shall be either to this gentleman
Or to her death, according to our law.

THESEUS

What say you, Hermia? Be advised, fair maid.
To you, your father should be as a god,
Demetrius is a worthy gentleman.

HERMIA

So is Lysander.
I would my father looked but with my eyes.

THESEUS

Rather your eyes must with his judgment look.

HERMIA

But I beseech your Grace that I may know
The worst that may befall me in this case
If I refuse to wed Demetrius.

THESEUS

Either to die the death or to abjure
Forever the society of men.
Therefore, fair Hermia, question your desires.

HERMIA

My soul consents not to give sovereignty.

THESEUS

Take time to pause, and by the next new moon
(The sealing day betwixt my love and me),
either prepare to die
For disobedience to your father's will,
Or else to wed Demetrius.

DEMETRIUS

Relent, sweet Hermia, and, Lysander, yield
to my certain right.

LYSANDER

You have her father's love, Demetrius.
Let me have Hermia's. Do you marry him.

EGEUS

Scornful Lysander, true, he hath my love;
And she is mine, and all my right of her
I do estate unto Demetrius.

LYSANDER, *to Theseus*

My love is more than his;
My fortunes every way as fairly ranked as Demetrius';
And I am beloved of beauteous Hermia.

WEEK ONE: LESSON 5

Midsummer Act 1, Scene 1 on Its Feet—Part 2

In our last class, students worked collaboratively to make meaning of the text, reading closely and looking for textual evidence. Today they'll use all of that discovery to put the scene "on its feet" in an informal performance. Everyone will participate in this performance, either as an actor or a director. Today students will decide how they want to perform it—and then they'll do so. Students will try out their various decisions on a character's tone, stress, sounds, and actions—all based on the text—on the 3D "stage" in your classroom.

- Set-up & Warm-up (3 minutes)

- Fifth Reading: On your feet (30 minutes)

- Closure (2 minutes)

- Reflection (10 minutes)

What Will I Need?

- Students need their scripts from yesterday – **RESOURCE #1.4**

- Students will need writing utensils

How Should I Prepare?

- Set up your classroom in a large circle with space in the middle.

- Copies of *A Midsummer Night's Dream*: Act 1, scene 1 for all students – **RESOURCE #1.4**

- Be ready to assign actors their parts and director groups.

Part One: Set-up & Warm-up

Let's review our scripts. Who can remind us of some of our observations from yesterday? Just a few as they come to mind?

Part Two: Getting the play on its feet

1. Let's put this scene on its feet! Based on all your knowledge so far, you're going to decide how to perform it. We're doing this to see how this scene might work in performance. We're not worried about where an audience might be sitting, or who can see . . . we're doing this for ourselves, to make it work for ourselves.

2. Where should this scene take place? Are there clues in the text that suggest where the action of this scene might occur? In Shakespeare, there's mostly no one right answer, but sometimes the text gives you clues. How can we arrange the classroom to set the stage? Let's use whatever we've got here to create the location or the setting.

3. I'm going to do the casting today. All of you will participate either as an actor or a director. Actors, you can ONLY speak words from the text—nothing else! And you need to follow the directions given to you by your directors. If you are uncomfortable with a direction, let your director know and why. Directors, I will put you in small groups, and each group will be assigned to direct a specific character. You're going to make the decisions about your assigned character.

[**TEACHER NOTE:** Since the actors can only speak Shakespeare's lines, and since the directors are the ones who will make suggestions about how this scene should go, you might want to give your more verbal or confident students acting parts; that will leave more room for directors to have their opinions known. If you have shy readers, then give them small acting parts. Even though Hippolyta doesn't have any lines, don't let the directors cut her part out. If you have props, you can offer them to the directors to incorporate into the scene.]

4. Okay, now that we have our parts for our actors, let's have the director groups start sitting together.

5. Directors, the decisions about ways to try out this scene are up to you. How should the characters enter the scene? What do they do when they enter? How do they speak their lines? How should certain characters relate to one another? You agree and then direct the actors. You know the text really well, so your knowledge will guide you. Actors, if you're delivering a line and you don't have direction on how to say it or what to do while you're speaking, make sure to ask your directors.

[**TEACHER NOTE:** Don't you direct. Don't even think about it. Encourage student decision-making from the sidelines. This is all about process and not one bit about the product. Use the questions in step 6 any time you feel like the characters are just reading off the page rather than putting the scene on its feet. This will encourage participation.]

6. Now we're about halfway through the scene. Do we need some adjustments? How are our characters doing? Any advice for them?

[**TEACHER NOTE:** Directors should be making decisions together as the actors work through the lines; however, we want to make sure we give each student-director a chance to input their voice in the decision-making. For quieter students, this might mean you have to step in a little to offer them the space to participate. Phrase your question with options incorporated in the questions. For example, should the character enter from left or right? Should the character do this or that?]

7. Okay. Where should we pick back up? Let's go, and run the scene to the end if we can. If not, that's okay too.

8. You did a great job putting Act 1, scene 1 of *Midsummer* on its feet! Let's have a round of enthusiastic applause for our actors and amazing directors!!! In the last two days, you have figured out a whole scene from Shakespeare yourselves—without any footnotes or any explanation from me.

Part Three: Checking for understanding one last time

Let's think about your understanding of this scene now. You can hold up *a closed fist*—that means "Zero, I have NO idea what I just read" OR you can hold up *all 5 fingers wagging*—that means "I understand every single word of what's going on in this scene" OR you can hold up any number of fingers in between. Let's see your hands and where your understanding might be now. How many of you improved your rating from the first read to now?

[**TEACHER NOTE:** Expect students to rate themselves 4 to 5. Really!]

Part Four: Wrap-up using Reflection Rounds

1. We will go around the circle and each person will take a turn finishing the sentence. Let's start with **"I was surprised that . . ."**

2. Now that everybody has done that round, let's go to **"I observed . . ."**

3. Last one: **"I learned . . ."**

Here's What Just Happened in the Last Two Classes

- Students collaborated to own and interpret an unfamiliar scene from *A Midsummer Night's Dream* with no explanation or translation from you.

- Students used the text to discover details of plot, character, setting, and conflict.

- Students used the reading round structure to read closely and question the text with their peers.

- Students saw how repeated close readings, discussions, and putting the text on its feet can help them build a collective understanding—with you out of the way.

- Students backed up their thinking with evidence from the text and negotiated ideas with each other to make decisions for Act 1, scene 1.

- Students monitored and saw their own growth in understanding throughout the process.

- Students created community in their classroom.

Helena's Decision: A Deeper Dive into 1.1

Here's What We're Doing and Why

Tossing Lines is a high-energy Folger Essential that puts the words into students' mouths right away without you having to give context to where the lines come from. As they're saying the lines and listening to each other, the puzzle pieces come together and they start building some ideas. Without your prompting, they use the language to make predictions about what's ahead in the reading. Lines gives kids the chance to notice important ideas in the language.

Cutting Text is a powerful tool to get kids working together to make choices and ultimately make meaning of the text. Cutting Text helps them to focus on what's important to them. We're expecting students to be able to do this independently in the next couple of weeks. So we'll start by working on Helena's inner monologue where she decides to go tell Demetrius that Hermia and Lysander are running away. This speech feeds conflict between the four lovers, and it gives us a look at an unhealthy relationship and how it can damage a person's self-worth. This is something that at least some of your students can relate to.

What Will I Need?

- Separate strips of lines for tossing—one line per student – **RESOURCE #2.1A**

- Lines from *A Midsummer Night's Dream* 1.1.232–257 to cut – **RESOURCE #2.1B**

- Beanbags, small stuffed animals, or other soft items for tossing

How Should I Prepare?

- Set up your classroom for students to work in small groups and also to stand in a circle.

- Make one or two copies of **RESOURCE #2.1A**, cut into separate strips—one line per student.

- Make enough copies of lines from *A Midsummer Night's Dream* 1.1.232–257 for all students – **RESOURCE #2.1B**.

- If you want to divide the class into cutting groups yourself, be ready with the groups.

Agenda (~ 45-minute class period)

❏ Part One: Set-up & Warm-up (5 minutes)

❏ Part Two: Tossing Lines (6 minutes)

❑ Part Three: Cutting Lines (15 minutes)

❑ Part Four: Sharing our cut versions and talking about them (18 minutes)

Here's What Students Hear (From You) and (Then What They'll) Do

Part One: Set-up & Warm-Up

1. Today we're going to toss Shakespeare around a bit. I'm giving you each a line.

[**TEACHER NOTE:** If students ask what their line means, don't explain what the text is about or define words. Direct them back to any words they DO know.]

And I'd like you to move around the room and read and reread your text aloud to yourself. Which word should you stress? What tone would make the most sense? Play with it a little. Keep walking around the room for a couple of minutes. [**TEACHER NOTE:** Encourage students to keep moving. You'll notice students' comfort level will grow as they speak their lines again and again. As always, don't correct the pronunciation or let them correct each other.]

Part Two: Tossing Lines

1. Please get into circles with five or six in a group. Here's a beanbag for each group.

2. The first person will read their line and then toss the beanbag to another person in the circle until everyone has had a turn. The person catching it says their line as they throw the beanbag to another student in the circle. Keep on with this for three minutes, and then I'll tell you to stop. Begin!

3. Great job, everyone! Now let's merge your circle with another circle to make a bigger circle. And we're going to do the same thing as we did before. You only need one beanbag per group.

4. That was great! So let's come together to talk about what we all did and heard.

5. First off, how did that feel . . . throwing Shakespeare lines and beanbags around together?

6. You all heard different lines in your group. And we worked some with *Midsummer* language last week. What do you think is going on in this world? And how do you know? Anything else that you notice about the words? [**TEACHER NOTE:** Please don't offer "answers" or comments. Don't expect students to make specific inferences about the text, but don't be surprised if they do!]

Part Three: Cutting Lines

1. We're going to read this scene in our large group first (**RESOURCE #2.1B**).

2. Now let's make groups of 3 to 4 students. Each group is going to cut this scene in half—there are 25 lines originally, so each group will cut at least 12 lines. And your cut text will make beautiful sense!

3. After 8 minutes or so, each group will share their cut version and explain why they made the cuts they did.

[**TEACHER NOTE:** Witness the groups working—there will be many options in play, so don't offer ideas. Let them work it out themselves. Also, don't mind if a group doesn't cut 50 percent—it's all about the process of collaborating and negotiating meaning.]

**For groups that finish early, I challenge you to cut the text in half again, to six lines. Can you do it?

Part Four: Sharing Our Versions of Helena

1. Cutting time is over! We'll all share our cuts and explain our decisions.

2. Take a few minutes to discuss in your groups about why you cut Helena's speech the way you did.

[**TEACHER NOTE:** Focus on the explanations, not the cut text.]

3. Okay! Let's hear from one of our groups! Who would like to be the first group to share? *(Take volunteers until everyone has had a chance to share.)* [**TEACHER NOTE:** Enthusiastic applause after each reading to celebrate each group's decisions and unique interpretation.]

4. What are your observations after listening to these different versions? Can you tell what Helena is *really* thinking and feeling? Were there any lines that everyone kept in, or that everyone cut? Why do you think that is?

Here's What Just Happened in Class

- All students engaged in Shakespeare's language through line tossing.

- Students used cutting to close-read a complex text.

- Students negotiated critical conversations about key elements of the text as they made their cuts.

- Students used textual evidence to support their cutting decisions.

- Students made inferences about Helena's motivations based on close reading of the text.

RESOURCE #2.1A

Lines for Tossing Lines for
A Midsummer Night's Dream

1.1.232–257

How happy
doting on Hermia's eyes
Wings, and no eyes
hail some heat
tomorrow night
waggish boys in game
He will not know
winged Cupid painted blind.
as fair as she
Things base and vile
unheedy haste
So he dissolved
Pursue her
I will go tell him
he was only mine
fair Hermia's flight
Demetrius thinks not so
Love looks not with the eyes
Love is perjured
show'rs of oaths did melt
enrich my pain
He hailed down oaths
have his sight
to the wood will he

RESOURCE #2.1B

A Midsummer Night's Dream

1.1.232–257

HELENA

How happy some o'er other some can be!
Through Athens I am thought as fair as she.
But what of that? Demetrius thinks not so.
He will not know what all but he do know.   235
And, as he errs, doting on Hermia's eyes,
So I, admiring of his qualities.
Things base and vile, holding no quantity,
Love can transpose to form and dignity.
Love looks not with the eyes but with the mind;   240
And therefore is winged Cupid painted blind.
Nor hath Love's mind of any judgment taste.
Wings, and no eyes, figure unheedy haste.
And therefore is Love said to be a child
Because in choice he is so oft beguiled.   245
As waggish boys in game themselves forswear,
So the boy Love is perjured everywhere.
For, ere Demetrius looked on Hermia's eyne,
He hailed down oaths that he was only mine;
And when this hail some heat from Hermia felt,   250
So he dissolved, and show'rs of oaths did melt.
I will go tell him of fair Hermia's flight.
Then to the wood will he tomorrow night
Pursue her. And, for this intelligence
If I have thanks, it is a dear expense.   255
But herein mean I to enrich my pain,
To have his sight thither and back again.

WEEK TWO: LESSON 2

Oberon and Titania's Conflict: A Deep Dive into 2.1

Here's What We're Doing and Why

This lesson is about exploring perspectives in a story, and cutting lines—your students are experts by now—will help us. Today, however, you'll ask them to cut with a focus—retaining either Titania's or Oberon's perspective. When they're finished and all versions have been shared, the students will be ready with their perspectives on Titania and Oberon's disagreements. Today's lesson is a combo of 3D Lit, Choral Reading, and Cutting Lines. Bonanza!

Act 2, scene 1, students will meet these magical forest royals and hear all the name-calling, ultimatums, and jealousies. And they will learn the source of their conflict: the Indian/Changeling Boy.

What Will I Need?

- Copies for all students of the scene between Oberon and Titania, 2.1.62–192 – **RESOURCE #2.2**

How Should I Prepare?

- Clear out enough space for all students to work in groups and to perform in a circle.

- Decide how you want to divide the class into 4 groups to work on the cutting.

Agenda (~ 45-minute class period)

- ❏ Part One: Reading Rounds (10 minutes)

- ❏ Part Two: Cutting Lines for Perspective (20 minutes)

- ❏ Part Three: Performing Your Cuts and Discussion (15 minutes)

Here's What Students Hear (From You) and (Then What They'll) Do

Part One: Getting to know the royalty

1. Let's get in a circle. Today we're going to meet the king and queen of the fairies.

2. As always, we want to get a feel for the language first, so we're going to read this scene together as a class. Read this fast, loud, and try to stay together as much as you can. Ready? Go.

3. That was a great first read! Let's try it again, reading around the circle, but read the character's whole speech before the next reader takes over.

4. Great! Let's talk about what we've picked up so far. Any observations? What's going on here and how do you know?

[**TEACHER NOTE:** By this time in the unit, you'll probably get some great observations. What you're after are the kind of observations they had last week as a result of these questions (included here in case you need them for prompts)]:

Who are these people? How do you know from the text? What is going on here? How do you know that from the text? Where are they? How do you know that from the text? How do these characters feel about each other? And how do you know that from the text? Who seems to have the most/least power? How do you know that from the text?

5. Great discussion, everyone. Take your scripts and get into Groups 1, 2, 3, and 4.

Part Two: Cutting Lines for Perspective

1. You are going to cut like crazy AND there's an additional challenge! You'll notice that your script divides the scene up into two parts. Two groups will work with lines 62 to 124 (Part 1), and 2 groups will work with lines 125 to 192 (Part 2). Your cutting assignments and extra challenge are these:

   Group 1: You will cut lines 62 to 124 (Part 1) in half, and you will cut to reflect *exactly* what Titania wants.

   Group 2: You will also work with lines 62 to 124 (Part 1), but you will cut to reflect *exactly* what Oberon wants.

   Group 3: You will cut lines 125 to 192 (Part 2) in half, and you will cut to reflect *exactly* what Titania wants.

   Group 4: You will also work with lines 125 to192 (Part 2), but you will cut to reflect *exactly* what Oberon wants.

2. Work together to figure out the words you don't know, or look them up if they seem essential to meaning. You own the text now, so get busy!

3. You'll have 20 minutes to cut and to think about how you'll perform your cut text.

4. In terms of sharing out, be ready to perform your cut text! And then we'll talk about this Fairy King and Queen and what your perspectives are!

Part Three: Performing Your Cuts and Discussion

1. Let's get back together so that we can share our cuts. Let's alternate so we hear first from a Titania perspective and then an Oberon perspective.

[**TEACHER NOTE:** Wild applause after each group's presentation to celebrate their choices.]

2. What are we thinking about these two? And what about the Indian boy? We'll talk more about him later, but do you have early thoughts?

3. Thanks for your hard work!

Here's What Just Happened in Class

- Students close-read the same piece of text to analyze multiple character perspectives and motivations.

- Students analyzed characters' perspectives to identify a key conflict in the play.

- Students read and heard a text through multiple modes, becoming comfortable with reading and performing the language aloud.

- Students negotiated with each other about essential ideas in the text.

RESOURCE #2.2

A Midsummer Night's Dream 2.1.62–192

PART ONE

OBERON

Ill met by moonlight, proud Titania.

TITANIA

What, jealous Oberon? Fairies, skip hence.
I have forsworn his bed and company.

OBERON

Tarry, rash wanton. Am not I thy lord?   65

TITANIA

Then I must be thy lady. But I know
When thou hast stolen away from Fairyland
And in the shape of Corin sat all day
Playing on pipes of corn and versing love
To amorous Phillida. Why art thou here,   70
Come from the farthest steep of India,
But that, forsooth, the bouncing Amazon,
Your buskined mistress and your warrior love,
To Theseus must be wedded, and you come
To give their bed joy and prosperity?   75

OBERON

How canst thou thus for shame, Titania,
Glance at my credit with Hippolyta,
Knowing I know thy love to Theseus?
Didst not thou lead him through the glimmering night   80
From Perigouna, whom he ravishèd,
And make him with fair Aegles break his faith,
With Ariadne and Antiopa?

TITANIA

These are the forgeries of jealousy;
And never, since the middle summer's spring,   85
Met we on hill, in dale, forest, or mead,
By pavèd fountain or by rushy brook,
Or in the beachèd margent of the sea,
To dance our ringlets to the whistling wind,
But with thy brawls thou hast disturbed our sport.   90

Therefore the winds, piping to us in vain,
As in revenge have sucked up from the sea
Contagious fogs, which, falling in the land,
Hath every pelting river made so proud
That they have overborne their continents.   95
The ox hath therefore stretched his yoke in vain,
The plowman lost his sweat, and the green corn
Hath rotted ere his youth attained a beard.
The fold stands empty in the drownèd field,
And crows are fatted with the murrain flock.   100
The nine-men's-morris is filled up with mud,
And the quaint mazes in the wanton green,
For lack of tread, are undistinguishable.
The human mortals want their winter here.
No night is now with hymn or carol blessed.   105
Therefore the moon, the governess of floods,
Pale in her anger, washes all the air,
That rheumatic diseases do abound.
And thorough this distemperature we see
The seasons alter: hoary-headed frosts   110
Fall in the fresh lap of the crimson rose,
And on old Hiems' thin and icy crown
An odorous chaplet of sweet summer buds
Is, as in mockery, set. The spring, the summer,
The childing autumn, angry winter, change   115
Their wonted liveries, and the mazèd world
By their increase now knows not which is which.
And this same progeny of evils comes
From our debate, from our dissension;
We are their parents and original.   120

OBERON

Do you amend it, then. It lies in you.
Why should Titania cross her Oberon?
I do but beg a little changeling boy
To be my henchman.

PART TWO

TITANIA

Set your heart at rest: 125
The Fairyland buys not the child of me.
His mother was a vot'ress of my order,
And in the spicèd Indian air by night
Full often hath she gossiped by my side
And sat with me on Neptune's yellow sands,   130
Marking th' embarkèd traders on the flood,

When we have laughed to see the sails conceive
And grow big-bellied with the wanton wind;
Which she, with pretty and with swimming gait,
Following (her womb then rich with my young   135
   squire),
Would imitate and sail upon the land
To fetch me trifles and return again,
As from a voyage, rich with merchandise.
But she, being mortal, of that boy did die,   140
And for her sake do I rear up her boy,
And for her sake I will not part with him.

OBERON

How long within this wood intend you stay?

TITANIA

Perchance till after Theseus' wedding day.
If you will patiently dance in our round   145
And see our moonlight revels, go with us.
If not, shun me, and I will spare your haunts.

OBERON

Give me that boy and I will go with thee.

TITANIA

Not for thy fairy kingdom. Fairies, away.
We shall chide downright if I longer stay   150
                        Titania and her fairies exit.

OBERON

Well, go thy way. Thou shalt not from this grove
Till I torment thee for this injury.—
My gentle Puck, come hither. Thou rememb'rest
Since once I sat upon a promontory
And heard a mermaid on a dolphin's back   155
Uttering such dulcet and harmonious breath
That the rude sea grew civil at her song
And certain stars shot madly from their spheres
To hear the sea-maid's music.

ROBIN I remember   160

OBERON

That very time I saw (but thou couldst not),
Flying between the cold moon and the Earth,
Cupid all armed. A certain aim he took
At a fair vestal thronèd by the west,

And loosed his love-shaft smartly from his bow   165
As it should pierce a hundred thousand hearts.
But I might see young Cupid's fiery shaft
Quenched in the chaste beams of the wat'ry moon,
And the imperial vot'ress passèd on
In maiden meditation, fancy-free.   170
Yet marked I where the bolt of Cupid fell.
It fell upon a little western flower,
Before, milk-white, now purple with love's wound,
And maidens call it "love-in-idleness."
Fetch me that flower; the herb I showed thee once.   175
The juice of it on sleeping eyelids laid
Will make or man or woman madly dote
Upon the next live creature that it sees.
Fetch me this herb, and be thou here again
Ere the leviathan can swim a league.   180

ROBIN
    I'll put a girdle round about the Earth
    In forty minutes.   *He exits.*

OBERON Having once this juice,
    I'll watch Titania when she is asleep
    And drop the liquor of it in her eyes.   185
    The next thing then she, waking, looks upon
    (Be it on lion, bear, or wolf, or bull,
    On meddling monkey, or on busy ape)
    She shall pursue it with the soul of love.
    And ere I take this charm from off her sight   190
    (As I can take it with another herb),
    I'll make her render up her page to me.

WEEK TWO: LESSON 3

Hermia and Helena: Friends? Frenemies?

Here's What We're Doing and Why

We're going to go back to a piece of 1.1 in order to learn more about what's going on with Helena and Hermia. They are dear friends, but Demetrius and Lysander have gotten everything all confused—who *does* love whom? And are Helena and Hermia still friends? There's a lot of back-and-forth in the dialogue between Helena and Hermia, and the Folger essential of Choral Reading will help highlight the conflict in this scene.

We've edited this scene so students can concentrate on what's going on between these two characters. As they have done earlier, students will read the text in a number of different ways, including some new ones that involve voice and action. This will allow them to notice some new things about the text each time. And they'll now be ready to say what they see and feel as they cite the text. They are practicing using these tools that they will employ throughout this unit, and that will be key to their ability to be successful in their final project/assessment. In addition, they will collaborate and build community with their classmates.

What Will I Need?

- Copies of 1.1.182–241, edited – **RESOURCE #2.3**

How Should I Prepare?

- Make enough copies of 1.1, edited for every student – **RESOURCE #2.3**.

- Make space for students to make a circle and also to stand opposite each other in parallel lines.

Agenda (~ 45-minute class period)

- ❏ Part One: Set-up (5 minutes)
- ❏ Part Two: Rounds of Choral Reading and Performing (35 minutes)
- ❏ Part Three: Fast Reflection Round (5 minutes)

Part One: Set-up

Today we're going to go back to the end of 1.1 because we want to focus on another relationship in this play. We're going to do some choral reading as we've done previously, and you'll have lots to say after that!

Part Two: Rounds of Choral Reading and Performing

1. So, for the first round, we're going to do the usual—read this as fast as we can while trying to stay together. As we've done before, just read Shakespeare's lines and not the names of the characters. As loud as you can!

2. Great first round! Let's read it again, fast and together, and try to read it as if you are ANGRY.

3. What's going on here?

[**TEACHER NOTE:** Give them a chance to come up with these questions—and textual support—themselves. Prompt a bit if they don't.

 – What's going on here? How do you know? What does the text say?

 – Who loves whom? How do you know? What does the text say?

 – Who doesn't love whom? What does the text tell you?]

4. Let's try it a different way: Form two parallel lines facing each other. You're going to have this Helena-and-Hermia conversation together. All of you on this side will read Hermia together. And all of you on the other side will read Helena. And we need one Lysander! Who will volunteer to be Lysander? Excellent! (Where should you stand, Lysander?) You'll have this conversation back and forth with each other.

5. Great job! Are there emotions involved here? Which ones? Let's hear some of them! Let's try it one more time. Let's switch parts for this one, so that if you were reading Helena before, you're now reading Hermia, and vice versa. And we need a new Lysander too. Let's read again. Any more observations? What are your thoughts about reading it this way?

6. Last version: Pair up in any way you'd like. Go off by yourselves for a few minutes so you can read it back and forth together. With action and gestures! With feeling! Then come up with two words that you feel describe Helena and Hermia's relationship at this point in the play.

7. Let's share those words, and if we have time, your pair performances!

Part Three: Fast Reflection Round

1. We'll just do one round: **"I observed . . ."**

Here's What Just Happened in Class

- Students close-read to analyze conflict between characters.

- Students performed opposing character perspectives to better understand character relationships.

- Students analyzed how tone impacts the mood of a text.

- Students really dived into a text together and, along with their peers, built their understanding.

- Students made discoveries about the text without teacher explanation.

- Students continued to back up their thinking with evidence from the text.

- Students added movement to their reading; this helps them continue to see these words as words in action.

RESOURCE #2.3

1.1.182–241, edited

LYSANDER

Look, here comes Helena.

HERMIA

Godspeed, fair Helena. Whither away?

HELENA

Call you me "fair"? That "fair" again unsay.
Demetrius loves your fair. O happy fair!
O, teach me how you look and with what art
You sway the motion of Demetrius' heart!

HERMIA

I frown upon him, yet he loves me still.

HELENA

O, that your frowns would teach my smiles such skill!

HERMIA

I give him curses, yet he gives me love.

HELENA

O, that my prayers could such affection move!

HERMIA

The more I hate, the more he follows me.

HELENA

The more I love, the more he hateth me.

HERMIA

His folly, Helena, is no fault of mine.

HELENA

None but your beauty. Would that fault were mine!

LYSANDER

Good luck grant thee thy Demetrius.—
As you on him, Demetrius dote on you!

HELENA
Through Athens I am thought as fair as she.
But what of that? Demetrius thinks not so.
He will not know what all but he do know.
Love can transpose to form and dignity.
Love looks not with the eyes but with the mind;
And therefore is winged Cupid painted blind.

Getting the Lovers Off the Page: Promptbooks!

Here's What We're Doing and Why

In this lesson, we will introduce the promptbook, a great Folger Essential that gets students to consider deeply—and record—all aspects of a scene. Creating a promptbook mirrors a practice that has been used in the world of theater for a long time—and we include some images of very early promptbooks from the Folger collection for you and your students to have a look at.

A promptbook is, at its core, a set of notes made directly on the text—in this case, the notes will be made by your students. These annotations give actors advice about how to convey meaning through the language, through their voices, gestures, and movements onstage. They also record cuts in the text (everybody cut the text!), entrances and exits of characters, and more. Because creating promptbooks brings students to consider all aspects of a scene deeply, we have found that it is an important process in connecting our students to Shakespeare.

Creating a first promptbook is a logical step at this point. Creating short promptbooks in small groups allows students to continue to take ownership of the language and the play, and this will also support their learning as they move toward the final assessment.

Their work today will focus on the lovers.

We'll begin our work with promptbooks by examining digital images of two rare *A Midsummer Night's Dream* promptbooks that are in the Folger collection.

What Will I Need?

- Promptbook image from the noted 1763 production of *A Midsummer Night's Dream* directed by David Garrick at the Drury Lane Theater in Covent Garden, London – **RESOURCE #2.4A**

- Promptbook image from Herbert Beerbohm Tree's lavish production of *A Midsummer Night's Dream,* onstage in Her Majesty's Theatre, London, in January 1900 – **RESOURCE #2.4B**

- Print copies of *A Midsummer Night's Dream,* 1.1.130–231, divided into four separate sections – **RESOURCE #2.4C**

    - 1.1.130–151
    - 1.1.152–181
    - 1.1.182–212
    - 1.1.213–231

How Should I Prepare?

- Set up your classroom in a large circle with space in the middle for action.

- Be ready to divide students into four groups. Each group will create a promptbook for their section of the scene.

Agenda (~ 45-minute class period)

❏ Review of promptbook pages from the Folger collection. Discuss promptbooks and outline the assignment (10 minutes)

❏ Reading of the scene as a whole class (10 minutes)

❏ Group work on the promptbook and quick performance (20 minutes)

❏ Reflection Rounds and discussion (5 minutes)

Here's What Students Hear (From You) and (Then What They'll) Do

Part One

1. Today, we will get to know the lovers a little better by creating promptbooks for *A Midsummer Night's Dream*, 1.1.130–231. Before we do, let's take a look at these images of rare promptbooks from the Folger collection – **RESOURCE #2.4A** and **RESOURCE #2.4B**

2. What do you notice, and what do you wonder, about these pages? On the board, let's gather some ideas about what else a promptbook might include.

[**TEACHER NOTE:** They may mention cut lines, tone, emotions, mood, pauses, whispers, exits, entrances, gestures, movements, laughter, lightning, hugs and handshakes, props, and more.]

Part Two: Read the Scene

1. Pass out copies of *A Midsummer Night's Dream* 1.1.130–231 (**RESOURCE #2.4C**).

2. As a class, let's read this whole scene aloud together. [**TEACHER NOTE:** Students can volunteer to read parts or you can assign them, or read it chorally.] Mark your script with anything that stands out or is interesting to you.

3. Now let's share with each other what we think is happening in this scene. Let's have volunteers share their thoughts on the scene.

Part Three: Create Your Promptbooks

1. You are going to form four groups, and I will assign each group a short section of the scene with which to create a promptbook. The handout is divided into four sections. Find the section assigned to your group and read through it as a group.
   - Group One: 1.1.130–151
   - Group Two: 1.1.152–181
   - Group Three: 1.1.182–212
   - Group Four: 1.1.213–231

2. In your groups, collaborate to make some annotations that show how your group would stage the text. All your choices must be supported by your understanding of the text. Write clear, detailed notes in the margins and on the

text, marking specific words and lines. Note your group decisions about these elements:

- **Mood / Tone**
    - Overall
    - Key moments
- **Acting:** Describe what each character is doing.
    - movement (gestures, exits, entrances, facial expressions)
    - voice (tone of voice, stress, volume)
    - emotion (nervous, angry, curious, elated, etc.)
    - nonverbal human sound (laughter, sigh, cry, scream, etc.)

3. Once you make decisions about your scene, choose group members to perform and run through your short scene a few times to practice your mood, tone, and **acting.** Your performance does not have to be perfect and you can read your **lines** from your script. There may be more students in your group than parts in your scene . . . and you will find creative ways to involve everyone in your performance. Or those of you without speaking parts, direct the scene like we did with 3D Lit.

4. Let's close out with a quick Reflection Round. Complete this sentence:

    a. "I noticed . . ."

    b. Let's do another round. Complete this sentence: **"I learned about myself . . ."**

Here's What Just Happened in Class

- Students had a chance to examine digitized versions of rare materials from the Folger collection, reading multimodal texts and placing their own work in a historical context.

- Students pulled together meaning, movement, vocal inflection, and more into a full treatment of the scene that revealed their close reading to the audience.

- Students made collaborative decisions about staging the play without your help.

- Students reflected on how their staging choices impacted the audience's interpretation of the scene.

RESOURCE #2.4A

From a Promptbook in the Folger Collection

Two pages from a promptbook created for a 1763 London production of *A Midsummer Night's Dream*. The printed book was published in 1734. This 1763 production used that text and marked up this copy to memorialize where cuts to the text should be made, where certain characters should move on stage, and where a few words should be changed.

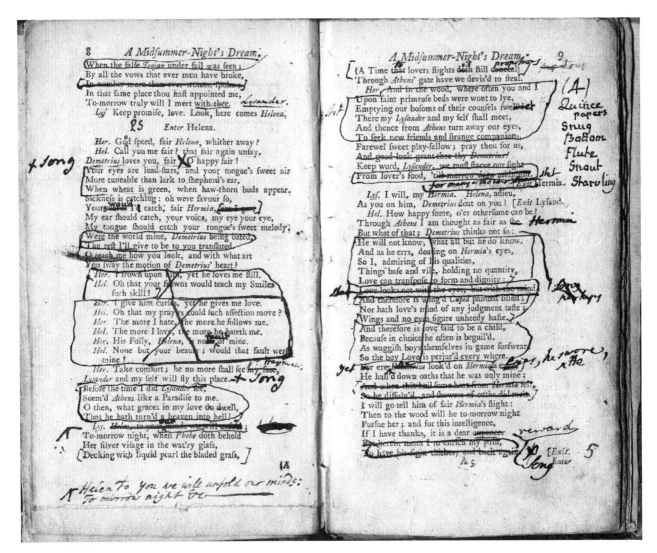

Preparation copy made by David Garrick (Burnim, Langhans, Shattuck). Promptbook for Drury Lane production of 23 Nov. 1763.

FROM THE COLLECTION OF THE FOLGER SHAKESPEARE LIBRARY IN WASHINGTON, DC.

RESOURCE #2.4B

From a Promptbook in the Folger Collection

Two pages from a promptbook created for a 1900 London production of *A Midsummer Night's Dream*. The printed book was published in 1888, and later marked up to serve as a promptbook for the 1900 production. You can see part of Act 2, scene 1—and cuts and notes—on the right-hand page. The left-hand page is full of extra stage directions that are very specific, pretty wonderful, and tell us how ornate this production was.

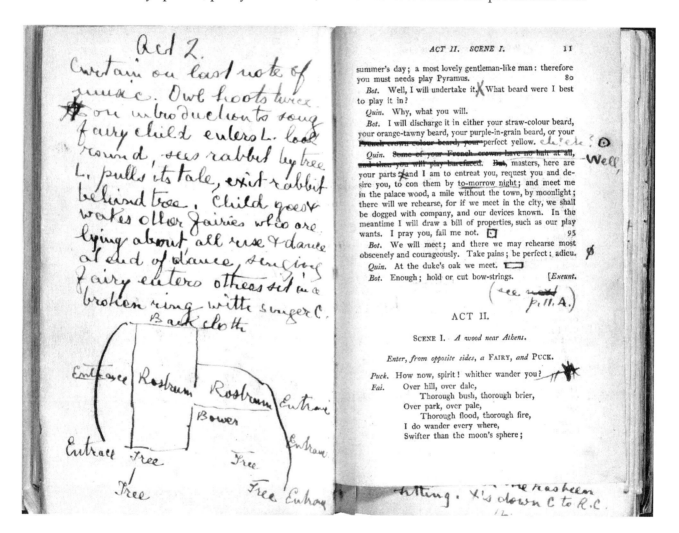

Palmer, F. Grove (Fred Grove), 1851–1927. Souvenir prompt book. Made by Fred Grove.
Records Herbert Beerbohm Tree's production.
FROM THE COLLECTION OF THE FOLGER SHAKESPEARE LIBRARY IN WASHINGTON, DC.

A Midsummer Night's Dream, 1.1.130–231

GROUP ONE: Lines 130–151

LYSANDER

    How now, my love? Why is your cheek so pale?   130
    How chance the roses there do fade so fast?

HERMIA

    Belike for want of rain, which I could well
    Beteem them from the tempest of my eyes.

LYSANDER

    Ay me! For aught that I could ever read,
    Could ever hear by tale or history,   135
    The course of true love never did run smooth.
    But either it was different in blood—

HERMIA

    O cross! Too high to be enthralled to low.

LYSANDER

    Or else misgraffèd in respect of years—

HERMIA

    O spite! Too old to be engaged to young.   140

LYSANDER

    Or else it stood upon the choice of friends—

HERMIA

    O hell, to choose love by another's eyes!

LYSANDER

    Or, if there were a sympathy in choice,
    War, death, or sickness did lay siege to it,
    Making it momentary as a sound,   145
    Swift as a shadow, short as any dream,
    Brief as the lightning in the collied night,
    That, in a spleen, unfolds both heaven and Earth,
    And, ere a man hath power to say "Behold!"

The jaws of darkness do devour it up.   150
So quick bright things come to confusion.

GROUP TWO: Lines 152–181

HERMIA

If then true lovers have been ever crossed,
It stands as an edict in destiny.
Then let us teach our trial patience
Because it is a customary cross,   155
As due to love as thoughts and dreams and sighs,
Wishes and tears, poor fancy's followers.

LYSANDER

A good persuasion. Therefore, hear me, Hermia:
I have a widow aunt, a dowager
Of great revenue, and she hath no child.   160
From Athens is her house remote seven leagues,
And she respects me as her only son.
There, gentle Hermia, may I marry thee;
And to that place the sharp Athenian law
Cannot pursue us. If thou lovest me, then   165
Steal forth thy father's house tomorrow night,
And in the wood a league without the town
(Where I did meet thee once with Helena
To do observance to a morn of May),
There will I stay for thee.   170

HERMIA My good Lysander,
I swear to thee by Cupid's strongest bow,
By his best arrow with the golden head,
By the simplicity of Venus' doves,
By that which knitteth souls and prospers loves,   175
And by that fire which burned the Carthage queen
When the false Trojan under sail was seen,
By all the vows that ever men have broke
(In number more than ever women spoke),
In that same place thou hast appointed me,   180
Tomorrow truly will I meet with thee.

GROUP THREE: Lines 182–212

LYSANDER

Keep promise, love. Look, here comes Helena.
                              Enter Helena.

HERMIA

Godspeed, fair Helena. Whither away?

HELENA

Call you me "fair"? That "fair" again unsay.
Demetrius loves your fair. O happy fair!   185
Your eyes are lodestars and your tongue's sweet air
More tunable than lark to shepherd's ear
When wheat is green, when hawthorn buds appear.
Sickness is catching. O, were favor so!
Yours would I catch, fair Hermia, ere I go   190
My ear should catch your voice, my eye your eye;
My tongue should catch your tongue's sweet
     melody.
Were the world mine, Demetrius being bated,
The rest I'd give to be to you translated.   195
O, teach me how you look and with what art
You sway the motion of Demetrius' heart!

HERMIA

I frown upon him, yet he loves me still.

HELENA

O, that your frowns would teach my smiles such
     skill!   200

HERMIA

I give him curses, yet he gives me love.

HELENA

O, that my prayers could such affection move!

HERMIA

The more I hate, the more he follows me.

HELENA

The more I love, the more he hateth me.

HERMIA

His folly, Helena, is no fault of mine.   205

HELENA

None but your beauty. Would that fault were mine!

HERMIA

Take comfort: he no more shall see my face.
Lysander and myself will fly this place.

Before the time I did Lysander see
Seemed Athens as a paradise to me.   210
O, **then**, what graces in my love do dwell
That he hath turned a heaven unto a hell!

GROUP FOUR: Lines 213–231

LYSANDER

Helen, to you our minds we will unfold.
Tomorrow night when Phoebe doth behold
Her silver visage in the wat'ry glass,   215
Decking with liquid pearl the bladed grass
(A time that lovers' flights doth still conceal),
Through Athens' gates have we devised to steal.

HERMIA

And in the wood where often you and I
Upon faint primrose beds were wont to lie,   220
Emptying our bosoms of their counsel sweet,
There my Lysander and myself shall meet
And thence from Athens turn away our eyes
To seek new friends and stranger companies.
Farewell, sweet playfellow. Pray thou for us,   225
And good luck grant thee thy Demetrius.—
Keep word, Lysander. We must starve our sight
From lovers' food till morrow deep midnight.

LYSANDER

I will, my Hermia   *Hermia exits.*
Helena, adieu.   230
As you on him, Demetrius dote on you!
                                             Lysander exits.

WEEK TWO: LESSON 5

Exploring Ideas of Beauty: Tagore's "Krishnakoli" Talks Back to Shakespeare *A Midsummer Night's Dream*, 3.2

Here's What We're Doing and Why

At the Folger, we often pair up texts when we teach Shakespeare—or any other author, for that matter. We teach two strong texts simultaneously, giving students the chance to see and make observations about differences and similarities in writing styles, belief sets, cultures, gender, religion and more. Studying texts in pairs is generative, and gives students more ways to look at both pieces of literature . . . and at life, too. It's across paired texts that students often recognize the presence of race, difference, identity, and power in Shakespeare and other authors. For more information and examples on two texts with students, find Donna Denizé's chapter on paired texts elsewhere in this book.

Today, students will consider writers of two different centuries, cultures, and religions and how they see beauty. Here we put a piece of Demetrius's speech to Helena in 3.2 (Shakespeare, 1564–1616) in conversation with "Krishnakoli," a poem by Rabindranath Tagore, India's celebrated poet and educator who lived from 1861–1941. Rabindranath Tagore was a poet, writer, playwright, composer, philosopher, social reformer and painter. He was known as the "Bard of Bengali" because of his beautiful poetry. He won the Nobel Prize for Literature in 1913, the first Indian to win this prize.

We dive into choral reading, stressing certain words in the rounds of reading. Students will see for themselves what's there, they'll question the language, and examine how each piece holds up when considered with the other. They will read and discuss the two texts separately, and then connect the two in a creative and exciting way. Considering these texts and their languages together will be useful as they work their way toward their final projects.

What Will I Need?

- *Midsummer*, 3.2.140–147 – **RESOURCE #2.5A**

- *Midsummer*, 3.2.140–147—for subsequent readings – **RESOURCE #2.5B**

- Tagore's "Krishnakoli" – **RESOURCE #2.5C**

- Tagore's "Krishnakoli"—for subsequent readings – **RESOURCE #2.5D**

- Tagore and Shakespeare in Conversation – **RESOURCE #2.5E**

How Should I Prepare?

- Copies of all these resources for each student

Agenda (~ 45-minute period, and a little longer if you have it)

❑ Part One: Shakespeare and Observations (10 minutes)

❑ Part Two: Tagore & Observations (10 minutes)

❑ Part Three: Tagore Talks Back to Shakespeare (15 minutes)

❑ Part Four: Reflection Rounds (10 minutes)

Here's What Students Hear (From You) and (Then What They'll) Do

Part One: Shakespeare and Observations

1. Today we're going to dig into different ideas of beauty: what *Midsummer* has to say about it, and the ideas of another, very different writer. We'll take a leap to 3.2 when Demetrius wakes up and sees Helena. As we know, Oberon put the love potion in Demetrius' eyes, so what's Demetrius going to do after seeing Helena? What do you think?

2. Let's look at **RESOURCE #2.5A**. Demetrius' reaction. First reading, we're going to read it together as a class. As usual, let's read it loud, fast, and try to stay together as much as we can. Ready?

3. Now that you've read it once, is there anything you don't understand? Let's try to figure it out or look it up. [**TEACHER NOTE:** Maybe "high Taurus' snow" and they can look that up.]

4. So let's make some observations. We know that this is Demetrius talking, and we know who he is talking to.

   – How do they feel? How do you know?

   – Who is not speaking? How do you know?

   – Is there power in having a voice? Explain your thinking or give examples.

5. Alright. We're going to read this text again. But this time, we'll move to **RESOURCE #2.5B**. We'll read it together, but whisper the words in regular print, and YELL out the bolded words. At the top of your lungs! Ready? Let's read it that way a couple of times.

[**TEACHER NOTE:** Hope that kids get loud for this round! Giggles and laughter will ensue.]

6. Let's talk some more about this text. Turn and talk to a partner close to you for a minute about the big ideas you see. According to Shakespeare in this speech:

   – What is beauty?

   – Who decides what's beautiful?

7. What did you and your partner talk about? Let's have some volunteers.

8. Okay, now we're going to read this speech again. This time, we're going to do the opposite of the last reading. You're going to YELL the regular words and whisper the bolded words. Ready?

9. Wonderful! What else do you notice about the words now that you've heard them in a couple of different ways? Turn and talk to your partner about the words, and what you noticed about them.

10. Will volunteers share what you and your partner talked about?

[**TEACHER NOTE:** Take their comments first. If they need prompting, go to these: How do the bolded words relate to each other? If you had to group them, how would you do that? What do these words imply?]

11. Thank you for the great insights, everyone! Now we're going to move to the next text.

Part Two: Tagore and Observations

1. Let's read the poem "Krishnakoli" by the famous Indian poet Rabindranath Tagore – **RESOURCE #2.5C**. For the first reading, we're going to read it together as we do. Let's read it loud, fast, and try to stay together as much as we can. Ready?

2. What initial observations do you have about this poem?

[**TEACHER NOTE:** Always ask students for their observations first.]

Let's think about this in the way we thought through Demetrius' speech:
   - Who is talking? How do you know?
   - Who are they talking about? How do you know?
   - How do they feel? How do you know?
   - Who is not speaking? How do you know?
   - Is there power in having a voice? Explain your thinking or give examples.
   - At this point, let's learn a little about Tagore. Can anyone tell us a little about him? Could someone quickly look him up?

[**TEACHER NOTE:** Share with students that Rabindranath Tagore (1861–1941) was a poet, writer, playwright, composer, philosopher, social reformer and painter from India. He was known as the "Bard of Bengali" because of his beautiful poetry. He won the Nobel Prize for Literature in 1913, the first Indian to win this prize.]

3. Let's do a second round of reading. Move on to **RESOURCE #2.5D**. This time, you're going to whisper the regular words and YELL out the bolded words. Let's do that twice too.

4. Great job, everyone. Let's talk about what else we picked up in this round. Turn and talk to your partner. In this poem:
   - What is beauty?
   - Who decides what's beautiful?

5. Any volunteers to share what you discussed?

6. Alright! Last round of reading. We're going to do the opposite of the last reading. You're going to YELL the regular words and whisper the bolded words.

7. Great! Let's talk about what else this reading might bring up for you. Turn and talk. [**TEACHER NOTE:** Take their comments first. If they need prompting, go to these: Do the bolded words relate to each other? If you had to group them, could you do that? What do these words imply?]

8. THE BIG QUESTION: Looking at these two texts together—what do they give us to think about? First, let's have everyone's thoughts on that.

[**TEACHER NOTE:** Give your students a chance to think or talk through similarities and differences. They may bring the differences between the writers into the mix. Your students may not bring up the white/dark comparison. If they don't, go to these questions: What do you notice about the descriptors of white and dark in each text? What do you think about those? What notions of beauty are not mentioned at all? What do you think about those?]

Part Three: Tagore Talks Back to Shakespeare

1. Now we're going to get Tagore and Shakespeare talking to each other:

If your birthday is January through June, gather on one side of the room. And if your birthday is July through December, gather on the other side of the room.

2. January-to-Junes, you are Shakespeare. All together, you read Shakespeare's words in bold. July-to-December, you are Tagore, and all together, you read Tagore's words in italics. Here is the mash-up (**RESOURCE #2.5E**). Let's hear it! Terrific, and let's hear it again. Now, switch parts: if you were reading Tagore, now you read Shakespeare, and vice versa.

3. Let's discuss this conversation between Tagore and Shakespeare.

[**TEACHER NOTE:**
   – What do these writers have to say to each other?
   – What is the definition of beauty of each?
   – Whose voice is missing?
   – How do *you* define beauty?]

Part Four: Reflection Rounds

1. First round, let's start with **"I was surprised that . . ."**

2. Next and last round: **"I learned about myself . . ."**

Here's What Just Happened in Class

- Students analyzed paired texts on a shared theme to note differences in figurative language.

- Students explored the smooth, sneaky, pretty, and complex ways in which two different writers present their notions about race and beauty.

- Students made connections across texts and between contrasting perspectives to consider their own perspectives on beauty.

A Midsummer Night's Dream, 3.2.140–147

DEMETRIUS

    O Helen, goddess, nymph, perfect, divine!
    To what, my love, shall I compare thine eyne?
    Crystal is muddy. O, how ripe in show
    Thy lips, those kissing cherries, tempting grow!
    That pure congealèd white, high Taurus' snow,
    Fanned with the eastern wind, turns to a crow
    When thou hold'st up thy hand. O, let me kiss
    This princess of pure white, this seal of bliss!

RESOURCE #2.5B

A Midsummer Night's Dream, 3.2.140–147

For subsequent readings . . .

DEMETRIUS

    O Helen, **goddess, nymph, perfect, divine!**
    To what, my **love**, shall I compare thine **eyne**?
    Crystal is muddy. O, how ripe in show
    Thy lips, those **kissing cherries**, tempting grow!
    That **pure** congealèd **white**, high Taurus' **snow**,
    Fanned with the eastern wind, turns to a **crow**
    When thou hold'st up thy **hand.** O, let me **kiss**
    This **princess** of **pure white**, this seal of **bliss!**

Tagore, "Krishnakoli"

(translated from the Bengali by Vidula Plante)

Though the villagers may call her dark,
I call her my dark flower.
It was a cloud-filled day when I beheld
this black beauty with dark doe eyes,
her veil askew,
her braided hair free to run down her back.
Dark?
So very dark she is;
I am captivated by the black beauty with dark doe eyes.

She is the northeast wind flowing from the dark clouds of May
She is the soft shadow blossoming on an early monsoon night
She is the joy gathering in the heart of a late monsoon night.
Dark?
So very dark she is;
I am captivated by the black beauty with dark doe eyes.

RESOURCE #2.5D

Tagore, "Krishnakoli"

(translated from the Bengali by Vidula Plante)

For subsequent readings . . .

Though the villagers may call her **dark**,
I call her my **dark flower**.
It was a cloud-filled day when I **beheld**
this **black beauty** with **dark doe eyes**,
her veil askew,
her **braided hair free** to run down her **back**.
Dark?
So **very dark** she is;
I am **captivated** by the **black beauty** with **dark doe eyes**.

She is the northeast wind **flowing** from the **dark** clouds of May
She is the **soft shadow blossoming** on an early monsoon **night**
She is the **joy** gathering in the **heart** of a late monsoon **night**.
Dark?
So **very dark** she is;
I am **captivated** by the **black beauty** with **dark doe eyes**.

TAGORE TALKS BACK TO SHAKESPEARE

Dark,
So very dark she is;
To what, my love, shall I compare thine eyne?
Crystal is muddy.
I am captivated by the black beauty with dark doe eyes.

She is the northeast wind flowing from dark clouds
That pure congealèd white high Taurus' snow,
Fanned with the eastern wind, turns to a crow
I call her my dark flower.

She is the joy gathering in the heart of a monsoon night
O goddess, nymph, perfect, divine!
Dark,
So very dark she is;
lips, tempting grow!

WEEK THREE: LESSON 1

Where Is the Indian Boy?:
Voice and/or the Lack of It in *Midsummer*

Here's What We're Doing and Why

The Indian Boy is mentioned in the play, but Shakespeare didn't write any lines for him, so in many productions he is talked about but not ever seen, because the director doesn't cast an actor for his part. In *A Midsummer Night's Dream*, a great deal occurs because of desire for the Indian Boy, but everybody is talking ABOUT him, and not TO him. Part of taking Shakespeare off his pedestal is challenging his text: *Whose story isn't being told here?* Today, students are going beyond the text. They will dig deeper to think about what's missing, just like scholars do. They'll explore and then give voice to that Boy!

Scholars generally agree that in Shakespeare's England, India was thought to be an exotic, magical place, and thus a Boy from India would be appealing and desirable.

Part of this lesson is a gallery walk. Please preview the images with attention to your comfort level and your students' maturity.

What Will I Need?

- Four printed images from the Folger collection – **RESOURCE #3.1A–RESOURCE #3.1D**

- Four segments of 2.1.1–192 for students to work with – **RESOURCES #3.1E–#3.1H**

How Should I Prepare?

- Print images of the Indian Boy **(RESOURCES #3.1A–D)** for groups to look at closely—hanging them on walls or putting them on tables in different parts of the room. Make several copies of the same image per station.

- Put the key image questions on the board:
    - Who is in this image? How can you tell?
    - What do you see that is interesting to you?
    - Who seems to have the most or least power? Why do you think?

- Be ready to put students in four groups—to review the images, work closely with pieces of 2.1, and then work together writing a monologue.

Agenda (~ 45-minute class period)

❏ Part One: Gallery walk and conversation (10 minutes)

❏ Part Two: Detective work in Act 2 and sharing out (20 minutes)

❏ Part Three: Create and perform a monologue (10 minutes)

❏ Part Four: Reflection Flash Round (5 minutes)

Here's What Students Hear (From You) and (Then What They'll) Do

Part One: Gallery Walk

1. Today, we're going to do some investigating about the Indian Boy, someone who is important to what happens in *A Midsummer Night's Dream*, but . . . is he? There are four images for you to look at from the Folger Shakespeare Library. In four groups, you're going to walk around the room to study these images closely – **RESOURCE #3.1A, #3.1B, #3.1C, and #3.1D.** You'll have two minutes to study each image. I will let you know when to move on to the next image. We'll continue until every group has studied each image. As you do, check out the questions on the board because they may help you observe:

    – Who is in this image? How can you tell?

    – What do you see that is interesting to you?

    – Who seems to have the most or least power? Why do you think?

2. Let's share some about what you observed.

[**TEACHER NOTE:** Students might notice that the Indian Boy is represented by a Caucasian child or one with a turban. They might notice Titania or a person with a donkey head. Just get the kids to keep talking about what they're seeing—there is no right answer. answer. You may have to help them with "changeling"—a child who is suspected to not be a couple's real child.]

Part Two: Some scholarly investigating about the Indian Boy

1. You've noticed that the Indian Boy appears in all the images, but he doesn't have any lines in the play. He has no voice. What's up with that? For the rest of this class, you will be detectives and writers. And by the end of class, the Indian Boy will have not just one voice but many.

2. In your groups, you will each investigate part of Act 2, scene 1, when we first hear about the Indian Boy. Each group will get a different part of Act 2, scene 1, and you will be detectives, finding what information you can about the Indian Boy from the lines in that section. (**RESOURCE #3.1E, RESOURCE #3.1F, RESOURCE #3.1G, RESOURCE #3.1H**)

3. Read your section of Act 2 together, as you know how to do. Then focus on the Indian Boy. What are you learning about him, about who feels in what way about him? Jot down the thoughts in your group. You have 10 minutes to do this work, and then we'll share out.

4. All-class share-out.

[**TEACHER NOTE:** Take student observations first. If they don't get to these, feel free to use prompts: What's the Indian Boy's story? What do we know has happened to him? Who wants what? Does Titania's interest in him seem the same as Oberon's, or different? Does the Indian Boy have any power? Can he choose?]

Part Three: Give this boy a voice

1. Now you're equipped to give the Indian Boy a voice—something that Shakespeare doesn't do. In your groups, write a speech for him of 10 to 15 lines. Say all the things you feel he'd like to say! Take a few minutes to do that, and then we'll perform the speeches for each other.

Part Four: Reflection Flash Round

1. You've done amazing work today!

2. A reflection flash round of only one sentence. Thoughts about the Indian Boy. **"About the Indian Boy, I'm wondering . . ."**

Here's What Just Happened in Class

- Students paired Shakespeare's text with images it inspired to engage in multimodal close reading.

- Students analyzed different representations of the same character to consider how other readers have imagined him.

- Students analyzed how a nonspeaking character is portrayed through other characters' perspectives.

- Students used textual evidence to compose an original monologue for a nonspeaking character.

RESOURCE #3.1A

Artist unknown, drawing, ink on paper, late 19th or early 20th century.

FROM THE COLLECTION OF THE FOLGER SHAKESPEARE LIBRARY IN WASHINGTON, DC.

RESOURCE #3.1B

George Romney, painting on cardboard,
Lady Hamilton as Titania with Puck and Changeling, 1793.
FROM THE COLLECTION OF THE FOLGER SHAKESPEARE LIBRARY IN WASHINGTON, DC.

RESOURCE #3.1C

W. Hay, engraving, *But she perforce witholds the loved boy,
Crowns him with flowers and makes him all her joy,* 19th century.

FROM THE COLLECTION OF THE FOLGER SHAKESPEARE LIBRARY IN WASHINGTON, DC.

RESOURCE #3.1D

"·SHE·NEVER· HAD ·ſo ·ſWEET· A · CHANGELING·"

Fanny Railton, *A Midsummer Night's Dream* (a set of 65 drawings), 1901.
FROM THE COLLECTION OF THE FOLGER SHAKESPEARE LIBRARY IN WASHINGTON, DC.

A Midsummer Night's Dream, 2.1.1–61

ROBIN
How now, spirit? Whither wander you?

FAIRY
Over hill, over dale,
Thorough bush, thorough brier,
Over park, over pale,
Thorough flood, thorough fire;   5
I do wander everywhere,
Swifter than the moon's sphere.
And I serve the Fairy Queen,
To dew her orbs upon the green.
The cowslips tall her pensioners be;   10
In their gold coats spots you see;
Those be rubies, fairy favors;
In those freckles live their savors.
I must go seek some dewdrops here
And hang a pearl in every cowslip's ear.   15
Farewell, thou lob of spirits. I'll be gone.
Our queen and all her elves come here anon.

ROBIN
The King doth keep his revels here tonight.
Take heed the Queen come not within his sight,
For Oberon is passing fell and wrath   20
Because that she, as her attendant, hath
A lovely boy stolen from an Indian king;
She never had so sweet a changeling.
And jealous Oberon would have the child
Knight of his train, to trace the forests wild.   25
But she perforce withholds the lovèd boy,
Crowns him with flowers and makes him all her
    joy.
And now they never meet in grove or green,
By fountain clear or spangled starlight sheen,   30
But they do square, that all their elves for fear
Creep into acorn cups and hide them there.

FAIRY
Either I mistake your shape and making quite,
Or else you are that shrewd and knavish sprite

Called Robin Goodfellow. Are not you he   35
That frights the maidens of the villagery,
Skim milk, and sometimes labor in the quern
And bootless make the breathless huswife churn,
And sometime make the drink to bear no barm,
Mislead night wanderers, laughing at their harm?   40
Those that "Hobgoblin" call you and "sweet Puck,"
You do their work, and they shall have good luck.
Are not you he?

ROBIN

Thou speakest aright.
I am that merry wanderer of the night.   45
I jest to Oberon and make him smile
When I a fat and bean-fed horse beguile,
Neighing in likeness of a filly foal.
And sometime lurk I in a gossip's bowl
In very likeness of a roasted crab,   50
And, when she drinks, against her lips I bob
And on her withered dewlap pour the ale.
The wisest aunt, telling the saddest tale,
Sometime for three-foot stool mistaketh me;
Then slip I from her bum, down topples she   55
And "Tailor!" cries and falls into a cough,
And then the whole choir hold their hips and loffe
And waxen in their mirth and neeze and swear
A merrier hour was never wasted there.
But room, fairy. Here comes Oberon.   60

FAIRY

And here my mistress. Would that he were gone!

A Midsummer Night's Dream, 2.1.62–124, edited

OBERON
    Ill met by moonlight, proud Titania.

TITANIA
    What, jealous Oberon? Fairies, skip hence.
    I have forsworn his bed and company.

OBERON
    Tarry, rash wanton. Am not I thy lord?   65

TITANIA
    Then I must be thy lady. But I know
    When thou hast stolen away from Fairyland
    And in the shape of Corin sat all day
    Playing on pipes of corn and versing love
    To amorous Phillida. Why art thou here,   70
    Come from the farthest steep of India,
    But that, forsooth, the bouncing Amazon,
    Your buskined mistress and your warrior love,
    To Theseus must be wedded, and you come
    To give their bed joy and prosperity?   75

OBERON
    How canst thou thus for shame, Titania,
    Glance at my credit with Hippolyta,
    Knowing I know thy love to Theseus?
      . . .

TITANIA
    These are the forgeries of jealousy;
    No night is now with hymn or carol blessed.   105
    Therefore the moon, the governess of floods,
    Pale in her anger, washes all the air,
    That rheumatic diseases do abound.
    And thorough this distemperature we see
    The seasons alter: hoary-headed frosts   110
    Fall in the fresh lap of the crimson rose,
    And on old Hiems' thin and icy crown
    An odorous chaplet of sweet summer buds
    Is, as in mockery, set. The spring, the summer,
    The childing autumn, angry winter, change   115

Their wonted liveries, and the mazèd world
By their increase now knows not which is which.
And this same progeny of evils comes
From our debate, from our dissension;
We are their parents and original.   120

OBERON

Do you amend it, then. It lies in you.
Why should Titania cross her Oberon?
I do but beg a little changeling boy
To be my henchman.

RESOURCE #3.1G

A Midsummer Night's Dream, 2.1.125–150

TITANIA Set your heart at rest: 125
   The Fairyland buys not the child of me.
   His mother was a vot'ress of my order,
   And in the spicèd Indian air by night
   Full often hath she gossiped by my side
   And sat with me on Neptune's yellow sands,   130
   Marking th' embarkèd traders on the flood,
   When we have laughed to see the sails conceive
   And grow big-bellied with the wanton wind;
   Which she, with pretty and with swimming gait,
   Following (her womb then rich with my young   135
     squire),
   Would imitate and sail upon the land
   To fetch me trifles and return again,
   As from a voyage, rich with merchandise.
   But she, being mortal, of that boy did die,   140
   And for her sake do I rear up her boy,
   And for her sake I will not part with him.

OBERON
   How long within this wood intend you stay?

TITANIA
   Perchance till after Theseus' wedding day.
   If you will patiently dance in our round   145
   And see our moonlight revels, go with us.
   If not, shun me, and I will spare your haunts.

OBERON
   Give me that boy and I will go with thee.

TITANIA
   Not for thy fairy kingdom. Fairies, away.
   We shall chide downright if I longer stay.   150
             Titania and her fairies exit.

RESOURCE #3.1H

A Midsummer Night's Dream, 2.1.151–192

OBERON

 Well, go thy way. Thou shalt not from this grove
 Till I torment thee for this injury.—
 My gentle Puck, come hither. Thou rememb'rest
 Since once I sat upon a promontory
 And heard a mermaid on a dolphin's back   155
 Uttering such dulcet and harmonious breath
 That the rude sea grew civil at her song
 And certain stars shot madly from their spheres
 To hear the sea-maid's music.

ROBIN I remember.   160

OBERON

 That very time I saw (but thou couldst not),
 Flying between the cold moon and the Earth,
 Cupid all armed. A certain aim he took
 At a fair vestal thronèd by the west,
 And loosed his love-shaft smartly from his bow   165
 As it should pierce a hundred thousand hearts.
 But I might see young Cupid's fiery shaft
 Quenched in the chaste beams of the wat'ry moon,
 And the imperial vot'ress passèd on
 In maiden meditation, fancy-free.   170
 Yet marked I where the bolt of Cupid fell.
 It fell upon a little western flower,
 Before, milk-white, now purple with love's wound,
 And maidens call it "love-in-idleness."
 Fetch me that flower; the herb I showed thee once.   175
 The juice of it on sleeping eyelids laid
 Will make or man or woman madly dote
 Upon the next live creature that it sees.
 Fetch me this herb, and be thou here again
 Ere the leviathan can swim a league.   180

ROBIN

 I'll put a girdle round about the Earth
 In forty minutes.   *He exits.*

OBERON Having once this juice,
 I'll watch Titania when she is asleep

And drop the liquor of it in her eyes.   185
The next thing then she, waking, looks upon
(Be it on lion, bear, or wolf, or bull,
On meddling monkey, or on busy ape)
She shall pursue it with the soul of love.
And ere I take this charm from off her sight   190
(As I can take it with another herb),
I'll make her render up her page to me.

WEEK THREE: LESSON 2

The Mechanicals' Path: Getting Them into the Action

Here's What We're Doing and Why

Students will launch into this group of tradesmen—or "the mechanicals" as they are sometimes called—and use their Choral Reading and 3D Lit tools to figure out what's up. Divided into two or three groups, they will get busy working through the scene, deciding how they will cut, cast, and perform it—and make notes about all of this in a promptbook. In class, they'll be using and practicing skills that are familiar. Your job is to set them off and let them go, cruising around, of course, as they work, but basically keeping out of the way. You've already taught them how to get this far!

What Will I Need?

- Copies of 1.2 for every student – **RESOURCE #3.2**

How Should I Prepare?

- Set up your room to facilitate group work and performance.

- Make copies of 1.2 – **RESOURCE #3.2** – one for each student.

- Decide how you'd like to divide your students into groups of at least five and no more than seven, and post the group lists somewhere visible.

Agenda (~ 45-minute class period)

- ❏ Part One: Set-up (5 minutes)

- ❏ Part Two: Group Work on 1.2 (30 minutes)

- ❏ Part Three: Share out the best 2 minutes of your work so far (10 minutes)

Here's What Students Hear (From You) and (Then What They'll) Do

Part One: Set-up

Today, you're going to work in groups and dive into 1.2 from *Midsummer*. You'll work together, using the tools you already know to figure out what's up—you'll be scholars, editors, directors, and actors. Some of the 3D Lit questions might help as you read together and get into it: Who are these folks? How do you know? What does the text tell you? What are they up to? What are they planning? How do you know?

Part Two: Get busy on 1.2

I've divided you into groups—check them out. You'll have 30 minutes to work. Each group will work on the same scene—1.2. You'll need to read it through a few times, figure out what's going on, have some thoughts about individual characters—and then talk about how you want to cut it, cast it (within your group), and perform it—creating a promptbook as you go, keeping track of all those decisions. Think about these things:

- Designate who will be keeping details in your promptbook. Make sure that the names of your group members are on it, and that you hand it to me at the end of class.

- You won't have the right number of actors to go around, though everyone must participate. How will you creatively solve this problem? (Shakespeare had to solve it all the time!)

Part Three: Let's have your best two minutes!

Let's have a two-minute share-out from each group: your best two minutes of process or performance!

Here's What Just Happened in Class

- Students applied the now-familiar Folger Method essentials of cutting to close read a scene.

- Students used their interpretations of the characters to make annotations and create a promptbook.

- Students annotated the text to make explicit connections between Shakespeare's words and their performance choices.

- Students built confidence in their ability to stage a scene on their own. (You can use this as a formative assessment at the halfway point of the play.)

RESOURCE #3.2

A Midsummer Night's Dream, 1.2

QUINCE Is all our company here?

BOTTOM You were best to call them generally, man by
man, according to the scrip.

QUINCE Here is the scroll of every man's name which
is thought fit, through all Athens, to play in our   5
interlude before the Duke and the Duchess on his
wedding day at night.

BOTTOM First, good Peter Quince, say what the play
treats on, then read the names of the actors, and so
grow to a point.   10

QUINCE Marry, our play is "The most lamentable
comedy and most cruel death of Pyramus and
Thisbe."

BOTTOM A very good piece of work, I assure you, and a
merry. Now, good Peter Quince, call forth your   15
actors by the scroll. Masters, spread yourselves.

QUINCE Answer as I call you. Nick Bottom, the weaver.

BOTTOM Ready. Name what part I am for, and
proceed.

QUINCE You, Nick Bottom, are set down for Pyramus.   20

BOTTOM What is Pyramus—a lover or a tyrant?

QUINCE A lover that kills himself most gallant for love.

BOTTOM That will ask some tears in the true performing
of it. If I do it, let the audience look to their
eyes. I will move storms; I will condole in some   25
measure. To the rest.—Yet my chief humor is for a
tyrant. I could play Ercles rarely, or a part to tear a
cat in, to make all split:
          The raging rocks
          And shivering shocks   30
          Shall break the locks

> *Of prison gates.*
> *And Phibbus' car*
> *Shall shine from far*
> *And make and mar*   35
> *The foolish Fates.*
This was lofty. Now name the rest of the players.
This is Ercles' vein, a tyrant's vein. A lover is more
condoling.

QUINCE Francis Flute, the bellows-mender.   40

FLUTE Here, Peter Quince.

QUINCE Flute, you must take Thisbe on you.

FLUTE What is Thisbe—a wand'ring knight?

QUINCE It is the lady that Pyramus must love.

FLUTE Nay, faith, let not me play a woman. I have a   45
    beard coming.

QUINCE That's all one. You shall play it in a mask, and
    you may speak as small as you will.

BOTTOM An I may hide my face, let me play Thisbe too.
    I'll speak in a monstrous little voice: "Thisne,   50
    Thisne!"—"Ah Pyramus, my lover dear! Thy Thisbe
    dear and lady dear!"

QUINCE No, no, you must play Pyramus—and, Flute,
    you Thisbe.

BOTTOM Well, proceed.   55

QUINCE Robin Starveling, the tailor.

STARVELING Here, Peter Quince.

QUINCE Robin Starveling, you must play Thisbe's
    mother.—Tom Snout, the tinker.

SNOUT Here, Peter Quince.   60

QUINCE You, Pyramus' father.—Myself, Thisbe's
    father.—Snug the joiner, you the lion's part.—
    And I hope here is a play fitted.

SNUG Have you the lion's part written? Pray you, if it
    be, give it me, for I am slow of study.   65

QUINCE You may do it extempore, for it is nothing but
    roaring.

BOTTOM Let me play the lion too. I will roar that I will
    do any man's heart good to hear me. I will roar that
    I will make the Duke say "Let him roar again. Let   70
    him roar again!"

QUINCE An you should do it too terribly, you would
    fright the Duchess and the ladies that they would
    shriek, and that were enough to hang us all.

ALL That would hang us, every mother's son.   75

BOTTOM I grant you, friends, if you should fright the
    ladies out of their wits, they would have no more
    discretion but to hang us. But I will aggravate my
    voice so that I will roar you as gently as any sucking
    dove. I will roar you an 'twere any nightingale.   80

QUINCE You can play no part but Pyramus, for Pyramus
    is a sweet-faced man, a proper man as one
    shall see in a summer's day, a most lovely gentlemanlike
    man. Therefore you must needs play
    Pyramus.   85

BOTTOM Well, I will undertake it. What beard were I
    best to play it in?

QUINCE Why, what you will.

BOTTOM I will discharge it in either your straw-color
    beard, your orange-tawny beard, your purple-in-grain   90
    beard, or your French-crown-color beard,
    your perfit yellow.

QUINCE Some of your French crowns have no hair at
    all, and then you will play barefaced. But, masters,
    here are your parts, *giving out the parts,* and I am   95
    to entreat you, request you, and desire you to con
    them by tomorrow night and meet me in the palace
    wood, a mile without the town, by moonlight. There
    will we rehearse, for if we meet in the city, we shall
    be dogged with company and our devices known. In   100

the meantime I will draw a bill of properties such as
our play wants. I pray you fail me not.

BOTTOM We will meet, and there we may rehearse
most obscenely and courageously. Take pains. Be
perfit. Adieu.   105

QUINCE At the Duke's Oak we meet.

BOTTOM Enough. Hold or cut bowstrings.

WEEK THREE: LESSON 3

Power and Representation Across the Sweep of Literature: Chimamanda Adichie and Shakespeare

Here's What We're Doing and Why

As we already know, pairing texts helps to expand students' knowledge and their sense of two very different writers. Today, Chimamanda Adichie helps to shine a light on some of the power dynamics in *Midsummer*, specifically Helena's feelings of self-worth. This is a chance to bring the Indian Boy into the mix as well, and to extend students' thinking and discussion into tomorrow's lesson too.

We start this lesson by giving the lines from both texts to the students to toss. And they will read each text in smaller groups. We've done some analyzing and practiced the steps to get them to this point of making **meaning of new text without** relying on you. Thinking about the big picture, this is what you'll be asking them to do for the final project at the end of the unit.

What Will I Need?

- A soft item to toss during activity (beanbag, stuffed toy, etc.)

- Handouts of:
    - Copies of Lines to Toss—**RESOURCE #3.3A**—cut apart, mixed up, and one line per student. Duplicated lines are fine.
    - Section of *A Midsummer Night's Dream*, 2.1.195–251 – **RESOURCE #3.3B**
    - Section of *We Should All Be Feminists* by Chimamanda Ngozi Adichie – **RESOURCE #3.3C**

How Should I Prepare?

- Set up your classroom in a large circle with space in the middle for large-group and small-group work.

- Copy and cut out the lines in **RESOURCE #3.3A** and mix them up for distribution to students. Make enough copies for each student of:
    - Section of *A Midsummer Night's Dream*, 2.1.195–251 – **RESOURCE #3.3B**
    - Section of *We Should All Be Feminists* by Chimamanda Ngozi Adichie – **RESOURCE #3.3C**

- Decide how you will divide your students into two groups.

Agenda (~ 45-minute class period)

❏ Part One: Tossing Lines (10 minutes)

❑ Part Two: Reading Shakespeare and Adichie (20 minutes)

❑ Part Three: All-class discussion on power and representation (15 minutes)

Here's What Students Hear (From You) and (Then What They'll) Do

Part One: Tossing Lines

1. We're going to start today with tossing lines, and then talking a little bit about them. I'm handing each of you a line. Have a look at it, don't show it to anybody, and be ready to shout it out when you toss.

2. Let's have circles with five or six in a group. Toss the beanbag to one another around your circle as you say your line. After a bit, let's join circles into one big one and toss around that circle.

3. Great work. Let's discuss for a bit:
   – What are your thoughts about these lines?

[TEACHER NOTE: As always, don't offer "answers" or comments. Don't expect students to make specific inferences about the text, but don't be surprised if they do!]

Part Two: Two different texts to get us thinking

1. These lines come from two different texts. Some are from *Midsummer* by Shakespeare, and some are from *We Should All Be Feminists* by Chimamanda Ngozi Adichie. Ms. Adichie is a celebrated writer who was born in Nigeria to an Igbo family. She has been awarded many prizes for her writing. Her second home is now in the United States. Feel free to look up more about her.

2. Now we're going to read the texts that your lines come from. We'll start with Shakespeare. Get into your groups and read through this in a few ways as we most often do.

   After you have a sense about what is going on in this scene, discuss in your group: How do you think Helena feels? How do you know? If you felt the way she does, what would you be saying? And what does Demetrius feel? How do you know? Who has the power here? How do you know? Who should have the power here? Is there a power struggle here? What else do you notice?

[TEACHER NOTE: Perhaps put these questions on the board if you need to prompt students as they discuss.]

   Hold on to your thoughts until we've read Adichie's piece.

3. Let's continue on, and read a selection from *We Should All Be Feminists* by Chimamanda Adichie. More than 400 years after Shakespeare, she is thinking about power too. Why do you think people have been talking about these kinds of power struggles for centuries?

4. You're going to read this section in your groups, and I'm going to ask you to read it around in your circle, paragraph-by-paragraph. Go to the next reader when you get to a double space before the next sentence begins. After you have

read through it several times, consider these questions with your group: Who does Ms. Adichie feel has the power? What words in her piece have power? Underline all that do!

5. We will continue to think about how both of these texts speak together tomorrow, but let's expand our thinking some too.

Part Three

1. Let's hear your thoughts and feelings on these two pieces, and bring the Indian Boy into the conversation now too. We talked about power with the Indian Boy, and now with Helena and Demetrius. What do you think this play might be telling us about power?

2. Where do we continue to see power struggles today?

3. Great work today!

Here's What Just Happened in Class

- Students used paired texts to explore ideas of power, gender, and representation across time and context.

- Students analyzed disturbing language about relationships with the help of a modern author's perspective on gender dynamics.

- Students made connections between the conflict between Helena and Demetrius and current social issues.

Lines to Toss . . .

I love thee not	die upon the hand I love	I am your spaniel
get thee gone	I love you the more	I am sick when I do look on thee
no power	I'll run from thee	I am sick when I look not on you
your power	unworthy as I am	strike me
neglect me	I'll follow thee	can I beg
We stifle the humanity of boys	Not too much ambition	We teach boys to be afraid of fear
We teach boys to be afraid of weakness	This is because of our culture	Girls shrink themselves
Girls make themselves smaller	A woman is more likely to compromise	

RESOURCE #3.3B

A Midsummer Night's Dream 2.1.195–251, edited

DEMETRIUS

    I love thee not; therefore pursue me not.   95
    Hence, get thee gone, and follow me no more.

HELENA

    Leave you your power to draw,
    And I shall have no power to follow you.   205

DEMETRIUS

    Do I entice you? Do I speak you fair?
    Or rather do I not in plainest truth
    Tell you I do not, nor I cannot love you?

HELENA

    And even for that do I love you the more.
    I am your spaniel, and, Demetrius,   210
    The more you beat me I will fawn on you.
    Use me but as your spaniel: spurn me, strike me,
    Neglect me, lose me; only give me leave
    (Unworthy as I am) to follow you.
    What worser place can I beg in your love   215
    Than to be usèd as you use your dog?

DEMETRIUS

    Tempt not too much the hatred of my spirit,
    For I am sick when I do look on thee.

HELENA

    And I am sick when I look not on you.   220

DEMETRIUS

    I'll run from thee and hide me in the brakes
    And leave thee to the mercy of wild beasts.   235

HELENA

    We cannot fight for love as men may do.
    We should be wooed and were not made to woo.   *Demetrius exits.*
    I'll follow thee and make a heaven of hell   250
    To die upon the hand I love so well.
                  Helena exits.

We Should All Be Feminists
by Chimamanda Ngozi Adichie

We do a great disservice to boys in how we raise them. We stifle the humanity of boys. We define masculinity in a very narrow way. Masculinity is a hard, small cage, and we put boys inside this cage.

We teach boys to be afraid of fear, of weakness, of vulnerability. We teach them to mask their true selves, because they have to be, in Nigerian-speak, a *hard man*.

And then we do a much greater disservice to girls, because we raise them to cater to the fragile egos of males.

We teach girls to shrink themselves, to make themselves smaller.

We say to girls, 'You can have ambition, but not too much. You should aim to be successful but not too successful, otherwise you will threaten the man. If you are the breadwinner in your relationship with a man, pretend that you are not, especially in public, otherwise you will emasculate him.'

But what if we question the premise itself? Why should a woman's success be a threat to a man?

A Nigerian acquaintance once asked me if I was worried that men would be intimidated by me. I was not worried at all—it had not even occurred to me to be worried, because a man who would be intimidated by me is exactly the kind of man I would have no interest in.

Still, I was struck by this. Because I am female, I'm expected to aspire to marriage. I am expected to make my life choices always keeping in mind that marriage is the most important. Marriage can be a good thing, a source of joy, love and mutual support. But why do we teach girls to aspire to marriage, yet we don't teach boys to do the same?

Our society teaches a woman at a certain age who is unmarried to see it as a deep personal failure. While a man at a certain age who is unmarried has not quite come around to making his pick.

It is easy to say, 'But women can just say no to all this.' But the reality is more difficult, more complex. We are all social beings. We internalize ideas from our socialization.

Even the language we use illustrates this. The language of marriage is often a language of ownership, not a language of partnership.

We use the word *respect* for something a woman shows a man, but not often for something a man shows a woman.

We teach females that in relationships, compromise is what a woman is more likely to do.

We raise girls to see each other as competitors—not for jobs or accomplishments, which in my opinion can be a good thing, but for the attention of men.

Other men might respond by saying, 'Okay, this is interesting, but I don't think like that. I don't even think about gender.'

Maybe not.

And that is part of the problem. That many men do not actively think about gender or notice gender. That many men say, like my friend Louis did, that things might have been bad in the past but everything is fine now. And that many men do nothing to change it. If you are a man and you walk into a restaurant and the waiter greets just you, does it occur to you to ask the waiter, 'Why have you not greeted her?' Men need to speak out in all of these ostensibly small situations.

Because gender can be uncomfortable, there are easy ways to close this conversation.

Some people will say a woman is subordinate to men because it's our culture. But culture is constantly changing. I have beautiful twin nieces who are fifteen. If they had been born a hundred years ago, they would have been taken away and killed. Because a hundred years ago, Igbo culture considered the birth of twins to be an evil omen. Today that practice is unimaginable to all Igbo people.

Culture does not make people. People make culture. If it is true that the full humanity of women is not our culture, then we can and must make it our culture.

Students Put Adichie and Shakespeare in Conversation

Here's What We're Doing and Why

Today, your students will take another step in the Shakespeare-Adichie conversation, this time adding Helena's self-worth into the mix, creating a conversation and a performance in an original mash-up. Then they'll decide how they will add gesture, tone, stress, and other physical action to their performance so that the back-and-forth of this conversation is as strong and clear as possible.

What Will I Need?

- Selection from *A Midsummer Night's Dream*, 2.2.90–105 – **RESOURCE #3.4A**

- Selection from *We Should All Be Feminists* – **RESOURCE #3.4B** (also in yesterday's lesson, same as yesterday's **RESOURCE #3.3C**)

How Should I Prepare?

- Set up your classroom for Choral Reading.

- Make copies for each student:
    - Selection from *A Midsummer Night's Dream*, 2.2.90–105 – **RESOURCE #3.4A**
    - Selection from *We Should All Be Feminists*—**RESOURCE #3.4B**—or maybe they have their copies from yesterday

- Plan how you'll put students in pairs or threes to create a mash-up.

Agenda (~ 45-minute class period)

- ❏ Part One: Choral Adichie (10 minutes)
- ❏ Part Two: Choral Shakespeare (10 minutes)
- ❏ Part Three: The Mash-up assignment and performances (20 minutes)
- ❏ Part Four: Reflection Flash Round (5 minutes)

Here's What Students Hear (From You) and (Then What They'll) Do

Part One: Let's get reacquainted with Adichie's text from yesterday

1. Let's get our copies of Adichie (**RESOURCE #3.4B**), stand in a circle, and first read the whole piece chorally. Then let's read it paragraph-by-paragraph as you did yesterday.

2. Any additional thoughts left over from our conversation yesterday?

Part Two: And dive into a new selection from Shakespeare

1. Let's move to **RESOURCE #3.4A**. Stay in our tight circle and let's read this chorally too.

2. First, let's read it as fast and as loud as we can while still trying to stay together.

3. Let's read it together again, this time switching readers at end punctuation.

4. Last reading—all of us together, but whisper the whole thing.

5. After all these readings—you are experienced readers and analyzers at this point—let's talk about it for a bit. What's going on here? What feelings and emotions can you sense?

Part Three: Creating and performing the mash-up

1. Now you'll work in pairs or threes. The assignment for each group is to create a mash-up in which Shakespeare and Chimamanda Adichie are talking to each other. You'll create the conversation between them, and then you'll perform that conversation!

2. In your smaller groups, read both pieces again. Do some thinking and talking about what the most powerful thoughts and words are in each piece. If the authors met in real life, what do you think they'd have to say to each other?

   – Your mash-up should include at least 10 lines (or parts of lines) from Adichie and 10 lines from Shakespeare.

   – Make sure they are having an interesting and compelling conversation!

3. Once you have created your mash-up, consider how you will perform it. How will physical action, tone of voice, and props (if you have them) add to the words here? Go for it!

Part Three: Mash-ups in performance

Let's share and celebrate these mash-ups. After each performance, let's have a few comments from the performing group—on anything about their process—and questions from the rest of the class.

Part Four: Reflection Flash Round

Let's go around the room and each of us finish this sentence: **"I noticed . . ."**

Here's What Just Happened in Class

- Students analyzed a character's feelings through a modern lens.

- Students used these two paired texts to explore ideas of power and gender across time and context.

- Students composed a conversation to explore the topic through multiple perspectives, and amplified that conversation through performance.

RESOURCE #3.4A

A Midsummer Night's Dream, 2.2.90–105

HELENA

    Stay, though thou kill me, sweet Demetrius.   90

DEMETRIUS

    I charge thee, hence, and do not haunt me thus.

HELENA

    O, wilt thou darkling leave me? Do not so.

DEMETRIUS

    Stay, on thy peril. I alone will go.   *Demetrius exits.*

HELENA

    O, I am out of breath in this fond chase.
    The more my prayer, the lesser is my grace.   95
    Happy is Hermia, wheresoe'er she lies,
    For she hath blessèd and attractive eyes.
    How came her eyes so bright? Not with salt tears.
    If so, my eyes are oftener washed than hers.
    No, no, I am as ugly as a bear,   100
    For beasts that meet me run away for fear.
    Therefore no marvel though Demetrius
    Do as a monster fly my presence thus.
    What wicked and dissembling glass of mine
    Made me compare with Hermia's sphery eyne?   105

We Should All Be Feminists
by Chimamanda Ngozi Adichie

From *We Should All Be Feminists*, edited for use in this lesson

We do a great disservice to boys in how we raise them. We stifle the humanity of boys. We define masculinity in a very narrow way. Masculinity is a hard, small cage, and we put boys inside this cage.

We teach boys to be afraid of fear, of weakness, of vulnerability. We teach them to mask their true selves, because they have to be, in Nigerian-speak, a *hard man*.

And then we do a much greater disservice to girls, because we raise them to cater to the fragile egos of males.

We teach girls to shrink themselves, to make themselves smaller.

We say to girls, 'You can have ambition, but not too much. You should aim to be successful but not too successful, otherwise you will threaten the man. If you are the breadwinner in your relationship with a man, pretend that you are not, especially in public, otherwise you will emasculate him.'

But what if we question the premise itself? Why should a woman's success be a threat to a man?

A Nigerian acquaintance once asked me if I was worried that men would be intimidated by me. I was not worried at all—it had not even occurred to me to be worried, because a man who would be intimidated by me is exactly the kind of man I would have no interest in.

Still, I was struck by this. Because I am female, I'm expected to aspire to marriage. I am expected to make my life choices always keeping in mind that marriage is the most important. Marriage can be a good thing, a source of joy, love and mutual support. But why do we teach girls to aspire to marriage, yet we don't teach boys to do the same?

Our society teaches a woman at a certain age who is unmarried to see it as a deep personal failure. While a man at a certain age who is unmarried has not quite come around to making his pick.

It is easy to say, 'But women can just say no to all this.' But the reality is more difficult, more complex. We are all social beings. We internalize ideas from our socialization.

Even the language we use illustrates this. The language of marriage is often a language of ownership, not a language of partnership.

We use the word *respect* for something a woman shows a man, but not often for something a man shows a woman.

We teach females that in relationships, compromise is what a woman is more likely to do.

We raise girls to see each other as competitors—not for jobs or accomplishments, which in my opinion can be a good thing, but for the attention of men.

Other men might respond by saying, 'Okay, this is interesting, but I don't think like that. I don't even think about gender.'

Maybe not.

And that is part of the problem. That many men do not actively think about gender or notice gender. That many men say, like my friend Louis did, that things might have been bad in the past but everything is fine now. And that many men do nothing to change it. If you are a man and you walk into a restaurant and the waiter greets just you, does it occur to you to ask the waiter, 'Why have you not greeted her?' Men need to speak out in all of these ostensibly small situations.

Because gender can be uncomfortable, there are easy ways to close this conversation.

Some people will say a woman is subordinate to men because it's our culture. But culture is constantly changing. I have beautiful twin nieces who are fifteen. If they had been born a hundred years ago, they would have been taken away and killed. Because a hundred years ago, Igbo culture considered the birth of twins to be an evil omen. Today that practice is unimaginable to all Igbo people.

Culture does not make people. People make culture. If it is true that the full humanity of women is not our culture, then we can and must make it our culture.

"Fetch Me That Flower": The Story of That Special Flower, in Relay!

Here's What We're Doing and Why

Today, students will explore some of the *Midsummer* magic by focusing on Oberon's magic flower and the mayhem and changes that it causes. Students will work in groups to read, prompt-book, and rehearse 4 different scenes that capture the path and varying perspectives of the flower with magic nectar. At the end of class, groups will perform their scenes in relay and tell the story of this special flower . . . almost completely. In their own scenes, they can divide up the speeches among more than one actor or more than one character, or they can add text if they can justify it well. They'll record all of these decisions in a promptbook and then perform their scenes for one another. (If you have more than 4 groups, that's okay. You can give the same scene to a couple of groups. Students will come up with very different interpretations, and that's always fascinating!)

They will perform their scenes in relay. When one scene finishes, the next one jumps right into action. A hat that the Oberons can pass from one to another could be helpful for continuity, or a bandana (or anything really) that can help the audience be able to identify Robin Goodfellow (Puck). What's powerful about this work is that students will realize in yet another way that there's no one right way or one single way to read or perform or interpret a text, and that this leads to the creation of their own interpretations. What they will do today prefigures a bit of what they will be doing for their final projects in Week Five.

What Will I Need?

- Speeches and scenes related to the magic flower, divided into 4 scripts – **RESOURCE #3.5**

How Should I Prepare?

- Clear out space for performances.

- Copies of a script related to the magic flower, made up of 4 sections. One script for each student – **RESOURCE #3.5**

- Be ready to divide the class into groups of 4 to 5.

Agenda (~ 45-minute class period)

- ❑ Set-up and directions (5 minutes)

- ❑ Reading and digging in (10 minutes)

- ❑ Rehearse, plan, perform (30 minutes)

Here's What Students Hear (From You) and (Then What They'll) Do

Part One: Setting up for scene work

1. Today you will all collaborate on telling the story of Oberon's special flower and the power it exerts throughout the play. You'll work in groups; each group will act a different scene. In your groups, you'll read the scene as we have many times, and then you'll use 3D Lit and other tools to put it on its feet, to perform, and to show us how the power of the magic flower potion impacts so much. Turn one of your scripts into a promptbook so that as you make decisions about entrances, exits, notes about actors' gestures, tone of voice, and more, they are recorded in the promptbook. You'll also record cuts or additions to the text, and indicate if you have divided one speech up among 2 or 3 actors.

2. I've set you up in the following groups: 1, 2, 3, and 4 . . . and here is **RESOURCE #3.5** that includes scripts for all groups.

Part Two: Reading and digging in

Let's start by reading all of these scenes, one after another, together, chorally. You're all experts now, so let's read them through once together so we can get a sense of what's happening.

Part Three: Rehearse, plan, perform

1. Get into your groups and read only your scene again. Try out various parts of your scene "on its feet" and record your decisions in your promptbook. Write actions, cues, and emotions where they should be performed within the lines. You can also use any props available in the classroom or on your person. Rehearse until your scene feels like it's headed in the right direction.

2. Let the magic relay begin! I will call out the groups in sequence; when it's your turn, run into the center of the circle, receive the hat, bandana, or whatever from the group ahead of you, and show us your stuff! Let us see your scene!

[**TEACHER NOTE:** Encourage enthusiastic applause! If you assigned the same scene to more than one group, they should perform right after each other.]

3. Your wonderful relay has provided us with the long story of that magical flower. Okay, let's talk about this scene quickly. What did you learn? What did you notice? Who has the power? Who doesn't? How do you know?

4. Great work this week! Next week, we'll do a few more deep dives as we head to the all-important Week Five!

Here's What Just Happened in Class

- Students narrowed in on a recurring element of the text—Oberon's magic flower—to show its impact on conflict.

- Students built their confidence as analysts of literature and as actors putting a play on its feet.

- Students close-read texts to analyze power dynamics.

- Students analyzed how performance choices impacted their scene.

RESOURCE #3.5

GROUP ONE
A Midsummer Night's Dream, 2.1.161–182

OBERON

That very time I saw (but thou couldst not),
Flying between the cold moon and the Earth,
Cupid all armed. A certain aim he took
At a fair vestal thronèd by the west,
And loosed his love-shaft smartly from his bow   165
As it should pierce a hundred thousand hearts.
But I might see young Cupid's fiery shaft
Quenched in the chaste beams of the wat'ry moon,
And the imperial vot'ress passèd on
In maiden meditation, fancy-free.   170
Yet marked I where the bolt of Cupid fell.
It fell upon a little western flower,
Before, milk-white, now purple with love's wound,
And maidens call it "love-in-idleness."
Fetch me that flower; the herb I showed thee once.   175
The juice of it on sleeping eyelids laid
Will make or man or woman madly dote
Upon the next live creature that it sees.
Fetch me this herb, and be thou here again
Ere the leviathan can swim a league.   180

ROBIN

I'll put a girdle round about the Earth
In forty minutes.   *He exits.*

GROUP TWO
A Midsummer Night's Dream, 2.1.183–192 and 2.2.33–40

OBERON Having once this juice,
I'll watch Titania when she is asleep
And drop the liquor of it in her eyes.   185
The next thing then she, waking, looks upon
(Be it on lion, bear, or wolf, or bull,
On meddling monkey, or on busy ape)
She shall pursue it with the soul of love.
And ere I take this charm from off her sight   190
(As I can take it with another herb),
I'll make her render up her page to me.

2.2.33–40

OBERON

    What thou seest when thou dost wake
    Do it for thy true love take.
    Love and languish for his sake.   35
    Be it ounce, or cat, or bear,
    Pard, or boar with bristled hair,
    In thy eye that shall appear
    When thou wak'st, it is thy dear.
    Wake when some vile thing is near.   40
                                He exits.

GROUP THREE
A Midsummer Night's Dream, 2.1.254–276 and 2.2.72–89

OBERON

    Hast thou the flower there? Welcome, wanderer.

ROBIN

    Ay, there it is.   255

OBERON I pray thee give it me.
                           Robin gives him the flower.
    I know a bank where the wild thyme blows,
    Where oxlips and the nodding violet grows,
    Quite overcanopied with luscious woodbine,
    With sweet muskroses, and with eglantine.   260
    There sleeps Titania sometime of the night,
    Lulled in these flowers with dances and delight.
    And there the snake throws her enameled skin,
    Weed wide enough to wrap a fairy in.
    And with the juice of this I'll streak her eyes   265
    And make her full of hateful fantasies.
    Take thou some of it, and seek through this grove.
                   He gives Robin part of the flower.
    A sweet Athenian lady is in love
    With a disdainful youth. Anoint his eyes,
    But do it when the next thing he espies   270
    May be the lady. Thou shalt know the man
    By the Athenian garments he hath on.
    Effect it with some care, that he may prove
    More fond on her than she upon her love.
    And look thou meet me ere the first cock crow.   275

ROBIN

Fear not, my lord. Your servant shall do so.

2.2.72–89

ROBIN

Through the forest have I gone,
But Athenian found I none
On whose eyes I might approve
This flower's force in stirring love. 75

He sees Lysander.

Night and silence! Who is here?
Weeds of Athens he doth wear.
This is he my master said
Despisèd the Athenian maid.
And here the maiden, sleeping sound 80
On the dank and dirty ground.
Pretty soul, she durst not lie
Near this lack-love, this kill-courtesy.—
Churl, upon thy eyes I throw
All the power this charm doth owe. 85

*He anoints Lysander's eyelids
with the nectar.*

When thou wak'st, let love forbid
Sleep his seat on thy eyelid.
So, awake when I am gone,
For I must now to Oberon. *He exits.*

GROUP FOUR
A Midsummer Night's Dream, 3.2.4–42 and 3.2.90–117

OBERON

Here comes my messenger. How now, mad spirit?
What night-rule now about this haunted grove? 5

ROBIN

My mistress with a monster is in love.
Near to her close and consecrated bower,
While she was in her dull and sleeping hour,
A crew of patches, rude mechanicals,
That work for bread upon Athenian stalls, 10
Were met together to rehearse a play
Intended for great Theseus' nuptial day.
The shallowest thick-skin of that barren sort,

Who Pyramus presented in their sport,
Forsook his scene and entered in a brake. 15
When I did him at this advantage take,
An ass's noll I fixèd on his head.
Anon his Thisbe must be answerèd,
And forth my mimic comes. When they him spy,
As wild geese that the creeping fowler eye, 20
Or russet-pated choughs, many in sort,
Rising and cawing at the gun's report,
Sever themselves and madly sweep the sky,
So at his sight away his fellows fly,
And, at our stamp, here o'er and o'er one falls. 25
He "Murder" cries and help from Athens calls.
Their sense thus weak, lost with their fears thus
   strong,
Made senseless things begin to do them wrong;
For briers and thorns at their apparel snatch, 30
Some sleeves, some hats, from yielders all things
   catch.
I led them on in this distracted fear
And left sweet Pyramus translated there.
When in that moment, so it came to pass, 35
Titania waked and straightway loved an ass.

OBERON

This falls out better than I could devise.
But hast thou yet latched the Athenian's eyes
With the love juice, as I did bid thee do?

ROBIN

I took him sleeping—that is finished, too— 40
And the Athenian woman by his side,
That, when he waked, of force she must be eyed.

3.2.90–117

OBERON, *to Robin*

What hast thou done? Thou hast mistaken quite 90
And laid the love juice on some true-love's sight.
Of thy misprision must perforce ensue
Some true-love turned, and not a false turned true.

ROBIN

Then fate o'errules, that, one man holding troth,
A million fail, confounding oath on oath. 95

OBERON

    About the wood go swifter than the wind,
    And Helena of Athens look thou find.
    All fancy-sick she is and pale of cheer
    With sighs of love that costs the fresh blood dear.
    By some illusion see thou bring her here.   100
    I'll charm his eyes against she do appear.

ROBIN I go, I go, look how I go,

    Swifter than arrow from the Tartar's bow.   *He exits.*

OBERON, *applying the nectar to Demetrius' eyes*

    Flower of this purple dye,
    Hit with Cupid's archery,   105
    Sink in apple of his eye.
    When his love he doth espy,
    Let her shine as gloriously
    As the Venus of the sky.—
    When thou wak'st, if she be by,   110
    Beg of her for remedy.

                     Enter Robin.

ROBIN

    Captain of our fairy band,
    Helena is here at hand,
    And the youth, mistook by me,
    Pleading for a lover's fee.   115
    Shall we their fond pageant see?
    Lord, what fools these mortals be!

WEEK FOUR: LESSON 1

Beginning to Weave It All Together— Part 1, Digging In

Here's What We're Doing and Why

In this lesson and in the next one, students will take on most of Act 3 by putting Folger Essentials 3D Lit, Choral Reading, and other Folger Method tools into action. Students will work in 5 groups on 5 different scenes—collaboratively reading for understanding, cutting, casting, and beginning to make performance decisions today. Tomorrow they will make more performance choices, rehearse, and perform. Though they have focused on selections from Act 3 in earlier lessons, this will offer them a chance to dive into the entire action-packed act. These two lessons will also provide them with a great warm-up for their final projects, which will start next week.

What Will I Need?

- Copies of each of the 5 scenes for each group – **RESOURCE #4.1A, RESOURCE #4.1B, RESOURCE #4.1C, RESOURCE #4.1D,** and **RESOURCE #4.1E**

- Your classroom arranged so that students can work in groups

How Should I Prepare?

- Decide how you will divide students into those five groups.

- Make enough copies of the **RESOURCES** so that each member of each group will have their own copy of their scene.

Agenda (~ 45-minute class period)

- ❏ Part One: Set-up of groups and work (5 minutes)
- ❏ Part Two: Read chorally and discuss (20 minutes)
- ❏ Part Three: Begin cutting and casting (15 minutes)
- ❏ Part Four: Flash Reflection Round (5 minutes)

Here's What Students Hear (From You) and (Then What They'll) Do

Part One

Today and tomorrow, you'll take on almost all of Act 3. You'll use many of the tools you've been using right along during these last few weeks to get into meaning and analysis. You'll have most of this period—35 minutes—to work together to read, understand, cut, and cast your scene. Each scene is about 100 lines; work to get it to about 50 lines. Once again, you will have will have too many actors or not enough actors for the parts in your scene, and you'll find creative ways to solve that dilemma. Gather into your groups. Here are your scripts—get busy!

Parts Two and Three

In your groups, start reading chorally, and try some different versions of choral reading too—character to character, or read to end punctuation. Decide collaboratively on the meaning of new words or complicated ideas. Be able to answer the foundational questions: Who are these folks? What do they want? How do you know? Then get busy. Some of you may want to start cutting as others might decide about casting. Feel free to use one of your scripts as a promptbook, marking all of your preferences there.

Part Four

Let's wrap up with a quick Reflection Round of only one sentence. Focused on the work we did today—partway through decision-making and rehearsal—let's go around our larger group and finish this sentence: **"I felt . . ."**

Here's What Just Happened in Class

- Students led their own close reading of a pivotal section of the play.
- Students independently worked through multiple reading rounds of a text and discussed the text.
- Students questioned the text to find meaning.
- Students negotiated promptbook annotations to stage their scene.
- Students made collaborative text-based staging decisions without teacher input.
- Students explained how their staging choices reflect the text's meaning.

A Midsummer Night's Dream, 3.1.1–106

BOTTOM Are we all met?

QUINCE Pat, pat. And here's a marvels convenient
place for our rehearsal. This green plot shall be
our stage, this hawthorn brake our tiring-house,
and we will do it in action as we will do it before   5
the Duke.

BOTTOM Peter Quince?

QUINCE What sayest thou, bully Bottom?

BOTTOM There are things in this comedy of Pyramus
and Thisbe that will never please. First, Pyramus   10
must draw a sword to kill himself, which the ladies
cannot abide. How answer you that?

SNOUT By 'r lakin, a parlous fear.

STARVELING I believe we must leave the killing out,
when all is done.   15

BOTTOM Not a whit! I have a device to make all well.
Write me a prologue, and let the prologue seem to
say we will do no harm with our swords and that
Pyramus is not killed indeed. And, for the more
better assurance, tell them that I, Pyramus, am not   20
Pyramus, but Bottom the weaver. This will put them
out of fear.

QUINCE Well, we will have such a prologue, and it shall
be written in eight and six.

BOTTOM No, make it two more. Let it be written in   25
eight and eight.

SNOUT Will not the ladies be afeard of the lion?

STARVELING I fear it, I promise you.

BOTTOM Masters, you ought to consider with yourself,
to bring in (God shield us!) a lion among ladies is a   30

most dreadful thing. For there is not a more fearful wildfowl than your lion living, and we ought to look to 't.

SNOUT Therefore another prologue must tell he is not a lion.   35

BOTTOM Nay, you must name his name, and half his face must be seen through the lion's neck, and he himself must speak through, saying thus, or to the same defect: "Ladies," or "Fair ladies, I would wish you," or "I would request you," or "I would   40 entreat you not to fear, not to tremble! My life for yours. If you think I come hither as a lion, it were pity of my life. No, I am no such thing. I am a man as other men are." And there indeed let him name his name and tell them plainly he is Snug the joiner.   45

QUINCE Well, it shall be so. But there is two hard things: that is, to bring the moonlight into a chamber, for you know Pyramus and Thisbe meet by moonlight.

SNOUT Doth the moon shine that night we play our   50 play?

BOTTOM A calendar, a calendar! Look in the almanac. Find out moonshine, find out moonshine.

Quince takes out a book.

QUINCE Yes, it doth shine that night.

BOTTOM Why, then, may you leave a casement of the   55 great chamber window, where we play, open, and the moon may shine in at the casement.

QUINCE Ay, or else one must come in with a bush of thorns and a lantern and say he comes to disfigure or to present the person of Moonshine. Then there   60 is another thing: we must have a wall in the great chamber, for Pyramus and Thisbe, says the story, did talk through the chink of a wall.

SNOUT You can never bring in a wall. What say you, Bottom?   65

BOTTOM Some man or other must present Wall. And

let him have some plaster, or some loam, or some
roughcast about him to signify wall, or let him
hold his fingers thus, and through that cranny shall
Pyramus and Thisbe whisper.   70

QUINCE If that may be, then all is well. Come, sit down,
every mother's son, and rehearse your parts. Pyramus,
you begin. When you have spoken your
speech, enter into that brake, and so everyone
according to his cue.   75
                              Enter Robin invisible to those onstage.

ROBIN, *aside*
What hempen homespuns have we swagg'ring here
So near the cradle of the Fairy Queen?
What, a play toward? I'll be an auditor—
An actor too perhaps, if I see cause.

QUINCE Speak, Pyramus.—Thisbe, stand forth.   80

BOTTOM, *as Pyramus*
Thisbe, the flowers of odious savors sweet—

QUINCE Odors, odors!

BOTTOM, *as Pyramus*
. . . odors savors sweet.
So hath thy breath, my dearest Thisbe dear.—
But hark, a voice! Stay thou but here awhile,   85
And by and by I will to thee appear.   *He exits.*

ROBIN, *aside*
A stranger Pyramus than e'er played here.   *He exits.*

FLUTE Must I speak now?

QUINCE Ay, marry, must you, for you must understand
he goes but to see a noise that he heard and is to   90
come again.

FLUTE, *as Thisbe*
Most radiant Pyramus, most lily-white of hue,
Of color like the red rose on triumphant brier,
Most brisky juvenal and eke most lovely Jew,
As true as truest horse, that yet would never tire.   95
I'll meet thee, Pyramus, at Ninny's tomb.

QUINCE "Ninus' tomb," man! Why, you must not

speak that yet. That you answer to Pyramus. You
speak all your part at once, cues and all.—Pyramus,
enter. Your cue is past. It is "never tire."   100

FLUTE O!
*As Thisbe. As true as truest horse, that yet would never
tire.*

> *Enter Bottom, and Robin as Pyramus with the
> ass-head.*

BOTTOM, *as Pyramus*
If I were fair, fair Thisbe, I were only thine.

QUINCE O monstrous! O strange! We are haunted. Pray,   105
masters, fly, masters! Help!

A Midsummer Night's Dream, 3.1.101–208

FLUTE O!
   As Thisbe. As true as truest horse, that yet would never
      tire.

                                    Enter Robin, and Bottom as Pyramus with the
                                    ass-head.

BOTTOM, *as Pyramus*
   If I were fair, fair Thisbe, I were only thine.

QUINCE O monstrous! O strange! We are haunted. Pray,   105
   masters, fly, masters! Help!

                             Quince, Flute, Snout, Snug, and Starveling exit.

ROBIN
   I'll follow you. I'll lead you about a round,
   Through bog, through bush, through brake,
      through brier.
   Sometime a horse I'll be, sometime a hound,   110
   A hog, a headless bear, sometime a fire,
   And neigh and bark and grunt and roar and burn,
   Like horse, hound, hog, bear, fire, at every turn.
                                    He exits.

BOTTOM Why do they run away? This is a knavery of
   them to make me afeard.   115

SNOUT O Bottom, thou art changed! What do I see on
      thee?

BOTTOM What do you see? You see an ass-head of your
   own, do you?

QUINCE Bless thee, Bottom, bless thee! Thou art   120
   translated!   *He exits.*

BOTTOM I see their knavery. This is to make an ass of
   me, to fright me, if they could. But I will not stir
   from this place, do what they can. I will walk up
   and down here, and I will sing, that they shall hear   125
   I am not afraid.
   He sings.
      The ouzel cock, so black of hue,

With orange-tawny bill,
The throstle with his note so true,
The wren with little quill—   130

TITANIA, *waking up*
   What angel wakes me from my flow'ry bed?

BOTTOM *sings*

   The finch, the sparrow, and the lark,
   The plainsong cuckoo gray,
   Whose note full many a man doth mark
   And dares not answer "nay"—   135
   for, indeed, who would set his wit to so foolish a
   bird? Who would give a bird the lie though he cry
   "cuckoo" never so?

TITANIA
   I pray thee, gentle mortal, sing again.
   Mine ear is much enamored of thy note,   140
   So is mine eye enthrallèd to thy shape,
   And thy fair virtue's force perforce doth move me
   On the first view to say, to swear, I love thee.

BOTTOM Methinks, mistress, you should have little
   reason for that. And yet, to say the truth, reason   145
   and love keep little company together nowadays.
   The more the pity that some honest neighbors will
   not make them friends. Nay, I can gleek upon
   occasion.

TITANIA
   Thou art as wise as thou art beautiful.   150

BOTTOM Not so neither; but if I had wit enough to get
   out of this wood, I have enough to serve mine own
   turn.

TITANIA
   Out of this wood do not desire to go.
   Thou shalt remain here whether thou wilt or no.   155
   I am a spirit of no common rate.
   The summer still doth tend upon my state,
   And I do love thee. Therefore go with me.
   I'll give thee fairies to attend on thee,
   And they shall fetch thee jewels from the deep   160
   And sing while thou on pressèd flowers dost sleep.
   And I will purge thy mortal grossness so

That thou shalt like an airy spirit go.—
Peaseblossom, Cobweb, Mote, and Mustardseed!

*Enter four Fairies: Peaseblossom, Cobweb,
Mote, and Mustardseed.*

PEASEBLOSSOM Ready.   165

COBWEB And I.

MOTE And I.

MUSTARDSEED And I.

ALL Where shall we go?

TITANIA
   Be kind and courteous to this gentleman.   170
   Hop in his walks and gambol in his eyes;
   Feed him with apricocks and dewberries,
   With purple grapes, green figs, and mulberries;
   The honey-bags steal from the humble-bees,
   And for night-tapers crop their waxen thighs   175
   And light them at the fiery glowworms' eyes
   To have my love to bed and to arise;
   And pluck the wings from painted butterflies
   To fan the moonbeams from his sleeping eyes.
   Nod to him, elves, and do him courtesies.   180

PEASEBLOSSOM Hail, mortal!

COBWEB Hail!

MOTE Hail!

MUSTARDSEED Hail!

BOTTOM I cry your Worships mercy, heartily.—I beseech   185
   your Worship's name.

COBWEB Cobweb.

BOTTOM I shall desire you of more acquaintance, good
   Master Cobweb. If I cut my finger, I shall make
   bold with you.—Your name, honest gentleman?   190

PEASEBLOSSOM Peaseblossom.

BOTTOM I pray you, commend me to Mistress Squash,

your mother, and to Master Peascod, your father.
Good Master Peaseblossom, I shall desire you of
more acquaintance too.—Your name, I beseech   195
you, sir?

MUSTARDSEED Mustardseed.

BOTTOM Good Master Mustardseed, I know your patience
well. That same cowardly, giantlike ox-beef
hath devoured many a gentleman of your house. I   200
promise you, your kindred hath made my eyes
water ere now. I desire you of more acquaintance,
good Master Mustardseed.

TITANIA
Come, wait upon him. Lead him to my bower.
The moon, methinks, looks with a wat'ry eye,   205
And when she weeps, weeps every little flower,
Lamenting some enforcèd chastity.
Tie up my lover's tongue. Bring him silently.
                              They exit.

A Midsummer Night's Dream, 3.2.1–103

OBERON

    I wonder if Titania be awaked;
    Then what it was that next came in her eye,
    Which she must dote on in extremity.
    Here comes my messenger. How now, mad spirit?
    What night-rule now about this haunted grove?   5

ROBIN

    My mistress with a monster is in love.
    Near to her close and consecrated bower,
    While she was in her dull and sleeping hour,
    A crew of patches, rude mechanicals,
    That work for bread upon Athenian stalls,   10
    Were met together to rehearse a play
    Intended for great Theseus' nuptial day.
    The shallowest thick-skin of that barren sort,
    Who Pyramus presented in their sport,
    Forsook his scene and entered in a brake.   15
    When I did him at this advantage take,
    An ass's noll I fixèd on his head.
    Anon his Thisbe must be answerèd,
    And forth my mimic comes. When they him spy,
    As wild geese that the creeping fowler eye,   20
    Or russet-pated choughs, many in sort,
    Rising and cawing at the gun's report,
    Sever themselves and madly sweep the sky,
    So at his sight away his fellows fly,
    And, at our stamp, here o'er and o'er one falls.   25
    He "Murder" cries and help from Athens calls.
    Their sense thus weak, lost with their fears thus
       strong,
    Made senseless things begin to do them wrong;
    For briers and thorns at their apparel snatch,   30
    Some sleeves, some hats, from yielders all things
       catch.
    I led them on in this distracted fear
    And left sweet Pyramus translated there.
    When in that moment, so it came to pass,   35
    Titania waked and straightway loved an ass.

OBERON

    This falls out better than I could devise.
    But hast thou yet latched the Athenian's eyes
    With the love juice, as I did bid thee do?

ROBIN

    I took him sleeping—that is finished, too—   40
    And the Athenian woman by his side,
    That, when he waked, of force she must be eyed.

                          Enter Demetrius and Hermia.

OBERON

    Stand close. This is the same Athenian.

ROBIN

    This is the woman, but not this the man.

                          They step aside.

DEMETRIUS

    O, why rebuke you him that loves you so?   45
    Lay breath so bitter on your bitter foe!

HERMIA

    Now I but chide, but I should use thee worse,
    For thou, I fear, hast given me cause to curse.
    If thou hast slain Lysander in his sleep,
    Being o'er shoes in blood, plunge in the deep   50
    And kill me too.
    The sun was not so true unto the day
    As he to me. Would he have stolen away
    From sleeping Hermia? I'll believe as soon
    This whole Earth may be bored, and that the moon   55
    May through the center creep and so displease
    Her brother's noontide with th' Antipodes.
    It cannot be but thou hast murdered him.
    So should a murderer look, so dead, so grim.

DEMETRIUS

    So should the murdered look, and so should I,   60
    Pierced through the heart with your stern cruelty.
    Yet you, the murderer, look as bright, as clear,
    As yonder Venus in her glimmering sphere.

HERMIA

    What's this to my Lysander? Where is he?
    Ah, good Demetrius, wilt thou give him me?   65

DEMETRIUS

    I had rather give his carcass to my hounds.

HERMIA

    Out, dog! Out, cur! Thou driv'st me past the bounds
    Of maiden's patience. Hast thou slain him, then?
    Henceforth be never numbered among men.
    O, once tell true! Tell true, even for my sake!   70
    Durst thou have looked upon him, being awake?
    And hast thou killed him sleeping? O brave touch!
    Could not a worm, an adder, do so much?
    An adder did it, for with doubler tongue
    Than thine, thou serpent, never adder stung.   75

DEMETRIUS

    You spend your passion on a misprised mood.
    I am not guilty of Lysander's blood,
    Nor is he dead, for aught that I can tell.

HERMIA

    I pray thee, tell me then that he is well.

DEMETRIUS

    An if I could, what should I get therefor?   80

HERMIA

    A privilege never to see me more.
    And from thy hated presence part I so.
    See me no more, whether he be dead or no.
                            She exits.

DEMETRIUS

    There is no following her in this fierce vein.
    Here, therefore, for a while I will remain.   85
    So sorrow's heaviness doth heavier grow
    For debt that bankrout sleep doth sorrow owe,
    Which now in some slight measure it will pay,
    If for his tender here I make some stay.
                 He lies down and falls asleep.

OBERON, *to Robin*

    What hast thou done? Thou hast mistaken quite   90
    And laid the love juice on some true-love's sight.
    Of thy misprision must perforce ensue
    Some true-love turned, and not a false turned true.

ROBIN

> Then fate o'errules, that, one man holding troth,
> A million fail, confounding oath on oath. 95

OBERON

> About the wood go swifter than the wind,
> And Helena of Athens look thou find.
> All fancy-sick she is and pale of cheer
> With sighs of love that costs the fresh blood dear.
> By some illusion see thou bring her here. 100
> I'll charm his eyes against she do appear.

ROBIN I go, I go, look how I go,
> Swifter than arrow from the Tartar's bow. *He exits.*

RESOURCE #4.1D

A Midsummer Night's Dream, 3.2.104–313, edited

OBERON, *applying the nectar to Demetrius' eyes*

    Flower of this purple dye,

    Hit with Cupid's archery,   105

    Sink in apple of his eye.

    When his love he doth espy,

    Let her shine as gloriously

    As the Venus of the sky.

                                Enter Robin.

ROBIN

    Captain of our fairy band,

    Helena is here at hand,

    And the youth, mistook by me,

    Pleading for a lover's fee.   115

    Shall we their fond pageant see?

    Lord, what fools these mortals be!

OBERON

    Stand aside. The noise they make

    Will cause Demetrius to awake.

ROBIN

    Then will two at once woo one.   120

    That must needs be sport alone.

    And those things do best please me

    That befall prepost'rously.

                         They step aside.

                         Enter Lysander and Helena.

LYSANDER

    Why should you think that I should woo in scorn?

    Scorn and derision never come in tears.   125

    Look when I vow, I weep; and vows so born,

    In their nativity all truth appears.

    How can these things in me seem scorn to you,

    Bearing the badge of faith to prove them true?

HELENA

    You do advance your cunning more and more.   130

    When truth kills truth, O devilish holy fray!

    These vows are Hermia's. Will you give her o'er?

Weigh oath with oath and you will nothing
   weigh.
Your vows to her and me, put in two scales, 135
Will even weigh, and both as light as tales.

LYSANDER

I had no judgment when to her I swore.

HELENA

Nor none, in my mind, now you give her o'er.

LYSANDER

Demetrius loves her, and he loves not you.

DEMETRIUS, *waking up*

O Helen, goddess, nymph, perfect, divine! 140
To what, my love, shall I compare thine eyne?
Crystal is muddy. O, how ripe in show
Thy lips, those kissing cherries, tempting grow!
That pure congealèd white, high Taurus' snow,
Fanned with the eastern wind, turns to a crow 145
When thou hold'st up thy hand. O, let me kiss
This princess of pure white, this seal of bliss!

HELENA

O spite! O hell! I see you all are bent
To set against me for your merriment.
   . . .
If you were men, as men you are in show,
You would not use a gentle lady so, 155
To vow and swear and superpraise my parts,
When, I am sure, you hate me with your hearts.
You both are rivals and love Hermia,
And now both rivals to mock Helena.

LYSANDER

You are unkind, Demetrius. Be not so, 165
For you love Hermia; this you know I know.
And here with all goodwill, with all my heart,
In Hermia's love I yield you up my part.

DEMETRIUS

Lysander, keep thy Hermia. I will none.
If e'er I loved her, all that love is gone.
My heart to her but as guest-wise sojourned,
And now to Helen is it home returned, 175
There to remain.

LYSANDER Helen, it is not so.

DEMETRIUS
    Disparage not the faith thou dost not know,
    Lest to thy peril thou aby it dear.
    Look where thy love comes. Yonder is thy dear.   180
                        Enter Hermia.

HERMIA, *to Lysander*

    . . .
    Thou art not by mine eye, Lysander, found;   185
    Mine ear, I thank it, brought me to thy sound.
    But why unkindly didst thou leave me so?

LYSANDER
    Why should he stay whom love doth press to go?

HERMIA
    What love could press Lysander from my side?

LYSANDER
    Why seek'st thou me? Could not this make thee
       know
    The hate I bear thee made me leave thee so?   195

HERMIA
    You speak not as you think. It cannot be.

HELENA
    Lo, she is one of this confederacy!
    Now I perceive they have conjoined all three
    To fashion this false sport in spite of me.—
    Injurious Hermia, most ungrateful maid,   200
    Have you conspired, have you with these contrived,
    To bait me with this foul derision?
    Is all the counsel that we two have shared,
    The sisters' vows, the hours that we have spent
    When we have chid the hasty-footed time   205
    For parting us—O, is all forgot?
    All schooldays' friendship, childhood innocence?

    . . .
    And will you rent our ancient love asunder,   220
    To join with men in scorning your poor friend?
    It is not friendly; 'tis not maidenly.
    Our sex, as well as I, may chide you for it,
    Though I alone do feel the injury.

HERMIA

    I am amazèd at your words.   225

    I scorn you not. It seems that you scorn me.

HELENA

    Have you not set Lysander, as in scorn,

    To follow me and praise my eyes and face,

    And made your other love, Demetrius,

    Who even but now did spurn me with his foot,   230

    To call me goddess, nymph, divine and rare,

    Precious, celestial? Wherefore speaks he this

    To her he hates? And wherefore doth Lysander

    Deny your love (so rich within his soul)

    And tender me, forsooth, affection,   235

    But by your setting on, by your consent?

HERMIA

    I understand not what you mean by this.

HELENA

    Ay, do. Persever, counterfeit sad looks,

    Make mouths upon me when I turn my back,

    Wink each at other, hold the sweet jest up.

    This sport, well carried, shall be chronicled.   245

    If you have any pity, grace, or manners,

    You would not make me such an argument.

    But fare you well. 'Tis partly my own fault,

    Which death or absence soon shall remedy.

LYSANDER

    Stay, gentle Helena. Hear my excuse,   250

    My love, my life, my soul, fair Helena.

HELENA

    O excellent!

HERMIA, *to Lysander*

    Sweet, do not scorn her so.

DEMETRIUS, *to Lysander*

    If she cannot entreat, I can compel.

LYSANDER

    Helen, I love thee. By my life, I do.

    I swear by that which I will lose for thee,

    To prove him false that says I love thee not.   260

DEMETRIUS
I say I love thee more than he can do.

LYSANDER
If thou say so, withdraw and prove it too.

DEMETRIUS
Quick, come.

HERMIA Lysander, whereto tends all this?

She takes hold of Lysander.

LYSANDER
Away, you Ethiop!   265

DEMETRIUS, *to Hermia*
No, no. He'll
Seem to break loose. *To Lysander.* Take on as you
would follow,
But yet come not. You are a tame man, go!

LYSANDER, *to Hermia*
Hang off, thou cat, thou burr! Vile thing, let loose,   270
Or I will shake thee from me like a serpent.

HERMIA
Why are you grown so rude? What change is this,
Sweet love?

LYSANDER Thy love? Out, tawny Tartar, out!
Out, loathèd med'cine! O, hated potion, hence!   275

HERMIA
Do you not jest?

HELENA Yes, sooth, and so do you.

LYSANDER
Demetrius, I will keep my word with thee.

DEMETRIUS
I would I had your bond. For I perceive
A weak bond holds you. I'll not trust your word.   280

LYSANDER
What? Should I hurt her, strike her, kill her dead?
Although I hate her, I'll not harm her so.

HERMIA

Am not I Hermia? Are not you Lysander?   285
I am as fair now as I was erewhile.
Since night you loved me; yet since night you left
  me.
Why, then, you left me—O, the gods forbid!—
In earnest, shall I say?   290

LYSANDER Ay, by my life,

And never did desire to see thee more.
Therefore be out of hope, of question, of doubt.
Be certain, nothing truer, 'tis no jest
That I do hate thee and love Helena.   295

Hermia turns him loose.

HERMIA

O me! *To Helena.* You juggler, you cankerblossom,
You thief of love! What, have you come by night
And stol'n my love's heart from him?

HELENA Fine, i' faith.

Have you no modesty, no maiden shame,   300
No touch of bashfulness? What, will you tear
Impatient answers from my gentle tongue?
Fie, fie, you counterfeit, you puppet, you!

HERMIA

"Puppet"? Why so? Ay, that way goes the game.
Now I perceive that she hath made compare   305
Between our statures; she hath urged her height,
And with her personage, her tall personage,
Her height, forsooth, she hath prevailed with him.
And are you grown so high in his esteem
Because I am so dwarfish and so low?   310
How low am I, thou painted maypole? Speak!
How low am I? I am not yet so low
But that my nails can reach unto thine eyes.

A Midsummer Night's Dream, 3.2.314–421

HELENA
I pray you, though you mock me, gentlemen,
Let her not hurt me. I was never curst;   315
I have no gift at all in shrewishness.
I am a right maid for my cowardice.
Let her not strike me. You perhaps may think,
Because she is something lower than myself,
That I can match her.   320

HERMIA "Lower"? Hark, again!

HELENA
Good Hermia, do not be so bitter with me.
I evermore did love you, Hermia,
Did ever keep your counsels, never wronged you—
Save that, in love unto Demetrius,   325
I told him of your stealth unto this wood.
He followed you; for love, I followed him.
But he hath chid me hence and threatened me
To strike me, spurn me, nay, to kill me too.
And now, so you will let me quiet go,   330
To Athens will I bear my folly back
And follow you no further. Let me go.
You see how simple and how fond I am.

HERMIA
Why, get you gone. Who is 't that hinders you?

HELENA
A foolish heart that I leave here behind.   335

HERMIA
What, with Lysander?

HELENA With Demetrius.

LYSANDER
Be not afraid. She shall not harm thee, Helena.

DEMETRIUS
No, sir, she shall not, though you take her part.

HELENA

    O, when she is angry, she is keen and shrewd.   340

    She was a vixen when she went to school,

    And though she be but little, she is fierce.

HERMIA

    "Little" again? Nothing but "low" and "little"?

    Why will you suffer her to flout me thus?

    Let me come to her.   345

LYSANDER Get you gone, you dwarf,

    You minimus of hind'ring knotgrass made,

    You bead, you acorn—

DEMETRIUS You are too officious

    In her behalf that scorns your services.   350

    Let her alone. Speak not of Helena.

    Take not her part. For if thou dost intend

    Never so little show of love to her,

    Thou shalt aby it.

LYSANDER Now she holds me not.   355

    Now follow, if thou dar'st, to try whose right,

    Of thine or mine, is most in Helena.

DEMETRIUS

    "Follow"? Nay, I'll go with thee, cheek by jowl.

                     Demetrius and Lysander exit.

HERMIA

    You, mistress, all this coil is long of you.

                       Helena retreats.

    Nay, go not back.   360

HELENA I will not trust you, I,

    Nor longer stay in your curst company.

    Your hands than mine are quicker for a fray.

    My legs are longer though, to run away.   *She exits.*

HERMIA

    I am amazed and know not what to say.   *She exits.*   365

OBERON, *to Robin*

    This is thy negligence. Still thou mistak'st,

    Or else committ'st thy knaveries willfully.

ROBIN

Believe me, king of shadows, I mistook.
Did not you tell me I should know the man
By the Athenian garments he had on?   370
And so far blameless proves my enterprise
That I have 'nointed an Athenian's eyes;
And so far am I glad it so did sort,
As this their jangling I esteem a sport.

OBERON

Thou seest these lovers seek a place to fight.   375
Hie, therefore, Robin, overcast the night;
The starry welkin cover thou anon
With drooping fog as black as Acheron,
And lead these testy rivals so astray
As one come not within another's way.   380
Like to Lysander sometime frame thy tongue;
Then stir Demetrius up with bitter wrong.
And sometime rail thou like Demetrius.
And from each other look thou lead them thus,
Till o'er their brows death-counterfeiting sleep   385
With leaden legs and batty wings doth creep.
Then crush this herb into Lysander's eye,

                                                    He gives a flower to Robin.

Whose liquor hath this virtuous property,
To take from thence all error with his might
And make his eyeballs roll with wonted sight.   390
When they next wake, all this derision
Shall seem a dream and fruitless vision.
And back to Athens shall the lovers wend,
With league whose date till death shall never end.
Whiles I in this affair do thee employ,   395
I'll to my queen and beg her Indian boy;
And then I will her charmèd eye release
From monster's view, and all things shall be peace.

ROBIN

My fairy lord, this must be done with haste,
For night's swift dragons cut the clouds full fast,   400
And yonder shines Aurora's harbinger,
At whose approach, ghosts wand'ring here and
    there
Troop home to churchyards. Damnèd spirits all,
That in crossways and floods have burial,   405
Already to their wormy beds are gone.
For fear lest day should look their shames upon,

They willfully themselves exile from light
And must for aye consort with black-browed night.

OBERON

But we are spirits of another sort.   410
I with the Morning's love have oft made sport
And, like a forester, the groves may tread
Even till the eastern gate, all fiery red,
Opening on Neptune with fair blessèd beams,
Turns into yellow gold his salt-green streams.   415
But notwithstanding, haste! Make no delay.
We may effect this business yet ere day.   *He exits.*

ROBIN

Up and down, up and down,
I will lead them up and down.
I am feared in field and town.   420
Goblin, lead them up and down.

Beginning to Weave It All Together—
Part 2, Acting Out

Here's What We're Doing and Why

Today student groups will keep their scene work moving toward performance, and they'll perform the scenes together—almost all of Act 3—at the end of class. Exciting! Every group member will participate in their group's performance. This will help them move toward their final projects next week.

What Will I Need?

- Students will need their scripts from yesterday, with promptbooking notes and other ideas that they generated – **RESOURCES #4.1A, #4.1B, #4.1C, #4.1D,** and **#4.1E**.

How Should I Prepare?

- Set up your classroom so that students can work in groups, and then perform for the rest of the class.

- Keep time pretty carefully so that kids will have a chance to work and perform.

Agenda (~ 45-minute class period)

- ❏ Reconvene and get clear on the timeline for this class (3 minutes)
- ❏ Last decisions and rehearsal (10 minutes)
- ❏ Performances! (25 minutes/5 minutes per scene)
- ❏ Reflection Rounds (10 minutes)

Here's What Students Hear (From You) and (Then What They'll) Do

Part One: Set-up & Warm-up

1. Today you'll have 10 minutes to whip your scenes into performance shape. Make final decisions and rehearse! Do your best! Keep your notes and directions promptbook-style on one of your scripts that has the names of everyone in your group.

2. When it's time to perform, we'll move into our performance space. Each scene should run 5 minutes, and we'll run them in order so we can get a sense of this big act!

Part Two: Group Scenes in Performance!

Perform for your delighted and enthusiastic classmates!

Part Three: Reflection Rounds

Two quick rounds today to help us gather our learnings:

- **From the preparation part of what we did (mostly yesterday), I learned . . .**

- **From the performance part of what we did (mostly today), I learned . . .**

Here's What Just Happened in Class

- Students took on a more complicated assignment, used their close reading to analyze a more complex scene, and as part of that analysis, created a usable promptbook.

- Students made decisions and staged their scene in front of the class.

- Students reflected on the practical aspects of the last two days' work, important in heading toward their final projects in Week Five.

Exploring 4.1 in Two Different Ways— Perspective #1

Here's What We're Doing and Why

Act 4 has only 2 scenes and in its entirety is only about 300 lines long, yet those lines contain important actions that move the story and the characters forward. Today's lesson and tomorrow's lesson are sequenced—quite deliberately—so that students will have a chance to experience 4.1 in two very different ways. Today, students will work in groups of 5. Each group will consider 4.1, read it together and take it in, and then, as a group, negotiate and make decisions as they ready the scene for performance. No time for a reflection today, as they will be squeezed to get through this scene during this class period.

What Will I Need?

- Set up your classroom for group work

- Copies of **RESOURCE #4.3** (all of Act 4, scene 1) for every student

- **RESOURCE #4.3** projected or on chart paper so that each group can use a large-scale copy on which to record their final promptbook choices

How Should I Prepare?

- Set up your room so groups can work separately and display their final choices in some way.

- Make copies of **RESOURCE #4.3** for everyone, and a large-scale printout of 4.1 for each group.

Agenda (~ 45-minute class period)

- ❏ Part One: Set up and get clear on the assignment and who's in which group (5 minutes)

- ❏ Part Two: Groups get busy, getting clear on the scene and on negotiating cutting, performance choices, etc. (30 minutes)

- ❏ Part Three: Groups note their final choices on their large-scale version of the scene (10 minutes)

Here's What Students Hear (From You) and (Then What They'll) Do

Part One: Set-up and get clear

Today and tomorrow, we'll focus on Act 4, scene 1—a key act—and the two lessons will be in sequence . . . exciting, and we'll see what we all will discover by the end of the lesson tomorrow. For both days, you'll work in the same groups of five.

Part Two: Groups get busy

In your groups, you'll do a read-through together but with no marking up or discussion yet. Then, begin to negotiate your choices for prompt-booking on your individual copies. You can cut up to half the scene if you choose to. All your suggestions and negotiating should be rooted in the text. Of course! Your groups will have today to negotiate and decide on your final promptbook notes.

Part Three: Note your final choices on your large-scale version of the scene

Mark up your large-scale copy with your **final promptbook notes**. No changes after today!

Here's What Just Happened in Class

- Students practiced and put to the test the ways that they have learned to get into Shakespeare's language and scenework throughout this unit.

- Students were in groups working more independently as they made meaning and suggested expansive performance possibilities in Act 4, scene 1.

- Students collaborated rather fiercely as they negotiated their final promptbook choices within their groups.

RESOURCE #4.3

A Midsummer Night's Dream, Act 4, scene 1

TITANIA
    Come, sit thee down upon this flow'ry bed,
    While I thy amiable cheeks do coy,
    And stick muskroses in thy sleek smooth head,
    And kiss thy fair large ears, my gentle joy.

BOTTOM Where's Peaseblossom? 5

PEASEBLOSSOM Ready.

BOTTOM Scratch my head, Peaseblossom. Where's
    Monsieur Cobweb?

COBWEB Ready.

BOTTOM Monsieur Cobweb, good monsieur, get you 10
    your weapons in your hand and kill me a red-hipped
    humble-bee on the top of a thistle, and, good
    monsieur, bring me the honey-bag. Do not fret
    yourself too much in the action, monsieur, and,
    good monsieur, have a care the honey-bag break 15
    not; I would be loath to have you overflown with a
    honey-bag, signior. *Cobweb exits.* Where's Monsieur
    Mustardseed?

MUSTARDSEED Ready.

BOTTOM Give me your neaf, Monsieur Mustardseed. 20
    Pray you, leave your courtesy, good monsieur.

MUSTARDSEED What's your will?

BOTTOM Nothing, good monsieur, but to help Cavalery
    Cobweb to scratch. I must to the barber's,
    monsieur, for methinks I am marvels hairy about 25
    the face. And I am such a tender ass, if my hair do
    but tickle me, I must scratch.

TITANIA
    What, wilt thou hear some music, my sweet love?

BOTTOM I have a reasonable good ear in music. Let's

have the tongs and the bones. 30

TITANIA

Or say, sweet love, what thou desirest to eat.

BOTTOM Truly, a peck of provender. I could munch
your good dry oats. Methinks I have a great desire
to a bottle of hay. Good hay, sweet hay, hath no
fellow. 35

TITANIA

I have a venturous fairy that shall seek
The squirrel's hoard and fetch thee new nuts.

BOTTOM I had rather have a handful or two of dried
peas. But, I pray you, let none of your people stir
me; I have an exposition of sleep come upon me. 40

TITANIA

Sleep thou, and I will wind thee in my arms.—
Fairies, begone, and be all ways away.
So doth the woodbine the sweet honeysuckle
Gently entwist; the female ivy so
Enrings the barky fingers of the elm. 45
O, how I love thee! How I dote on thee!

Enter Robin Goodfellow.

OBERON

Welcome, good Robin. Seest thou this sweet sight?
Her dotage now I do begin to pity.
For, meeting her of late behind the wood,
Seeking sweet favors for this hateful fool, 50
I did upbraid her and fall out with her.
For she his hairy temples then had rounded
With coronet of fresh and fragrant flowers;
And that same dew, which sometime on the buds
Was wont to swell like round and orient pearls, 55
Stood now within the pretty flouriets' eyes,
Like tears that did their own disgrace bewail.
When I had at my pleasure taunted her,
And she in mild terms begged my patience,
I then did ask of her her changeling child, 60
Which straight she gave me, and her fairy sent
To bear him to my bower in Fairyland.
And now I have the boy, I will undo
This hateful imperfection of her eyes.
And, gentle Puck, take this transformèd scalp 65

From off the head of this Athenian swain,
That he, awaking when the other do,
May all to Athens back again repair
And think no more of this night's accidents
But as the fierce vexation of a dream.   70
But first I will release the Fairy Queen.
                        He applies the nectar to her eyes.
            Be as thou wast wont to be.
            See as thou wast wont to see.
            Dian's bud o'er Cupid's flower
            Hath such force and blessèd power.   75
Now, my Titania, wake you, my sweet queen.

TITANIA, *waking*
    My Oberon, what visions have I seen!
    Methought I was enamored of an ass.

OBERON
    There lies your love.

TITANIA How came these things to pass?   80
    O, how mine eyes do loathe his visage now!

OBERON
    Silence awhile.—Robin, take off this head.—
    Titania, music call; and strike more dead
    Than common sleep of all these five the sense.

TITANIA
    Music, ho, music such as charmeth sleep!   85

ROBIN, *removing the ass-head from Bottom*
    Now, when thou wak'st, with thine own fool's eyes
        peep.

OBERON
    Sound music.   *Music.*
    Come, my queen, take hands with me,
    And rock the ground whereon these sleepers be.   90
                        Titania and Oberon dance.
    Now thou and I are new in amity,
    And will tomorrow midnight solemnly
    Dance in Duke Theseus' house triumphantly,
    And bless it to all fair prosperity.
    There shall the pairs of faithful lovers be   95
    Wedded, with Theseus, all in jollity.

ROBIN

> Fairy king, attend and mark.
> I do hear the morning lark.

OBERON

> Then, my queen, in silence sad
> Trip we after night's shade.   100
> We the globe can compass soon,
> Swifter than the wand'ring moon.

TITANIA

> Come, my lord, and in our flight
> Tell me how it came this night
> That I sleeping here was found   105
> With these mortals on the ground.

> > *Oberon, Robin, and Titania exit.*
> > *Wind horn. Enter Theseus and all his train,*
> > *Hippolyta, Egeus.*

THESEUS

> Go, one of you, find out the Forester.
> For now our observation is performed,
> And, since we have the vaward of the day,
> My love shall hear the music of my hounds.   110
> Uncouple in the western valley; let them go.
> Dispatch, I say, and find the Forester.
> We will, fair queen, up to the mountain's top
> And mark the musical confusion
> Of hounds and echo in conjunction.   115

HIPPOLYTA

> I was with Hercules and Cadmus once,
> When in a wood of Crete they bayed the bear
> With hounds of Sparta. Never did I hear
> Such gallant chiding, for, besides the groves,
> The skies, the fountains, every region near   120
> Seemed all one mutual cry. I never heard
> So musical a discord, such sweet thunder.

THESEUS

> My hounds are bred out of the Spartan kind,
> So flewed, so sanded; and their heads are hung
> With ears that sweep away the morning dew;   125
> Crook-kneed, and dewlapped like Thessalian bulls;
> Slow in pursuit, but matched in mouth like bells,
> Each under each. A cry more tunable
> Was never holloed to, nor cheered with horn,

In Crete, in Sparta, nor in Thessaly.   130
Judge when you hear.—But soft! What nymphs are
    these?

EGEUS

My lord, this is my daughter here asleep,
And this Lysander; this Demetrius is,
This Helena, old Nedar's Helena.   135
I wonder of their being here together.

THESEUS

No doubt they rose up early to observe
The rite of May, and hearing our intent,
Came here in grace of our solemnity.
But speak, Egeus. Is not this the day   140
That Hermia should give answer of her choice?

EGEUS It is, my lord.

THESEUS

Go, bid the huntsmen wake them with their horns.
                              A servant exits.
               Shouts within. Wind horns. They all start up.

THESEUS

Good morrow, friends. Saint Valentine is past.
Begin these woodbirds but to couple now?   145
               Demetrius, Hermia, and Lysander kneel.

LYSANDER

Pardon, my lord.

THESEUS I pray you all, stand up.
I know you two are rival enemies.
How comes this gentle concord in the world,
That hatred is so far from jealousy   150
To sleep by hate and fear no enmity?

LYSANDER

My lord, I shall reply amazèdly,
Half sleep, half waking. But as yet, I swear,
I cannot truly say how I came here.
But, as I think—for truly would I speak,   155
And now I do bethink me, so it is:
I came with Hermia hither. Our intent
Was to be gone from Athens, where we might,
Without the peril of the Athenian law—

EGEUS

Enough, enough!—My lord, you have enough. 160
I beg the law, the law upon his head.
They would have stol'n away.—They would,
    Demetrius,
Thereby to have defeated you and me:
You of your wife and me of my consent, 165
Of my consent that she should be your wife.

DEMETRIUS

My lord, fair Helen told me of their stealth,
Of this their purpose hither to this wood,
And I in fury hither followed them,
Fair Helena in fancy following me. 170
But, my good lord, I wot not by what power
(But by some power it is) my love to Hermia,
Melted as the snow, seems to me now
As the remembrance of an idle gaud
Which in my childhood I did dote upon, 175
And all the faith, the virtue of my heart,
The object and the pleasure of mine eye,
Is only Helena. To her, my lord,
Was I betrothed ere I saw Hermia.
But like a sickness did I loathe this food. 180
But, as in health, come to my natural taste,
Now I do wish it, love it, long for it,
And will forevermore be true to it.

THESEUS

Fair lovers, you are fortunately met.
Of this discourse we more will hear anon.— 185
Egeus, I will overbear your will,
For in the temple by and by, with us,
These couples shall eternally be knit.—
And, for the morning now is something worn,
Our purposed hunting shall be set aside. 190
Away with us to Athens. Three and three,
We'll hold a feast in great solemnity.
Come, Hippolyta.

DEMETRIUS

These things seem small and undistinguishable,
Like far-off mountains turnèd into clouds. 195

HERMIA

Methinks I see these things with parted eye,
When everything seems double.

HELENA   So methinks.
And I have found Demetrius like a jewel,
Mine own and not mine own.   200

DEMETRIUS Are you sure
That we are awake? It seems to me
That yet we sleep, we dream. Do not you think
The Duke was here and bid us follow him?

HERMIA
Yea, and my father.   205

HELENA   And Hippolyta.

LYSANDER
And he did bid us follow to the temple.

DEMETRIUS
Why, then, we are awake. Let's follow him,
And by the way let us recount our dreams.
                                    Lovers exit.

BOTTOM, *waking up* When my cue comes, call me,   210
and I will answer. My next is "Most fair Pyramus."
Hey-ho! Peter Quince! Flute the bellows-mender!
Snout the tinker! Starveling! God's my life! Stolen
hence and left me asleep! I have had a most rare
vision. I have had a dream past the wit of man to say   215
what dream it was. Man is but an ass if he go about
to expound this dream. Methought I was—there
is no man can tell what. Methought I was and
methought I had—but man is but a patched fool if
he will offer to say what methought I had. The eye of   220
man hath not heard, the ear of man hath not seen,
man's hand is not able to taste, his tongue to
conceive, nor his heart to report what my dream
was. I will get Peter Quince to write a ballad of this
dream. It shall be called "Bottom's Dream" because   225
it hath no bottom; and I will sing it in the
latter end of a play, before the Duke. Peradventure,
to make it the more gracious, I shall sing it at her
   death.
                                    He exits.

Exploring 4.1 in Two Different Ways—Perspective #2

Here's What We're Doing and Why

The second lesson in this sequence gives students a chance to broaden their thinking about both meaning and performance choices—all while learning from one another. On this second day, they will rotate and focus on another group's final set of promptbook choices. Each group will work with an entirely "new" promptbook scene (prepared in **final** yesterday by another group), and they will perform that scene for the class. The rules are strict—no changes on the script they've been given to perform. All groups will be enacting *someone else's ideas*! These two lessons together expand students' awareness of and sensibilities about meaning, interpretation, performance possibilities . . . and control! The longer and deeper reflection session will be lively, and ought to be a helpful send-off into Week Five and final projects.

What Will I Need?

- Each group's large-scale printout or projected **final promptbook version** from yesterday's class. (These were **RESOURCE #4.3**—Act 4, scene 1—projected or on chart paper; groups recorded their final promptbook choices on these.)

How Should I Prepare?

- Set up your classroom for group work that allows for the display of the large-scale **final promptbooks** from yesterday (now working scripts for each group) as well as for performance.

Agenda (~ 45-minute class period)

- ❏ Part One: Set-up and the task at hand (3 minutes)
- ❏ Part Two: Groups rehearse (10 minutes)
- ❏ Part Three: Each group will present a short scene from their "today script" (20 minutes)
- ❏ Part Four: Robust reflection (12 minutes)

Here's What Students Hear (From You) and (Then What They'll) Do

Part One: Set-up and the task at hand

We're going to continue our work from yesterday . . . and that means that you will rotate to the **final promptbook** prepared by another group, and you will perform *their* script, not the one you prepared yesterday. This means that you **cannot change or add** any prompts to the new scene that you've been given. This also means that another group will be performing your **final promptbook**. How exciting is that?!

Parts Two and Three

You will have **10 minutes** to rehearse the scene from your new promptbook, and as a class, you'll perform excerpts from your new scene over 20 minutes after that. Each group will present their performance based on the new promptbook.

Part Four

1. One quick Reflection Round around the whole group: **"Watching all of these performances, I observed that . . ."**

2. The following questions may come quite naturally from students' reflections, but in case they don't:
   – What was the difference between the promptbook you created yesterday and the one you performed from today?
   – Were there similarities in promptbooks across all groups?
   – How did you feel about performing the scene without control over any of the decisions?
   – What did the different interpretations make you realize or think about Shakespeare, this play, and/or performance?

Here's What Just Happened in Class

- Students expanded their experiences and sensibilities by engaging with an interpretation of Act 4, scene 1 completely different from their own.

- Students' energy and familiarity with tools for understanding Shakespeare's language brought these "new" scenes to life.

- Students engaged in analyses of differences and similarities across the range of scenes, just as scholars, editors, actors, and directors do.

Refresher on the Power of Movement:
The Dumb-Show

Here's What Will Happen Today and Why

Today students will be introduced to the historical theater convention of a dumb-show, and at the same time, they'll explore and relearn the power of movement—how movement allows them to understand the language more deeply, and really take ownership of the text.

Early medieval plays would often be performed without actors speaking, and this tradition continued into the Early Modern period when Shakespeare was writing. They were called dumb-shows, short plays performed without words that were often inserted into a longer play with spoken parts. Characters in the play mimed what was about to happen, so audiences would be ready for the action when it took place. "The Murder of Gonzago" dumb-show is a key element of *Hamlet*.

It is important for students to know that in Shakespeare's time, the word *dumb* had only one meaning: "without words" or "silent." We don't use that definition for *dumb* anymore; if we could go backwards in history, we would call what happens in a dumb-show a "mime" or "pantomime."

In this lesson, while actually paying very close attention to language, students will create and then perform a dumb-show. Ironically, they'll focus on language as they strip away both language and voice, and have to convey the meaning of words only through movement, facial expressions, and gestures. This is a great reminder as they gear up for their final projects and their own Act 5!

At the end of this lesson, you'll find your own path through Week 5. Check out **RESOURCE #4.5B** . . . it's all for you!

What Will I Need?

- Copies of *Midsummer* 4.2 – **RESOURCE #4.5A**

How Should I Prepare?

- Divide the class into groups of six. The *Midsummer* scene has six parts and they'll need a narrator, but they'll be ready to figure that out.

- Be ready to explain the idea of a dumb-show and the directions.

Agenda (~ 45-minute class period)

❏ Intro to dumb-show and today's project (5 minutes)

❏ Groups get into the scene by choral reading several times, then create and rehearse their dumb-shows (20 minutes)

❑ Performance of all dumb-shows (10 minutes)

❑ Reflection (10 minutes)

Here's What Students Hear (From You) and (Then What They'll) Do

- Today, we're going to learn a little about something that often appeared in medieval and Early Modern plays—and that's a dumb-show. Shakespeare's *Hamlet* even has a dumb-show written right into the play. We're going to create and share dumb-shows based on 4.2 of *A Midsummer Night's Dream.*

  - Medieval plays were often performed with silent actors, and this tradition continued into the Early Modern period when Shakespeare was writing. They were called dumb-shows, short plays performed without words and inserted into a longer play with spoken parts. Characters in the play mimed what was about to happen, so audiences would be ready for the action when it took place.

  - In Shakespeare's time, the word *dumb* had only one meaning: "without words" or "silent." We don't use that definition for *dumb* anymore; if we could go backwards in history, we would call what happens in a dumb-show a "mime" or "pantomime."

- Today, in groups, you will start with 4.2, the spoken scene. You will read and get a sense of the language, and then you'll create a dumb-show that depicts the moments when the mechanicals learn that they will be able to perform their play.

  - In dumb-shows, there is one speaker—the narrator who reads the text— but for the rest of you, there is NO SPEAKING, so you'll be using ONLY body movements, facial expressions, and gestures to tell the story.

  - As the narrator reads, the others in the group act out what is being described.

  - You will still pay extremely close attention to the words, though, because you'll need to use movement accurately. NO SPEAKING, but you may improvise with furniture and props available in the classroom.

- You'll have 20 minutes to create and rehearse your dumb-shows. And then we'll see and celebrate all of them!

Reflection Round

Discuss in the last lively few minutes:

- How did removing most of the language from the scene change the way we approached performance?

- Were we successful in conveying a creative interpretation? Why or why not?

- How did we do at conveying elation and excitement?

Here's What Just Happened in Class

- Students had to leave speaking behind for this class, and were made to embody

Shakespeare's language through making text-based visual choices.

- Students, because they could not speak, had to go beyond the words to make some creative visual choices that more strongly conveyed the action and/or emotion.

- Students created a dumb-show and observed the dumb-shows of other groups as well—a great chance for multiple scene analysis!

RESOURCE #4.5A

A Midsummer Night's Dream, Act 4, scene 2

Enter Quince, Flute, Snout, and Starveling.

QUINCE Have you sent to Bottom's house? Is he come
    home yet?

STARVELING He cannot be heard of. Out of doubt he
    is transported.

FLUTE If he come not, then the play is marred. It goes   5
    not forward, doth it?

QUINCE It is not possible. You have not a man in all
    Athens able to discharge Pyramus but he.

FLUTE No, he hath simply the best wit of any handicraftman
    in Athens.   10

QUINCE Yea, and the best person too, and he is a very
    paramour for a sweet voice.

FLUTE You must say "paragon." A "paramour" is (God
    bless us) a thing of naught.
                Enter Snug the joiner.

SNUG Masters, the Duke is coming from the temple,   15
    and there is two or three lords and ladies more
    married. If our sport had gone forward, we had all
    been made men.

FLUTE O, sweet bully Bottom! Thus hath he lost sixpence
    a day during his life. He could not have   20
    'scaped sixpence a day. An the Duke had not given
    him sixpence a day for playing Pyramus, I'll be
    hanged. He would have deserved it. Sixpence a day
    in Pyramus, or nothing!
                Enter Bottom.

BOTTOM Where are these lads? Where are these   25
    hearts?

QUINCE Bottom! O most courageous day! O most happy
    hour!

BOTTOM Masters, I am to discourse wonders. But ask
    me not what; for, if I tell you, I am not true   30
    Athenian. I will tell you everything right as it fell
    out.

QUINCE Let us hear, sweet Bottom.

BOTTOM Not a word of me. All that I will tell you is that
    the Duke hath dined. Get your apparel together,   35
    good strings to your beards, new ribbons to your
    pumps. Meet presently at the palace. Every man
    look o'er his part. For the short and the long is, our
    play is preferred. In any case, let Thisbe have clean
    linen, and let not him that plays the lion pare his   40
    nails, for they shall hang out for the lion's claws.
    And, most dear actors, eat no onions nor garlic, for
    we are to utter sweet breath, and I do not doubt but
    to hear them say it is a sweet comedy. No more
    words. Away! Go, away!   45
                                    They exit.

Teacher's Overview

Introducing the Final Week and the Final Project:
Make *A Midsummer Night's Dream* Your Own

Final Project's Learning Goals

This project is the culmination of everything your students have been doing all unit long. Students will work in groups to make a scene from *A Midsummer Night's Dream* entirely their own.

By the end of this project, every student will have:

- Pulled together all the pieces of this unit, particularly essential practices like Cutting a Scene and Creating a Promptbook and 3D Lit, in order to get inside of and create a scene from *A Midsummer Night's Dream.*

- Moved collaboratively through a complex process of reading, rereading, editing, adapting, embodying, imagining, re-editing, rehearsing, performing, deciding, and defending.

- Used the text to make choices about how to edit, adapt, and stage the scene.

- Performed their original interpretation of an *A Midsummer Night's Dream* scene for an audience.

- Written and presented a group rationale for the text-based decisions that led to this performance (edits, additions, staging, etc.).

- Written a brief personal reflection on the experience of completing this project.

- Grappled with the whole play through work in class up to now and more collaborative work across the whole play during this week.

Both the students and you, the teacher, should walk away with resounding evidence that everyone in your class can make meaning from Shakespeare's language—from complex texts—on their own.

Advice and reminders

Time. This learning experience is designed to take roughly 5 class periods of 45 minutes each. However, depending on your teaching context, it might take a longer or shorter time. For example, this plan is written with one day for final performance, but if you need more time and have the time, take more time!

Chaos. Since it's all about turning the language and the learning over to the students, you can expect the process to get somewhat messy and noisy. As long as students are making *their own way* through their scenes, it's all good. As you have been doing right along, resist the urge to explain the text to your students. Trust the process—and trust your students to ask questions, find answers, create interpretations, and make meaning on their own, as they have been doing. (If they don't do this, then they're missing the point of the project.) Throughout this process and this week, students are tracking their cutting, adding, making promptbooking decisions and preparing to present, along with their scene performance, an oral defense of their key decisions.

Time and Less Chaos. It works out best if you can decide how much time your schedule allows you for the final performances and scene rationales on the final day of the project. Then work backwards to schedule your groups within that time.

An example: If you have 45 minutes of class time and 20 students, you might have 5 performing groups each with 4 students each. That could mean that each group would have 7 to 8 minutes to share their work (their performance + then defense of their decisions). 8 minutes x 5 groups = 40 minutes, leaving 5 minutes for a whole-class reflection round. If this feels tight to you, give each group 7 minutes.

Flexibility and Creativity. You'll see that on the menu of scenes for this project, some scenes involve more than 4 actors, and some fewer than 4 actors. Students will add their own creativity to the mix by double-casting parts, or using other means to make sure they have full participation.

Suggested Guidance For You on Assessing the Final Projects: A Seven-Point Checklist

1. Does the performance demonstrate a grasp of what the characters are saying and wanting?

2. Does the performance make strategic use of voice and body to convey effective tone and feeling?

3. Does the defense summarize the scene clearly, concisely, and accurately?

4. Does the defense comment on the scene's importance in the overall play and our world today?

5. Does the defense justify key decisions to cut, add, and perform language in this particular way? Is there strong and relevant textual evidence for this performance overall?

6. Does the defense describe how this process shaped new or different understandings of this play?

7. Does the personal reflection consider specific things that the student has learned, contributed, and discovered?

WEEK FIVE: LESSON 1

Your Final Projects!

Here's What We're Doing This Week and Why

Today kicks off the culminating project, the student-driven process of making Shakespeare thoroughly their own, by collaborating on creating for each other great scenes from *A Midsummer Night's Dream*. By the end of this lesson, students will understand what's expected of them and why—both as individuals and as project groups. They will also have gathered with their group-mates and have their assigned scene for this project. Although we've divided the final project into 5 days, it's really one unified, cumulative process, so please make whatever pacing adjustments your students need. Different groups might be at different steps of the process on different days, and that's okay.

What Will I Need?

- Final Project: The Teacher Overview – **RESOURCE #5.1A** (Perhaps you got an early start and have read this already because we attached it to last week's final lesson too!)

- Final Project: The Student Overview and Assignment – **RESOURCE #5.1B**

- The menu of *Midsummer* scenes for you to assign from, or for groups to choose from – **RESOURCE #5.1C**

How Should I Prepare?

- Make copies of the student's overview and assignment for everyone in class.

- Make a plan for grouping students.

- Make a plan for matching groups to scenes. (It's up to you whether you want to assign them scenes that you feel are key to the play or allow them to make their own choices.)

- Figure out how much time students will have for their scenes and their defense so you can let them know today. (See Teacher Overview, **RESOURCE #5.1A**.)

- Prepare yourself to get out of the way and let students figure things out on their own. You're assessing their ability to do exactly that.

Agenda (~ 45-minute class period)

- ❏ Part One: Intro to the assignment and scene menu: 20 minutes
- ❏ Part Two: Groups meet for the first time: 25 minutes

Here's What Students Hear (From You) and (Then What They'll) Do

Part One: Project Introduction

1. Give students the project assignment and go through the directions with them.

2. Check for understanding with reflection rounds:

   I notice . . .

   I wonder . . .

3. Assign scenes, answer any wonderings, and fill in any details that students missed.

Part Two: Group work

Students work in their groups and get started!

Here's What Just Happened in Class

- Students met their final project and started working in groups to tackle the assignment!

- Every student read out loud some *A Midsummer Night's Dream* new to them as groups started to befriend their scenes.

Teacher's Overview

Introducing the Final Week and the Final Project: Make *A Midsummer Night's Dream* Your Own

The Final Project's Learning Goals

This project is the culmination of everything your students have been doing all unit long. Students will work in groups to make a scene from *A Midsummer Night's Dream* entirely their own.

By the end of this project, every student will have:

- Pulled together all the pieces of this unit, particularly essential practices like cutting a scene, creating a promptbook, and 3D Lit, in order to get inside of and create a scene from *A Midsummer Night's Dream.*

- Moved collaboratively through a complex process of reading, rereading, editing, adapting, embodying, imagining, re-editing, rehearsing, performing, deciding, and defending.

- Used the text to make choices about how to edit, adapt, and stage the scene.

- Performed their original interpretation of an *A Midsummer Night's Dream* scene for an audience.

- Written and presented a group rationale for the text-based decisions that led to this performance (edits, additions, staging, etc.).

- Written a brief personal reflection on the experience of completing this project.

- Grappled with the whole play through work in class up to now and more collaborative work across the whole play during this week.

Both the students and you, the teacher, should walk away with resounding evidence that everyone in your class can make meaning from Shakespeare's language—from complex texts—on their own.

Advice and reminders

Time. This learning experience is designed to take roughly 5 class periods of 45 minutes each. However, depending on your teaching context, it might take a longer or shorter time. For example, this plan is written with one day for final performance, but if you need more time and have the time, take more time!

Chaos. Since it's all about turning the language and the learning over to the students, you can expect the process to get somewhat messy and noisy. As long as students are making *their own way* through their scenes, it's all good. As you have been doing right along, resist the urge to explain the text to your students. Trust the process—and trust your students to ask questions, find answers, create interpretations, and make meaning on their own, as they have been doing. (If they don't do this, then they're missing the point of the project.) Throughout this process and this week, students are tracking their cutting, adding, making promptbooking decisions and preparing to present, along with their scene performance, an oral defense of their key decisions.

Time and Less Chaos. It works out best if you can decide how much time your schedule allows you for the final performances and scene rationales on the final day of the project. Then work backwards to schedule your groups within that time.

An example: If you have 45 minutes of class time and 20 students, you might have 5 performing groups each with 4 students each. That could mean that each group would have 7 to 8 minutes to share their work (their performance + then defense of their decisions). 8 minutes x 5 groups = 40 minutes, leaving 5 minutes for a whole-class Reflection Round. If this feels tight to you, give each group 7 minutes.

Flexibility and Creativity. You'll see that on the menu of scenes for this project, some scenes involve more than 4 actors, and some fewer than 4 actors. Students will add their own creativity to the mix by double-casting parts, or using other means to make sure they have full participation.

Suggested Guidance on Assessing the Projects: A Seven-Point Checklist

1. Does the performance demonstrate a grasp of what the characters are saying and wanting?

2. Does the performance make strategic use of voice and body to convey effective tone and feeling?

3. Does the defense summarize the scene clearly, concisely, and accurately?

4. Does the defense comment on the scene's importance in the overall play and our world today?

5. Does the defense justify key decisions to cut, add, and perform language in this particular way? Is there strong and relevant textual evidence for this performance overall?

6. Does the defense describe how this process shaped new or different understandings of this play?

7. Does the personal reflection consider specific things that the student has learned, contributed, and discovered?

Student's Overview and Assignment

Introducing the Final Week and the Final Project:
Make *A Midsummer Night's Dream* Your Own

You will work in groups to make a scene from *A Midsummer Night's Dream* entirely your own. This project is the culmination of everything you have been doing all unit long, and this week you will be demonstrating all that you have learned!

By the end of this project, you will have:

- Put together all the pieces of this unit, particularly essential practices like choral reading, cutting a scene, creating promptbooks, and 3D Lit, in order to get inside of and create a scene from *A Midsummer Night's Dream*.

- Moved collaboratively through a complex process of reading, rereading, editing, adapting, embodying, imagining, re-editing, rehearsing, performing, deciding, and defending.

- Used the text to make choices about how to edit, adapt, and stage the scene.

- Performed your original interpretation of the scene for an audience.

- Written and presented a group rationale for the text-based decisions that led to this performance (edits, additions, staging, etc.).

- Written a brief personal reflection on the experience of completing this project.

- Grappled with the whole play (Acts 1–5) through work in class up to now and collaborative work on scenes throughout the play this week.

You, your classmates, and your teacher will walk away with resounding evidence that YOU can make meaning from Shakespeare's language—from complex texts—on your own.

What You Will Produce

1. A performed scene from *A Midsummer Night's Dream* (in a group)

2. A defense of your scene, delivered orally and in writing (in a group)

3. A personal reflection on this project (from you, as an individual)

Your Action Steps

1. Get your group and scene assignment from your teacher.

2. Next, before anything else: With your group, dive deeply into your scene. Read it out loud as a group, just as we have done in class. Take notes on all of this— these will come in handy later. Collaboratively as a group, figure out:

   – What's happening in the scene?

   – What are the characters saying?

> – What does each of the characters want?
>
> – Why is the scene important in the play?
>
> – Why should someone care about this scene today?

3. Next, **consider the end goal**: Your group is making a scene of _____ minutes and an oral defense of the scene that is no longer than _____ minutes. Your teacher will tell you the timing that you—like any group of actors—must work with. Keep this in mind as you work through the scene.

4. Next, work to **be directors and put the scene on its feet**. Each member of the group should be **creating a promptbook** for the scene along the way so that you're all working from the same script with the same notes. Together, make—and note—decisions about the following and be prepared to explain to your audience what in the text (and in your personal experience of reading it) motivated you to cut, add, and perform as you did:

   - **Cutting the scene.** Perhaps you must cut it so that it fits your time limit and still makes sense. What must stay? What can go?

   - **Locating the scene.** Where is it happening? What does this place look like? Feel like? Smell like? Sound like? How do you know this?

   - **Adding to the scene.** You may want to choose 1–2 outside texts to mash-up with your scene. If you do, what is gained by putting these texts into your Shakespeare scene? What made you choose this text/these texts? Why and where do they work best? If you choose to add outside texts, be sure that at least 80 percent of your scene is *A Midsummer Night's Dream*.

   - **Getting ready to perform the scene.** Cast the parts. Which of you plays whom? Every group member must speak. What does each character want and think and feel? How can the audience tell? Who is moving where on what line, and why? Get on your feet and start moving, because some of these questions are answered when you get a scene on its feet. As you know, this is not about acting talent; it is about knowing what you are saying and doing as you bring life to this scene.

   - **As you go, you're documenting your decisions and preparing your oral defense of the scene.** What are the most significant or original decisions your group made? What drove those decisions? Let the audience into your interpretive process, your minds, ever so concisely. Your defense should involve every group member and do the following:

     – Summarize your scene

     – Comment on the scene's importance in the overall play

     – Justify your cutting, adding, and performing choices with textual evidence

     – Conclude by describing how the process of preparing this performance shaped new or different understandings of *A Midsummer Night's Dream*.

5. **Rehearse.** Yes, you should memorize your lines, though you can ask someone to serve as your prompter, as we think Shakespeare's company might have done. *Repeat: This is not about acting talent.*

6. **Perform your scene and present your scene rationale** during your scheduled class period. After your performance, present your rationale for your scene. As with your performance, every group member must speak. Focus on just the most significant decisions and stick to your time limit. We will all watch all the final project scenes together so that we can celebrate wrapping up *A Midsummer Night's Dream* with YOUR voices.

7. At that time, you will **submit the 2 written documents**:
   – The written version of your group's defense of your scene
   – An individual reflection (400–500 words) reflecting on the experience— both the process and what you feel were your own contributions to the project.

Menu: *A Midsummer Night's Dream* – 6 Options

ACTS & SCENES	LINES	# OF CHARACTERS
4.1	1–106	5–8
4.1	107–209	7
4.1 and 4.2	210–229, 1–45	5
5.1	114–199	5
5.1	200–277	9
5.1	278–379	7

Your Final Project: Making *A Midsummer Night's Dream* Your Own

Here's What We're Doing and Why

We're here! Groups are making their way through the final project this week. They are working on scenes from *Midsummer,* demonstrating as they go what they have learned in terms of making the language, characters, and action their own—all infused with their own energy and creativity. They are also presenting scenes to each other as we wrap up *A Midsummer Night's Dream.*

Agenda for Lessons 2, 3, and 4

Lesson 2:

❏ Introduction: 10 minutes

❏ Cutting the Scene: 35 minutes

Lesson 3:

❏ Introduction: 10 minutes

❏ Adding outside texts if you choose to, and promptbook the newly edited scene: 35 minutes

Lesson 4:

❏ Warm-up of choice: 10 minutes

❏ Rehearsing the scene and writing the scene rationale: 35 minutes

What Will I Need for These Lessons?

- Some print copies of the Folger Shakespeare edition of the play for student reference

- A few dictionaries or Shakespeare glossaries for student reference

- Space and time for students to make their way through this project

- Strength to resist the urge to explain or interpret the text for students (you're a pro by now)

- Access to outside books, songs, poems, films, etc. if they choose to add outside material to their scene

- A discreet eye to observe students as they work

How Should I Prepare for These Lessons?

- Arrange your room to facilitate group work (desks in groups or spaces opened up for students to meet, work, and perform together).

- As long as every student understands the task at hand, you're good. Students are doing the hard work now!

Lesson 2: Here's What Students Hear (From You) and (Then What They'll) Do

Part One: Introduction/Warm-up

1. Choose your favorite line from your scene.

2. Count off by 4. Meet with the other students with the same number.

3. Toss your lines in a circle; everyone should say their line three times (say it differently each time!).

4. Discuss as a class: Given the lines you heard in your circle, what do you think is happening in the scenes we are performing? Which delivery of your line felt like the best fit for your character or scene? Why?

Part Two: Group work

1. Groups are reading, rereading, and cutting their final scenes.

   a. They are also cooperating to compose a rationale for their unique performance of the scene.

   b. For a closer look at the steps in this process, please refer to the Student Overview and Assignment – **RESOURCE #5.1B**.

[**TEACHER NOTE:** Students typically need to take this work home with them, especially the 2 writing tasks: the group rationale and the personal reflection. Check in with your students each class to see where they are in the process and help them set realistic goals for homework and classwork.]

Lesson 3: Here's What Students Hear (From You) and (Then What They'll) Do

Part One: Warm-up

1. In your groups, agree on a song that best represents your scene.

2. Discuss with your small group. Share with the class.

Part Two: Group work

1. Groups are cutting, adapting, promptbooking, and rehearsing their final scenes.

    a. If they are including an outside text(s), they should decide what and how today.

    b. For a closer look at the steps in this process, please refer to the Student Overview and Assignment—**RESOURCE #5.1B**.

[**TEACHER NOTE:** Once again, check in with your students each class to see where they are in the process, and help them set realistic goals for homework and classwork and that they have a plan to complete the 2 writing tasks.]

Lesson 4: Here's What Students Hear (From You) and (Then What They'll) Do

Part One: Warm-up

1. Decide on a great warm-up.

2. Either use it yourselves or pass it on to another group to do!

Part Two: Group work

1. Groups are rehearsing their final scenes.

    a. They are also cooperating to compose a rationale for their unique performance of their scene.

    b. For a closer look at the steps in this process, please refer to the Student Overview and Assignment – **RESOURCE #5.1B**.

[**TEACHER NOTE:** Students typically need to work at home on these, especially the 2 writing tasks: the group rationale and the personal reflection. Check in with your students each class to see where they are in the process and help them set realistic goals for homework and classwork.]

Here's What Just Happened in These Three Classes

- You observed a class full of students in a state of flow, deeply engaged in the process of making a scene from *A Midsummer Night's Dream* their own!

- You watched peers help one another by asking good questions, building comprehension, citing textual evidence, and encouraging creativity.

The Final Project: Your Own *A Midsummer Night's Dream*, Performed!

Here's What We're Doing and Why

It's showtime! Watch and listen as your students demonstrate their ability to grapple with, respond to, and perform Shakespeare's language. Hear why they staged things as they did. Celebrate how far your students have come, not just as Shakespeareans but as thinkers and readers and makers. Don't forget to save time for a whole-class Reflection Round after all the performances. This is often just as enlightening as the scenes themselves, if not more so.

What Will I Need?

- Space and time for all groups to present their performances and rationales

- A notepad or digital doc to take notes on all the great learning you're witnessing. These notes will come in handy when you provide student feedback. (Revisit the 7-point checklist and the learning goals of the final project when it's time for feedback.)

- Space and time for everyone to gather in a circle for a reflection round

How Should I Prepare?

- Create and share the "run of show" for today. At the beginning of class, groups should know when they're on.

- Arrange your space so everyone can see each scene. A giant circle is our favorite.

- It's always nice to have a lighthearted but clear way to call "time" on a scene, too. Some teachers rely on a phone timer. Your call.

Agenda (45-minute class period)

- ❏ Groups get organized: 5 minutes
- ❏ Scenes performed and defenses presented: 40 minutes
- ❏ Whole-class reflection: 10 minutes

Here's What Students Will Do

Part One: Groups Get Organized

Students meet in their groups to organize props or make quick, last-minute changes to their scene.

Part Two: Performances

- Each group presents their work to thunderous applause.

- Collect whatever project documentation you need to assess student learning.

Part Three: Reflection Round

To conclude the performances, respond to the following prompts *thinking just about your work this week, including this performance experience.*

[**TEACHER NOTE:** Don't forget to participate in this process, too!]

    I noticed . . .

    I learned . . .

    I wondered . . .

If responses stay focused on the language and activities, teachers should add: What did you learn about yourself this week?

Here's What Just Happened in Class

- Massive learning in action, all set up by you. WOW!

Teaching Shakespeare—and
A Midsummer Night's Dream—
with English Learners

Christina Porter

I am Christina Porter and for the past 20 years I have worked in an urban school community right outside of Boston, Massachusetts. I began as an English teacher, then a literacy coach, and currently I am the district curriculum director for the humanities. I first started working with English Learners in 2006 when I became the literacy coach. Prior to that, I had little experience with these phenomenal students.

Also prior to working with them, I knew the general assumptions about ELs. For as long as they have sat in U.S. classrooms, ELs most often have been considered "other," having many "deficits" that need to be overcome. The "deficits" tend to be their native language and culture—seen as roadblocks that should be surmounted so that EL students can more closely match prevailing assumptions of "American" culture—white, middle-class, and English-speaking. In my work with EL students, I soon learned that this mindset can manifest itself in many ugly ways in schools, and it is both culturally and academically destructive.

Something I observed early on was that while our white, middle-class, English-speaking students were reading Shakespeare—the real thing, not that watered-down summarized stuff—our English Learners were not. Not even a watered-down version of Shakespeare! By "real Shakespeare" I mean *his* words in all their glorious, Early Modern English (both with the full text of a play as well as in edited scenes from a play). Initially, I had the incorrect assumption myself: I *assumed*, like so many others, that because students were developing English, Shakespeare was probably too difficult for them to handle. I *learned* that this is incorrect. What I learned instead was that once we adults dismissed our own deficit-based thinking—and allowed our EL students to read, create, design, and imagine—the results were tremendous. With Shakespeare as well as many other complex texts.

Coinciding with my start as literacy coach, I spent a summer at the Folger Library's Teaching Shakespeare Institute. I learned about so many of the student-centered, get-them-on-their-feet methods that are one of the backbones of this book. As the new literacy coach at the high school, I was so excited to get into a classroom and use these, especially because I had the unique opportunity to work with many teachers in the building. One of the first colleagues to reach out was an English as a Second Language (ESL) teacher. We met to brainstorm, and I described how I had spent my summer at the Folger Library learning all of these innovative methods of engaging students. She was immediately onboard. Specifically, she wanted to tackle Shakespeare (again, REAL Shakespeare). Over the course of several years, we taught many plays together, and I did the same with other colleagues in the ESL department. Our ELs consistently destroyed any concern I or others could have had about their ability to read and perform something as intricate and as complex as Shakespeare. Just one example: One of the first things I learned was that these students are uniquely attuned to the intricacy of language; it's how they exist on a daily basis! Sometimes when teaching a play with my native speakers, I found that they would want to rush. In this rushing, they would miss the depth and beauty of the words. ELs, on the other hand, take time with language, with the word, the line, the speech, and the scene. This is only one of the many strengths these students bring to working with Shakespeare, and other authors too.

Because the Folger understands the importance of ELs, I have been asked to share some of the knowledge I've gained working with these unique, intelligent, and resilient EL students *and* Shakespeare. My suggestions are based on years of scholarly research regarding second language acquisition coupled with my knowledge and experience in working with ELs, Shakespeare, and the Folger Method. I am excited to share both what I've taught and what I've learned from EL students!

One important and perhaps obvious note here is that English Learners *are not* a monolith. You may have students in your class who have had exposure to English in their native country; you may also have students who have experienced gaps in schooling, and more. Though most of this chapter is focused on ELs generally, when I have found an approach that is particularly helpful for a specific subgroup of ELs, I point that out.

I build here on principles and classroom practices that you will find throughout this book and this series. Since teachers are the busiest people on the planet, this material is organized so that you can find what you need quickly:

❑ **Part One: ELs at Home in the Folger Method**

❑ **Part Two: Shakespeare with English Learners**

❑ **Part Three:** *A Midsummer Night's Dream* **with English Learners**

Part One: ELs at Home in the Folger Method

Many of the Folger Essentials are *already* excellent supports for ELs. Folger Essentials like choral reading, rereading, focusing on single words and lines and then building to speeches and scenes—all of these support fluency and comprehension. In addition, these *Teaching Guides* include plot summaries and play maps, and the lesson plans include lots of other active instructional approaches.

When reading Shakespeare with ELs, I always give the option to read the scene summary in advance. I do this because it balances accessibility with giving them a chance to grapple with a complex text. Remember, Shakespeare borrowed most of his plots, so the plot is the least of our concern. We never want the story to become the roadblock to working with the words. The Folger Shakespeare, both in print and online, includes brief play and scene synopses for all of the plays. The play maps may be helpful to ELs who may have had interruptions in their prior schooling or ELs who have not previously read a drama. It can be another structural support to "unveil" the characters and plot. You may choose to spend some time deconstructing the structure of a piece of drama—discussing, for example, scenes, acts, and character lists. For some students, drama may be completely new; for others, this quick activity can serve as an activator of prior knowledge.

Understanding text features is a solid support for comprehension. It is easy to assume that by high school, when most students are reading this play, they have been exposed to drama, but this is not always the case, depending on the backgrounds of individual students.

Part Two: Shakespeare with English Learners

With the Folger Method as my base, I build in additional resources to support English Learners in my urban school. This is because working with ELs *is* different from working with native English speakers. Equity is removing barriers. Equity is giving students what *they* need to be successful. Thus, I have come to four Truths that prevail when diving into Shakespeare—and other complex texts too—with EL students:

- TRUTH #1: **ELs need support with classroom practices.** We cannot assume that our ELs have had the same experience in classrooms as our other students. We need to offer specific guidance and support for common classroom practices such as having a small-group discussion, acting out a piece of drama, or other Folger Essentials. Being clear in our expectations, our directions, and offering scaffolds (for example, sentence starters for small group discussions) is good for all students and essential for ELs.

- TRUTH #2: **ELs need additional support in order to grapple with complex texts.** ELs are capable of reading Shakespeare. ELs also need supports for language comprehension. Important supports include chunking a scene/speech into smaller parts and using edited scenes or plays. To be clear, we always use Shakespeare's text (rather than the "simplified" versions) and we want to offer accessibility to those words through appropriate support for students who are in the process of acquiring English.

- TRUTH #3: **ELs need to have space for their unique language and culture to live in our classrooms.** Students' funds of knowledge are an asset, not a deficit. They need to bring their selves and their whole native culture to Shakespeare. This truth echoes the Folger principle about the importance of student voice.

- TRUTH #4: **ELs need support with the specific aspects of the English language and how words function** (individually, in a sentence, and more). This helps them to build academic vocabulary, in written as well as oral language.

Continuing from Truth #4 and parts of the Folger Method, I introduce my students to what I call the "actor's arsenal"—a toolbox of five elements of communication that actors (and all of us) have at their disposal in English: stress, inflection, pause, nonverbal communication, and tone. At its simplest, it looks like this, and my students appreciate this visual:

STRESS: Emphasis placed on a **WORD** (or word, or word)

INFLECTION: The way the voice goes ^{up} or _{down} when a word is pronounced

PAUSE: A break ..... in reading for emphasis

NONVERBAL COMMUNICATION: Without words, the gestures, posture, presence or absence of eye contact

TONE: The *emotional* sound in your voice

These five tools deserve attention because *they are not the same in all languages*. In some languages, some of these tools are nonexistent or used in different ways than they are in English. I have a distinct memory of teaching a lesson on tone for the first time to a class of ELs. Generally, students really enjoy practicing a word/line with varying tones of voice. In this class, I couldn't help but notice one student who had a puzzled look on his face. I didn't want to embarrass him in his small group, so I sought guidance from the ESL teacher I was working with. She explained to me that tone did not work the same way in his native language as it did in English. In some languages—Hmong, for example—tone alone literally changes the meaning of a word, while in other languages—English, for one—tone accompanied by nonverbal communication alters the subtext of a word/phrase.

When working with students who have varying language backgrounds, additional attention to tone and nonverbal communication is very helpful. I typically introduce this "arsenal" as a part of our pre-reading. Tone and Stress, the first Folger Essential, includes visuals and practice rounds, and is recommended for all students beginning their journey with Shakespeare's language. Learn more about it in the Folger Method chapter. What I describe here can be an additional and introductory support for EL students.

I often begin this communication work by asking students to consider a universal teenage dilemma—having a disagreement with your parents or caregivers. (I have found, after working with students from all over the world, this is one of the few situations that transcends language and culture for most adolescents.) I then ask them to brainstorm all the different ways they can "show" their displeasure with words or actions. The list they generate generally includes items like volume, eye rolling, silence, additional gestures, and tone of voice. I then introduce the concept of tone vocabulary and include visuals with each element to further support comprehension. We pay particular attention to tone, as the English language offers infinite options for impacting the meaning of a word or phrase with tone alone. We define tone as the emotional sound in your voice, and I offer a specific list of tones for students' reference: love, hate, anger, joy, fear, and sorrow. While certainly not comprehensive of all the tones available in English, these six seem to capture the fundamentals. Students always enjoy taking a phrase like "That's great!" and applying these tones in small groups. For students coming from language backgrounds where tone is not utilized in the same way as it is in English, this activity offers additional practice in and added awareness of how tone functions in English. Using the Folger Essential, students practice with the word *Oh!*, saying it in a variety of tones (happy, sad, angry, surprised, and more). Students on their own will automatically add accompanying nonverbal communication, crossing their arms if the tone is angry, for example.

In addition, you can use a film clip of a scene from a Shakespeare play to further explore tone. (There is a wide variety of clips on sites like YouTube, or check out folger.edu.) Initially, I hand out to the students a copy of the scene, and I play the clip *audio only*. Students can work individually or they can work in small groups. They listen to the audio only, following along with the lines. As they listen, I instruct them to focus on one character and note any tone of voice they hear (anger, love, joy, and more). Next, we watch the scene *video only*, with no audio at all. They continue to track the same character and note any nonverbal communication. Finally, we watch the scene *with audio and video*, and add any additional notes on tone, stress, nonverbal communication, inflection, or pause. After this, students share their notes and findings either in a pair (if they have been working individually) or with another small group. Later, when we get up on our feet as a class, we are able to draw upon this kind of analysis to support our version of the play!

Part Three: *A Midsummer Night's Dream* with English Learners

Teaching a play about a dream immediately opens the door to collecting students' experiences and beliefs about dreaming! When you are working with students from a variety of cultural backgrounds, this is such an interesting way to begin this play and also aligns with my Truth #3 (**ELs need to have space for their unique language and culture to live in our classrooms**). Before we begin reading it, I display the title of the play and the following parable:

If I wake from a dream that I am a butterfly, am I a man who has dreamed he was a butterfly, or a butterfly dreaming that I am a man?
  —Chinese philosopher Chuang Tzu

I then give students the opportunity to discuss this parable in a pair or a triad. While students generally agree that the dreamer is indeed still a man, it begins our conversation on the beliefs around dreams. I then pose the question, "Are our dreams real or important?" Students have small-group discussions again before we share as a whole class. I have learned so many interesting takes on the concept of dreaming from these conversations! These have ranged from dreams as a form of supernatural knowledge, to predicting the future, to omens (good and bad). The idea of recurring dreams is also a fascinating topic, with some students viewing these as elements of the subconscious (very Freudian)! I remember one student sharing her belief that if you have a dream about your own death, this is actually predicting a long life. When we arrive at scene 4.1 (Bottom waking up from his "dream"), we revisit the parable above about the butterfly. Most students agree that, for Bottom, he was a man dreaming he was an ass. I invite you to try this beginning approach with your multicultural students!

In looking at the play as a whole, one of the challenging pieces of the structure and plot are the three groupings of characters: the Athenian Court, the Mechanicals, and the Fairies. While they do interact, they also have unique subplots. To support ELs' comprehension, I adapted an organizer from one of my brilliant colleagues and Folger teacher Mary Ellen Dakin (FIGURE 1). The organizer arranges the three groups of characters with their unique subplots. You can add some color-coding for the different characters to support readability.

FIGURE 1.

THE ATHENIAN COURT	THE MECHANICALS (workers who put on a play)	THE FAIRIES
Theseus, *Duke of Athens; engaged to Hippolyta*	**Nick Bottom**, *a weaver who plays Pyramus*	**Oberon**, *King of the fairies*
Hippolyta, *Queen of the Amazons*	**Peter Quince**, *a carpenter who directs the play and speaks the Prologue*	**Titania**, *Queen of the fairies*
Egeus, *father of Hermia*	**Francis Flute**, *a bellows-mender who plays Thisbe*	**Puck**, *Oberon's attendant*
Hermia, *in love with Lysander*	**Tom Snout**, *a tinker who plays Wall*	Peaseblossom, Cobweb, Moth, and Mustardseed, *Titania's fairy attendants*
Lysander, *in love with Hermia*	**Robin Starveling**, *a tailor who plays Moonshine*	
Helena, *in love with Demetrius*	**Snug**, *a joiner who plays Lion*	
Demetrius, *Egeus's choice as a husband for Hermia*		
THE PLOT	**THE PLOT**	**THE PLOT**
As Athens prepares to celebrate the upcoming wedding of **Theseus** and **Hippolyta**, an angry father named **Egeus** demands that **Theseus** force his daughter **Hermia** to marry the man he has chosen for her (**Demetrius**), but **Hermia** loves someone else. The laws of Athens are on the father's side, so **Theseus** reluctantly tells **Hermia** that she must obey her father, or choose between death and a convent.	In preparation for the marriage celebration of **Theseus** and **Hippolyta**, the workmen rehearse a play about forbidden love called *Pyramus and Thisbe*. They meet at night in the Athenian woods to plan their production.	**Oberon** and **Titania**, who hold court in the Athenian woods, love each other but are battling over a mortal child, "adopted" by **Titania**. **Oberon** is somewhat jealous of the child and wants to take him from **Titania** and keep him as his attendant. **Titania**, who is also jealous of **Oberon's** many love affairs, refuses to give him the child.

Hermia and Lysander (the man she loves) plan to meet in the Athenian woods and run away. A jealous Helena overhears this, and tells Demetrius. At night, the four young lovers wander through the woods, arguing. They attract the attention of the Fairies, then fall asleep. When they awake, nothing is the same!	Though Peter Quince is older and wiser, Nick Bottom is a bossy show-off who tries to "run the show." As they rehearse, they attract the attention of the Fairies, who decide to have some fun at their expense. Nick Bottom is magically "transformed" into a different shape, though he doesn't know it. The other players run away, leaving Nick to fall asleep in the woods. When he awakes, nothing is the same!	Oberon decides to use magic on Titania to get his way. Meanwhile, he overhears the lovers quarreling in his woods and orders his attendant Puck to use more magic to set things right for the lovers. Puck prefers mischief, so he sets about following Oberon's orders in his own way. Once he begins to meddle in the affairs of the mortals, nothing is the same!

Students see that the play has three groups of characters and while they do interact, they each have their own story. The play map earlier in this book is helpful in this way, too, and gives my students a visual way to see the connections between these groups. If you're worried about students knowing the plot before they dive into the play, please don't be! Shakespeare wrote plays based on stories that were already familiar to his audiences, so we assume that lots of people in the Globe Theatre knew the story before they got there.

My students read through this organizer and then process it in small groups using a tool I call the S.W.B.S.—"Somebody Wanted But So"—FIGURE 2 here. Students identify some of the conflicts that are present in the play. They name a character or characters (**Somebody**), describe a want or a need (**wanted**), describe the conflict or the problem that prevented them from meeting their need (**but**), and then describe what they do to solve the problem (**so**). There is an example below from 1.1: **SOMEBODY** Egeus **WANTED** to have his daughter marry Demetrius **BUT** she is in love with Lysander, **SO** he asks Theseus to order her to **marry Demetrius (or be killed or sent to a nunnery)**.

FIGURE 2. S.W.B.S.

Somebody . . . (Name the character/s)	Wanted . . . (What does the character/s want or what is their need?)	But . . . (What is the problem OR what is keeping the character/s from their goal?)	So . . . (What is the solution to the problem or how does the character/s reach their goal?)
Example . . . 1. Egeus	2. **wanted** to have his daughter marry Demetrius	3. **but** she is in love with Lysander,	4. **so** he asks Theseus to order her to marry Demetrius (or be killed or sent to a nunnery).

When I am teaching a play for the first time, I consider *what* about that particular play's complexity would be something that ELs would need additional support with. This could range from the structure of the sentences to the staging, etc. Because I am not a Shakespearean scholar, I look to the experts! An easy way to do that is to look to the *Midsummer* material on folger.edu/a-midsummer-nights-dream or the introductory pieces in the *Folger Shakespeare,* either online (and free) or in paperback. When I was new to *Midsummer,* I learned from these sources that this play has a lot of scenes where you can have some "imaginative staging." This includes Oberon and Robin anointing the eyes of the sleeping characters, Robin "mocking" the fighting between Demetrius and Lysander, the chaotic opening scene, or the mechanicals' play. My EL Truth #1 is that ELs need support with classroom practices. You may have students in front of you who have extensive experience in reading and acting drama. You may have others for whom this is totally new. Before they move on to the Folger Essential 3D Lit—beautifully detailed in the teaching unit earlier in this book (with step-by-step instructions!)—my students practice staging a scene at their desks. For *Midsummer,* I have used these scenes for desktop staging:

- 1.1 – At the Athenian court, Egeus asks the duke to force his daughter to marry Demetrius.

- 1.2 – The Mechanicals practice their play.

- 3.2 – Robin and Oberon try to anoint the "correct" Athenian after the mix-up with Lysander and Demetrius.

- 5.1 – The Performance of *Pyramus and Thisbe* for the Athenian court.

Working in small groups, students read through the scene using the Folger Essentials you have been using thus far. As they do that, I distribute a pile of buttons to each group. I ask them to choose a point in the scene that they want to "freeze"—and use the buttons to indicate where their characters or actors are and, based on the lines they are working from, why they made those choices. All of the scenes and rationales are shared and discussed enthusiastically. From there, we then move on to 3D Lit—a deeper dive into the scenes in which they work together as actors and directors, acting out a section of their scene themselves.

The Folger Method is an excellent pathway for ELs into not just Shakespeare but other complex texts as well. I hope these specific *Midsummer* thoughts will send both you and your students into a wonderful learning experience.

Teaching Shakespeare—including *A Midsummer Night's Dream*—to Students with Learning Differences

Roni DiGenno

I am Roni DiGenno, a special education teacher with 10 years' experience teaching ninth- through twelfth-grade English in a District of Columbia public high school. My students' reading levels range from pre-primer to college level, and their special education classifications include specific learning disabilities, ADHD, auditory disabilities, autism, as well as intellectual and emotional disabilities. I teach self-contained pull-out classes, each of about fifteen students, all with IEPs. Sometimes I have a teaching assistant, but most often I do not.

I love teaching. I love my students. And I love teaching Shakespeare to my students. I put to use what I have learned at the Folger; I use Shakespeare to inspire my students to believe in themselves. Most importantly, my students begin to see themselves as learners because I trust them with the hard stuff, the challenging content. I believe we can do it together, and my students know this. My passion for teaching these kids, who at times seem unreachable, comes from my own experience growing up with a reading difficulty. I could not sound out words, but this had nothing to do with my value or my intellect. My students, and all students, deserve the best, most engaging, most intellectually stimulating lessons possible.

Shakespeare Rewrites How Students See Themselves as Learners

For the past several years, I have taught exclusively some of the most difficult students in my school—those with very large learning gaps, usually reading 5–8 years below grade level, and with emotional disturbances that make it difficult to build positive peer and adult relationships. They arrive in my classroom plagued with low expectations of themselves and of school, because for years other people have had low expectations of them. They are used to passing just by showing up and doing minimal work. Some have been through the criminal justice system, which adds another layer of low expectations. My first priority is to help my students see themselves as capable and valued members of our classroom community. I do this by teaching lessons that empower them—lessons based on the Folger's philosophy. As a result, my students grow in exciting and surprising ways that no one could have anticipated.

I teach students like Armando, who had serious trust issues. He cut class frequently and was involved in groups that negatively influenced him in school. He repeated grades because he refused to do the work and he cursed teachers out regularly. In addition to being in and out of the criminal justice system, he was also a target of violent crime, which left him hospitalized for weeks and suffering from post-traumatic stress disorder. Through our class's collaborative work using Folger methods, Armando slowly began to discover and enjoy his strengths. He felt welcomed into the learning process and started to trust himself and others. He eventually became a peer leader who helped facilitate lessons.

I also taught Martin, a student who had such severe dyslexia that early on in my class he was reading at a kindergarten level. He was withdrawn and shied away from participating for fear of judgment. Here again, by incorporating Folger principles and practices, I was able to give Martin the safe learning environment he needed and the confidence to try reading aloud. He learned to trust his peers and began to take risks—reading parts, participating, and giving amazing insight into discussion topics.

The Folger Method supports students like Armando and Martin, who have vastly different learning needs but who may also be in the same class. The teaching strategies offer students multiple entry points—tactical, visual, and aural—through which to engage and enjoy complex texts. Differentiation and scaffolding are built into the Folger's interactive lessons so students build a positive association with challenging texts. This is hugely important for students with learning differences and emotional difficulties. If content or concepts are overwhelming, or not taught in a way that they can grasp them, students will build a negative association. No one wants to struggle or feel like they can't learn something, which is often the root cause of behavior issues within classrooms. The Folger Method meets students' social and emotional learning needs through building a supportive and collaborative classroom community. Through the process, students begin to work through conflict, solve problems, and accept and support one another's learning differences.

How the Folger Method Works for Students with IEPs

In the Folger Method and *Midsummer* lessons in this book, you'll find that the Folger Essentials will throw your students right into the text through powerful practices like tossing words and phrases, two-line scenes, choral reading, and 3D Lit. Each Essential gives students exposure to the language and removes a barrier to learning and comprehension. Each builds on the others, increasing cognitive demand. Students master each step before moving to the next—words before lines, lines before scenes, choral reading before acting and reading parts solo. They don't feel left behind because they learn the content and the skills to understand it simultaneously.

Every year, my students look forward to my unit on Shakespeare. Typically about ten weeks long, the unit allows us to slow down and dig into the text. Instead of skipping over difficult parts, we want to conquer them! It is important for us to embrace the struggle because it is an inevitable part of the learning process. In the Folger work, struggle is about joyful investigation and thinking hard together rather than a feeling of inadequacy. Students question, try out, and connect with the words and each other and so they learn that there is no one right answer, but rather a whole new way to discover a text. The Essentials get the language in the students' mouths, encourage collaboration, and shift focus away from the teacher so that students can practice navigating themselves through their learning. It's a different way of teaching and a different way of learning. At first, they are hesitant: they resist, they laugh, they feel weird, they are unsure, they can't believe they are talking this much in class—and I am encouraging all of it. Within a week or two, students are more willing to experiment and take risks with the language by reading really strange words they have never seen or heard before. And soon, students are reading Shakespeare and enjoying it.

Reading Shakespeare can be a great equalizer. While scholars and directors and actors never tire of decoding, interpreting, and defining Shakespeare, the truth is that no one knows exactly what Shakespeare really meant. He left no diary or notes. Everyone is entitled to their own interpretation. We also have no idea how the words were spoken, because we have no audio recordings of the play performances in the Globe Theatre in 1600. The "funny" English (my students' term) in Shakespeare's works puts us all on the same playing field. Be vulnerable, mess up some words, and have fun! The students will ask, "How do you say this word?" and my only response is, "Not sure, let's figure it out." It's okay to do your best and sound "funny." We are all in this together, and repeating that idea to students builds bridges.

The Folger Method gives students the scaffolding and tools needed to launch them from struggling readers to invested readers. Martin, my student with severe dyslexia and on a Beginning Reader level, struggled with sight words. As the rest of his class became more comfortable reading Shakespeare's words, he remained unsure. Could he read and understand Shakespeare? But he can't read! But he has a learning disability! But . . . nothing! Martin found his voice and his courage to try to read, and read he did. One day we were using the Folger Essential 3D Lit to explore a scene, and when his turn came to read, he chose not to pass. Previously, he had always politely declined to read aloud, and the class and I obliged. On this day, though, he did not pass. Slowly, he began to read the words. Fumbling often, he kept reading, with the encouragement and support of his peers. They helped him sound out words when he didn't know how to start. He finished reading, and the room applauded him. Martin entered center stage that day because he had developed both belief in himself and trust in his peers. He wanted to join them and believed he could do it. Shakespeare is truly for everyone, and everyone is capable of "getting it." Martin "got it," not because he read the text flawlessly and was able to analyze the motifs in an essay. He got it because he was able to understand the text through a series of activities that led to his comprehension.

Shakespeare and other excellent complex texts are so important, especially for students who have IEPs, because they deserve an enriching learning experience with real, challenging content. Giving students access to appropriate, grade-level material is essential to meeting their IEP goals, regardless of the educational setting (resource, pull-out, or inclusion). More than teaching Shakespeare, the Folger Method is also about instilling confidence in the students about the reality that they can do much of this work themselves. Even if it takes a while, even if they need a little help here and there—they can do it.

My Students and *A Midsummer Night's Dream*

Connecting the Play to Their Own Lives

In general, multiple connections to any text build interest and improve comprehension. I have found that when my students connect elements of Shakespeare's plays to their own lives, they become more engaged in what they read and build stronger bonds to the text. In my classes, through the Folger approach, we have been building a safe, trusting community all along that makes it possible to explore these big ideas in the text.

A Midsummer Night's Dream offers students any number of connections to their own lives. Here are a few, and ways in which you might use these in class:

Jealousy. Jealousy is a common and complicated emotion that moves from rage to suspicion to anger and then to fear and humiliation. *A Midsummer Night's Dream* starts with Helena's jealousy of Hermia and Lysander's love. This is followed by Titania's jealousy of Oberon's attraction/lust for Hippolyta and then Oberon's jealousy toward Titania's actions. These revolving doors of pain and jealousy rotate to different characters, just as the feeling of jealousy can be fed back and forth in any relationship.

Idea for class: Students can engage in a talk show where certain characters share their points of view and explain how they feel according to what is in the text. The main characters of the talk-show could be Titania, Oberon, and Helena, along with a host to ask questions. As a class, students will craft questions for each of the characters. Next, students will be assigned to a team in which they will work on answering each of the questions for an assigned character using information from the text. Lastly, students then participate in a talk-show format where some students elect to play the roles of the characters with the answered questions and at least one student will act as the talk-show host asking the questions. This will encourage students to use the text to answer questions, work cooperatively, and then engage in a discussion about a theme of the text.

Deceit/Trickery: Puck is the ultimate trickster of *A Midsummer Night's Dream*. As a common motif, he creates confusion through his mischievous actions. Puck also gets confused and gives the wrong potion to the wrong couples, which adds to the comedy. However, there is a fine line between the comedic trickery and the deep deceit Oberon orders Puck to do to Titania by putting the love potion in her eyes.

Idea for class: A tableau is a "living picture" in which players pose stationary a scene from a play or story. After reading the scene in which Puck puts the potion in Titania's eyes, first, students will closely read the scene and then annotate the text during a second reading. Next, in teams of 3, students will figure out what they would like their tableaux to look like and practice getting into the poses for the scene. Lastly, student teams can compete for the best tableau in the class and use evidence from the text to support that decision.

Men vs. Women: The characters in *A Midsummer Night's Dream* live in a patriarchal society when they are in Athens, but upon entering the woods they assume different roles. In a time when women were expected to be docile and obedient, several women defy their stereotypes. Titania, Hermia, and Helena pursue love instead of waiting to be chosen. The play reverses expectations only in the woods in the company of fairies, which calls into question its application in the "real world."

Idea for class: To investigate the gender roles and expectations in the play, students can track how women and men behave differently throughout the play. The purpose is to recognize that when the characters enter the woods, they are allowed to act in ways that were not reinforced by the cultural norms in Athens. Starting with a two-column chart and Act 1, scene 1, students can write on one side how the women are treated and/or what they are allowed to do and then on the other side what it says in the text. Once the characters leave the city, another chart can be made describing how the women assume more dominant roles and evidence from the text that supports that.

Focus on Key Scenes

The lessons in this book focus on key scenes and use the Folger Essentials to actively and immediately involve students. These scenes work really well with my students: The lovers plan to flee (1.1), Preparing for the play-within-a-play (1.2), Titania is given a love potion (2.1), Lovers' mistakes (3.2), Lovers unite and blessings are given (4.1), *Pyramus and Thisbe* play (5.1).

I pay attention to these important guidelines:

Prioritize depth over breadth. It is more important that students learn the skills to dig deep into a text, especially independently, than it is to read every line in the play. It may take your class of students with IEPs the same amount of time to analyze 4 key scenes as it takes your general education class to analyze 7. That's okay. Give your students the time they need to do this important work rather than rush through the text. The scripts we create and use in class are without footnotes or explanatory glosses. This allows students to decipher meaning on their own or collaboratively and removes distractions that impede their understanding.

Keep the original language. Always use Shakespeare's original language and not the modernized, made-easy versions. Do not substitute simplified language to make it easier. For one thing, it doesn't make it easier. More importantly, students with IEPs need to be given access to the original language and be able to make sense of it. And they can.

Shorten the scenes if you need to. You can cut key scenes to include just the most important information. Don't worry about cutting Shakespeare. For as long as Shakespeare's been performed, his plays have been cut by directors and editors. To guide you, ask yourself these questions: What do I want students to understand from this scene? In what part of the scene does that idea happen? Below is a cut version of 1.1 that I have used in my class. (The *Midsummer* teaching unit elsewhere in this book begins with students diving right into what's going on in this same scene.)

The cut version of *A Midsummer Night's Dream* 1.1 below is about 101 lines; the original scene is 257 lines. You can find the full text here: folger .edu/a-midsummer-nights-dream and you can download it for your own editing. Because the scene is brief, students can focus on meaning, setting, and characters on their own without getting lost. The cutting keeps the most important parts of plot and character. Using Folger Shakespeare on- line makes finding and cutting scenes easy.

ACT 1

Scene 1, edited

Enter Theseus, Hippolyta, and Philostrate, with others.

THESEUS Now, fair Hippolyta, our nuptial hour
Draws on apace.

HIPPOLYTA Four days will quickly steep themselves in night.

THESEUS Hippolyta, I wooed thee with my sword
But I will wed thee in another key,
With pomp, with triumph, and with reveling.

> *Enter Egeus and his daughter Hermia, and Lysander and Demetrius.*

THESEUS Good Egeus. What's the news with thee?

EGEUS Full of vexation come I, with complaint
Against my child, my daughter Hermia.—
Stand forth, Demetrius.—
This man hath my consent to marry her.—
Stand forth, Lysander.—
This man hath bewitched the bosom of my child.—
And interchanged love tokens with my child.
Turned her obedience (which is due to me)
To stubborn harshness.—
As she is mine, I may dispose of her,
Or to her death, according to our law.

THESEUS What say you, Hermia? Be advised, fair maid.
To you, your father should be as a god.

HERMIA So is Lysander.

THESEUS In himself he is,
But the other must be held the worthier.

HERMIA I do entreat your Grace to pardon me.
   The worst that may befall me in this case
   If I refuse to wed Demetrius.

THESEUS Either to die the death or to abjure
   Forever the society of men.
   Therefore, fair Hermia, question your desires,
   Know of your youth, examine well your blood,
   Whether (if you yield not to your father's choice)
   You can endure the livery of a nun,
   To live a barren sister all your life.

HERMIA So will I grow, so live, so die, my lord,
   My soul consents not to give sovereignty.

THESEUS Take time to pause, and by the next new moon
   Upon that day either prepare to die
   For disobedience to your father's will,
   Or else to wed Demetrius, as he would,
   Or on Diana's altar to protest
   For aye austerity and single life.

DEMETRIUS Relent, sweet Hermia, and, Lysander, yield.

LYSANDER You have her father's love, Demetrius.
   Let me have Hermia's. Do you marry him.

LYSANDER, *to Theseus*
   I am, my lord, as well derived as he,
   As well possessed. My love is more than his;
   I am beloved of beauteous Hermia.
   Why should not I then prosecute my right?

THESEUS I must confess that I have heard so much,
   But, Demetrius, come,
   I have some private schooling for you both.—
   For you, fair Hermia, look you arm yourself
   To fit your fancies to your father's will,
   To death or to a vow of single life.—
   Come, my Hippolyta.

                                 All but Hermia and Lysander exit.

LYSANDER How now, my love? Why is your cheek so pale?

HERMIA O hell, to choose love by another's eyes!

LYSANDER A good persuasion. Therefore, hear me, Hermia:

I have a widow aunt, a dowager
From Athens is her house remote seven leagues,
There, gentle Hermia, may I marry thee;
And to that place the sharp Athenian law
Cannot pursue us. If thou lovest me, then
Steal forth thy father's house tomorrow night.

HERMIA My good Lysander,
I swear to thee by Cupid's strongest bow,
Tomorrow truly will I meet with thee.

LYSANDER Keep promise, love. Look, here comes Helena.

Enter Helena.

HERMIA Godspeed, fair Helena. Whither away?

HELENA Call you me "fair"? That "fair" again unsay.
Demetrius loves your fair.
O, teach me how you look and with what art
You sway the motion of Demetrius' heart!

HERMIA I frown upon him, yet he loves me still.

HELENA O, that your frowns would teach my smiles such
skill!

HERMIA I give him curses, yet he gives me love.

HELENA O, that my prayers could such affection move!

HERMIA Take comfort: he no more shall see my face.
Lysander and myself will fly this place.
And in the wood where
There my Lysander and myself shall meet
And good luck grant thee thy Demetrius.—
Keep word, Lysander. We must starve our sight
From lovers' food till morrow deep midnight.

LYSANDER I will, my Hermia.   *Hermia exits.*
Helena, adieu.
As you on him, Demetrius dote on you!   *Lysander exits.*

HELENA How happy some o'er other some can be!
Love looks not with the eyes but with the mind;
And therefore is winged Cupid painted blind.
Nor hath Love's mind of any judgment taste.
Wings, and no eyes, figure unheedy haste.

And therefore is Love said to be a child
Because in choice he is so oft beguiled.
I will go tell him of fair Hermia's flight.
Then to the wood will he tomorrow night
Pursue her. And, for this intelligence
If I have thanks, it is a dear expense.
But herein mean I to enrich my pain,
To have his sight thither and back again.

She exits.

Annotate the Text

When I say "annotate," I mean making any notes about what is happening in the text; this practice helps students remember what is happening. Some may call this "marking the text." It's all the same. Encourage students to take notes directly on the text during discussions because it leads them to analysis. **Make it purposeful.** Ensure that each time students annotate, they relate the underlined parts of the text to what is happening in the discussion. The annotations can be used for writing assignments.

Show them what an annotated scene or speech looks like and how it's useful. Model for students by annotating and thinking aloud with them. You can do this by using the tech in your classroom or by distributing copies of your own annotations. The example below is a student's annotation of Act 1, Scene 2.

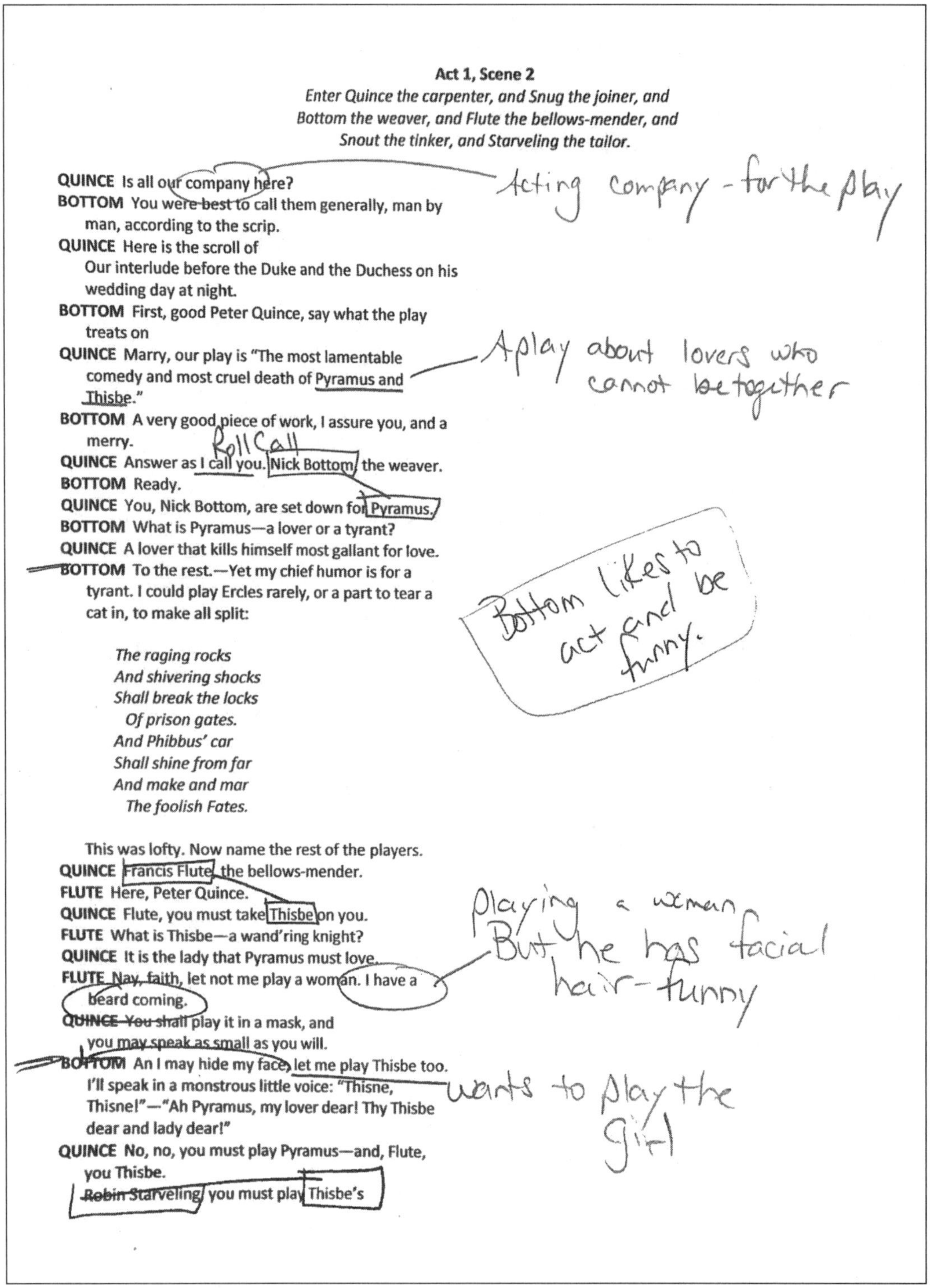

Act 1, Scene 2

Enter Quince the carpenter, and Snug the joiner, and
Bottom the weaver, and Flute the bellows-mender, and
Snout the tinker, and Starveling the tailor.

QUINCE Is all our company here?

BOTTOM You were best to call them generally, man by
man, according to the scrip.

QUINCE Here is the scroll of
Our interlude before the Duke and the Duchess on his
wedding day at night.

BOTTOM First, good Peter Quince, say what the play
treats on

QUINCE Marry, our play is "The most lamentable
comedy and most cruel death of Pyramus and
Thisbe."

BOTTOM A very good piece of work, I assure you, and a
merry.

QUINCE Answer as I call you. Nick Bottom, the weaver.

BOTTOM Ready.

QUINCE You, Nick Bottom, are set down for Pyramus.

BOTTOM What is Pyramus—a lover or a tyrant?

QUINCE A lover that kills himself most gallant for love.

BOTTOM To the rest.—Yet my chief humor is for a
tyrant. I could play Ercles rarely, or a part to tear a
cat in, to make all split:

> The raging rocks
> And shivering shocks
> Shall break the locks
>   Of prison gates.
> And Phibbus' car
> Shall shine from far
> And make and mar
>   The foolish Fates.

This was lofty. Now name the rest of the players.

QUINCE Francis Flute, the bellows-mender.

FLUTE Here, Peter Quince.

QUINCE Flute, you must take Thisbe on you.

FLUTE What is Thisbe—a wand'ring knight?

QUINCE It is the lady that Pyramus must love.

FLUTE Nay, faith, let not me play a woman. I have a
beard coming.

QUINCE You shall play it in a mask, and
you may speak as small as you will.

BOTTOM An I may hide my face, let me play Thisbe too.
I'll speak in a monstrous little voice: "Thisne,
Thisne!"—"Ah Pyramus, my lover dear! Thy Thisbe
dear and lady dear!"

QUINCE No, no, you must play Pyramus—and, Flute,
you Thisbe.

Robin Starveling, you must play Thisbe's

[Handwritten annotations:]
Acting company - for the play
A play about lovers who cannot be together
Roll Call
Bottom likes to act and be funny.
Playing a woman But he has facial hair - funny
wants to play the girl

mother.—Tom Snout the tinker.
You, Pyramus' father.—Myself, Thisbe's
father.—Snug the joiner, you the lion's part.—

SNUG Have you the lion's part written,
Give it me, for I am slow of study. ——— Not Smart

QUINCE it is nothing but roaring.

BOTTOM Let me play the lion too. I will roar that
I will make the Duke say "Let him roar again. Let
him roar again!"

QUINCE An you should do it too terribly, you would
fright the Duchess and the ladies that they would
shriek, and that were enough to hang us all.
You can play no part but Pyramus.

BOTTOM Well, I will undertake it. What beard were I
best to play it in? your straw-color
beard, your orange-tawny beard, your purple-in-grain
beard, or your French-crown-color beard,
your perfit yellow.

QUINCE masters, here are your parts, *giving out the parts,* and I am
to entreat you, request you, and desire you to con
them by tomorrow night and meet me in the palace
wood, a mile without the town, by moonlight. There
will we rehearse,

BOTTOM We will meet, and there we may rehearse
most obscenely and courageously.

QUINCE At the Duke's Oak we meet.

will practice the next night to surprise everyone.

They exit.

Spread the Shakespeare love

You and your students are on a Shakespeare journey together. As with everything you teach, the energy you give is the energy you get back. The more you LOVE teaching Shakespeare, the more your students will love it too. Keep in mind that it may take time, so fake it until you make it. When I started using the Folger Method, my students thought I was way too excited about Shakespeare. Over time, the energy is contagious, and now they are just as excited to learn as I am to teach. Shakespeare has always been my favorite unit because it demonstrates that powerful literature belongs to them, and my students look forward to it because it is fun. From calling each other "greasy onion-eyed nut-hook" and "rank rump-fed giglet" to fake swordplay and adding "thee" and "thou" to those words, I can see through their actions that they have fallen for Shakespeare as well.

Starting this journey with your students isn't always easy, but it is worth it. You are expecting more from them and teaching them more. Believe they can do the work and they will start to believe in themselves. Forgive yourself if a day does not work out. We are all works in progress, and it may take some tweaking to find out what extra things your students may need. Teaching Shakespeare or any other complex text using the Folger Method may be an adjustment to the way you teach now, so the more you do it, the better you will get at it. Students will become the drivers of the classroom, so get yourself ready for the show.

So, to my students who pop in to ask, "Hey Ms. DiGenno, you still doing that Shakespeare thing?" "Yes, I am, and so are you," I always say back as they rush out of the class again. Usually their last word: "Cool!"

Paired Texts: *A Midsummer Night's Dream* Off the Pedestal and in Conversation with Other Voices

Donna Denizé

Something wildly important happens when we teach two very different works or authors together—like *Macbeth* and writings of Frederick Douglass; *Hamlet* and something by Claudia Rankine; *Othello* and the poetry of George Moses Horton, or *The Taming of the Shrew* and the poems of Audre Lorde.

Paired texts are two texts that you and your students dive into at the same time. Both texts have equal weight; each is strong and can stand fully on its own. You can pair whole works or segments of works, selected narratives, scenes, or stanzas. But there is no "primary" and "secondary" or "supplemental" hierarchy—ever. Two voices, two points of view, two writing styles, two characters . . . and each will illuminate the other.

It's important to note here, since we are in the world of Shakespeare, that a Shakespeare play and an adaptation of a Shakespeare play or plot are *not* paired texts. That's a primary text and most often some kind of supplemental one. Together, they don't have the power or the payoff of a set of paired texts.

Why pair texts? Because, taken together, they illuminate each other in powerful and surprising ways. Looking closely at paired works gives kids a sense of the sweep of literature and allows them to consider together two authors who wrote in vastly different times, places, cultures, genders, races, religions—you name it. These juxtapositions allow them to notice that in many cases, writers have been asking the same big questions for some time: about human identity—how we define ourselves through culture, our moral choices, or how we navigate power or powerlessness, and more. In other instances, they are on very different wavelengths and . . . what might be the reasons for that?

I developed my love for paired texts in my thirty-eight years teaching in a variety of secondary school settings—public, private, urban, and rural—and in serving a term on the advisory board for all vocational schools in the state of Virginia. I currently teach at St. Albans School for Boys in Washington, DC, where I chair the English department. I love working with paired texts because two strong texts working together produce something marvelous in class: they create a space for meaningful conversations that come from students' experiences and questions, and this creates not just good analysis but empathy. Since students today must navigate an incredibly complex global society, they can only benefit by considering a sweep of literature that helps them deepen their empathy for others.

I've found that the more specific or particular the pairing, the better, since this inspires students' creativity and establishes new ways of thinking about both texts. It also strengthens students' analytical skills and increases their capacity for understanding complexity—qualities that are essential for navigating current human challenges and the promise of an ever-evolving world—and the worlds students inhabit.

The following section is designed in two parts: the first to give you an example and a fuller sense of how paired texts work, and the second to specifically recommend two text pairs that in my experience have worked very well with *A Midsummer Night's Dream*.

Part One: An Example of a Pair of Texts and How They Have Worked in Class

1. Pairing **Macbeth's "If it were done" soliloquy** (1.7.1–28, Macbeth weighs plans to murder King Duncan) with the passage from **Frederick Douglass's *Narrative of the Life of Frederick Douglass: An American Slave*** in which Douglass sits on a hillside watching freely moving ships while his movement is confined by slavery and its laws and customs.

Macbeth 1.7.1–28	*Narrative of the Life of Frederick Douglass*
MACBETH If it were done when 'tis done, then 'twere well It were done quickly. If th' assassination Could trammel up the consequence and catch With his surcease success, that but this blow Might be the be-all and the end-all here, But here, upon this bank and shoal of time, We'd jump the life to come. But in these cases We still have judgment here, that we but teach Bloody instructions, which, being taught, return To plague th' inventor. This even-handed justice Commends th' ingredience of our poisoned chalice To our own lips. He's here in double trust: First, as I am his kinsman and his subject, Strong both against the deed; then, as his host, Who should against his murderer shut the door, Not bear the knife myself. Besides, this Duncan Hath borne his faculties so meek, hath been So clear in his great office, that his virtues Will plead like angels, trumpet-tongued, against The deep damnation of his taking-off;	Our house stood within a few rods of the Chesapeake Bay, whose broad bosom was ever white with sails from every quarter of the habitable globe. Those beautiful vessels, robed in purest white, so delightful to the eye of freemen, were to me so many shrouded ghosts, to terrify and torment me with thoughts of my wretched condition. I have often, in the deep stillness of a summer's Sabbath, stood all alone upon the lofty banks of that noble bay, and traced, with saddened heart and tearful eye, the countless number of sails moving off to the mighty ocean. The sight of these always affected me powerfully. My thoughts would compel utterance; and there, with no audience but the Almighty, I would pour out my soul's complaint, in my rude way, with an apostrophe to the moving multitude of ships:— "You are loosed from your moorings, and are free; I am fast in my chains, and am a slave! You move merrily before the gentle gale, and I sadly before the bloody whip! You are freedom's swift-winged angels, that fly round the world; I am

And pity, like a naked newborn babe
Striding the blast, or heaven's cherubin horsed
Upon the sightless couriers of the air,
Shall blow the horrid deed in every eye,
That tears shall drown the wind. I have no spur
To prick the sides of my intent, but only
Vaulting ambition, which o'erleaps itself
And falls on th' other—

confined in bands of iron! O that I were free! O, that I were on one of your gallant decks, and under your protecting wing! Alas! betwixt me and you, the turbid waters roll. Go on, go on. O that I could also go! Could I but swim! If I could fly! O, why was I born a man, of whom to make a brute. The glad ship is gone; she hides in the dim distance. I am left in the hottest hell of unending slavery. O God, save me! God, deliver me! Let me be free! Is there any God? Why am I a slave? I will run away. I will not stand it. Get caught, or get clear, I'll try it. I had as well die with ague as the fever. I have only one life to lose. I had as well be killed running as die standing. Only think of it; one hundred miles straight north, and I am free! Try it? Yes! God helping me, I will. It cannot be that I shall live and die a slave. I will take to the water. This very bay shall yet bear me into freedom. The steamboats steered in a north-east course from North Point. I will do the same; and when I get to the head of the bay, I will turn my canoe adrift, and walk straight through Delaware into Pennsylvania. When I get there, I shall not be required to have a pass; I can travel without being disturbed. Let but the first opportunity offer, and, come what will, I am off. Meanwhile, I will try to bear up under the yoke. I am not the only slave in the world. Why should I fret? I can bear as much as any of them. Besides, I am but a boy, and all boys are bound to some one. It may be that my misery in slavery will only increase my happiness when I get free. There is a better day coming."

Thus I used to think, and thus I used to speak to myself; goaded almost to madness at one moment, and at the next reconciling myself to my wretched lot.

In class, we started with a definition of *ambition*. Kids looked it up in various dictionaries. They came up with definitions like these:

- an earnest desire for some type of achievement or distinction, as power, honor, fame, or wealth, and the willingness to strive for its attainment

- the object, state, or result desired or sought after

- to seek after earnestly

- aspire to

I asked a few simple questions to start them off:

1. What is the ambition of each man? What is it driving him toward? What is he seeking?

2. What are they both wrestling against and with—morally and socially?

3. What solutions, if any, does each one reach?

A discussion developed that connected the word *ambition* with some of the other topics that they found in both texts: isolation; self-perception; moral dilemmas; questions about freedom and justice. My students came up with valuable comparisons and contrasts that I list here in no particular order:

- Both are wrestling in the mind, the imagination alive, the struggle with consequences, moral right and wrong.

- In *Macbeth,* the moral wrong is in the individual; in the Douglass text, the moral wrong is in the larger society.

- Both bring isolation, pain, and suffering. Macbeth's isolation leads to his destruction; Douglass's isolation leads him to being an orator and a major voice in the cause for the abolition of slavery.

- Macbeth's ambition has a negative outcome, while Douglass's has a positive outcome.

- Both search for justice—Macbeth to avoid it and Douglass to have justice manifest.

- Macbeth has social and political power, while Douglass—a slave—is marginalized, without social and political power.

- Both are seeking freedom. Macbeth imagines freedom from consequences. Douglass imagines the consequences of freedom.

These two texts—Shakespeare's *Macbeth* and Frederick Douglass's *Narrative of the Life of Frederick Douglass: An American Slave*—are separated by time, space, culture, and geopolitics, and yet my students made wonderful connections between both texts, identifying isolation, self-perception, and moral dilemmas. They also asked big questions about freedom and justice, the function of human imagination, and ambition.

Part Two: Two *A Midsummer Night's Dream* Text Pairs

1. Pairing **Bottom's dream** (4.1.210–229; awakened from the spell of Puck's magic potion, Bottom believes that the brief time he shared in love with Titania was only a dream) with **Eamon Grennan's poem "Look Out"** (Nature's freshness and beauty reveals love as light, and like lovers waking from a dream, the speaker realizes that love is the only reality). Eamon Grennan is an Irish poet; this poem was published in 2008.

A Midsummer Night's Dream, 4.1.210–229 by William Shakespeare	*"Look Out"* by Eamon Grennan
BOTTOM, *waking up* When my cue comes, call me, and I will answer. My next is "Most fair Pyramus." Hey-ho! Peter Quince! Flute the bellows-mender! Snout the tinker! Starveling! God's my life! Stolen hence and left me asleep! I have had a most rare vision. I have had a dream past the wit of man to say what dream it was. Man is but an ass if he go about to expound this dream. Methought I was—there is no man can tell what. Methought I was and methought I had—but man is but a patched fool if he will offer to say what methought I had. The eye of man hath not heard, the ear of man hath not seen, man's hand is not able to taste, his tongue to conceive, nor his heart to report what my dream was. I will get Peter Quince to write a ballad of this dream. It shall be called "Bottom's Dream" because it hath no bottom; and I will sing it in the latter end of a play, before the Duke. Peradventure, to make it the more gracious, I shall sing it at her death.	This morning it's our bare, moist, muscular masters, the trees, that have to stand in shadowy majesty for something. No stopping the colour-stuff in pussy willows, or what happens to any stem this weather reddens, thickens, fills with only its own happening. The needle pumping nothing through your tongue but pristine numbness has you walking around mid-day, sun blazing, dumb as a fish being filleted for tomorrow's dinner—not sole on the bone but some slow simmered thing that leaches all its life-juices out and sets them one against the other, to teach you again how in the end good ends depend on death to begin with. Turning the other cheek is not the answer: didn't the shadow of the turkey vulture—itself a black shadow stapled to the blank blue sky-face—only yesterday cross the path you were tracing, and didn't your blood skitter for an instant, sensing its thwart and pitiless intention? But could words like *relish*, *savour*, or *abide* strike a right note to end on? Now clouds are brazen radiance, are scarcely matter—only thick light, white brilliance against blue. Later they'll grow a heart-fraught leaden grey, day dimming—though a still fierce gleam to the west makes one small nimbus melting in the blue, transfiguring birches and leftover snow to this deep, meditative rose. Another time it's a word like *roofbeam* brings you out of emptiness: you picture the nestle of it, light smearing its grain, the long silence before sleep, your father finding a fresh unclouded residence in the offing—a sort of guardian, different but reliable. Then sleep makes a clean sweep of things, the ceiling of your head a crown of stars, their names unknown, a realm away from impermanence—though that's your main address now, the word *home* cropping up only here and there. Because—as the maker of mists remarked that first morning—*Love is not consolation, it is light.*

We read these in class, using many of the Folger Essentials that you have explored elsewhere in this book.

To begin discussion, I asked my students to list some of the qualities of dreams, and they came up with these:

- They are not logical, they are irrational, and so anything can happen.

- We can do extraordinary things in our dreams (i.e., one can fly or have superpowers).

- Dreams are uncontrollable, and time is different (not bound by chronological time).

- They seem very real sometimes, and it's difficult to tell what was dream and what was waking reality, so they are connected in some way.

- Maybe they revive our energy, mind, and imagination.

- Maybe they can show our deepest fears and desires.

Then, I ask them for initial separate observations—of any kind—about each text so we can get them out there.

Next, I ask them a few questions:

- Looking at this list, which of these seem to apply to Bottom when he "wakes"?

- Once awakened from his "dream" of love, how are Bottom's senses confused—his eyes, ears, and taste? And how has love affected Bottom's imagination, or his willingness to work with others?

- In the poem "Look Out," where do we find mention of human senses—seeing, tasting, and hearing?

- Looking at the opening stanzas of this poem, how have the speaker's senses been changed in the morning after waking from sleep?

- In the poem's final stanza, how is love like a dream?

The lively conversation that followed led them to these topics:

- In both works, the world looks different after sleep, and the previous cares or day's realities can be swept away, making room for new possibilities—in the imagination.

- In both works, love is transforming and brings new understandings.

- Bottom's "dream" of love improved his relationships with others and his own identity more clearly: Bottom is much more open to others' suggestions, and he no longer wants to play every part.

- In Grennan's poem, sleep reawakened the senses and the imagination to the reality of love.

Diving into these two texts separately and then as a pair offered students the chance to see each of them, the pair, and themselves more deeply. Based on what they found in the texts, my students ended up in a lively discussion about both the power of love to transform our perceptions and ourselves, and the connections between dreams and waking reality.

2. Pairing **Helena's speech** (1.1.238–257; Helena loves Demetrius and is upset that he loves her friend Hermia) with **Mona Van Duyn's poem "Letter From a Father"** (an adult daughter's love brings her aging, despondent parents back to life through a gift). For this pairing, students read and discussed each text separately, and then looked at them together as a pair. Mona Van Duyn was an American poet who was US poet laureate in 1992. This poem was published in 1982.

A Midsummer Night's Dream, 1.1.238–257

HELENA
Things base and vile, holding no quantity,
Love can transpose to form and dignity.
Love looks not with the eyes but with the mind;
And therefore is winged Cupid painted blind.
Nor hath Love's mind of any judgment taste.
Wings, and no eyes, figure unheedy haste.
And therefore is Love said to be a child
Because in choice he is so oft beguiled.
As waggish boys in game themselves forswear,
So the boy Love is perjured everywhere.
For, ere Demetrius looked on Hermia's eyne,
He hailed down oaths that he was only mine;
And when this hail some heat from Hermia felt,
So he dissolved, and show'rs of oaths did melt.
I will go tell him of fair Hermia's flight.
Then to the wood will he tomorrow night
Pursue her. And, for this intelligence
If I have thanks, it is a dear expense.
But herein mean I to enrich my pain,
To have his sight thither and back again.

Again, I began by asking students for a definition of *love*, and a few of their definitions were as follows:

- A strong attraction for someone

- Uncontrollable joy

- Feeling like you can't live without seeing that person

The definitions led to a discussion about the difference between infatuation and true love, and the difference between sympathy (to feel sorry for) and empathy (to feel with). Eventually, students settled on this definition for *love*:

- Strong feelings of empathy (to feel with) for someone or something

Next, they described how love behaves, or rather what its distinguishing qualities are, and here were a few of their responses:

- Love is patient; enduring, and it doesn't abandon a person when troubles occur.

- Love is an action, not just words.

- Love is not hasty; that is, it takes its time, so it's a process.

- Love is kind, generous, not jealous, and it doesn't value superficial things/qualities (looks, social class).

All of this was a lively conversation . . .

Then I asked the class a few questions:

- How does Helena describe love? And please list 3 or 4 qualities in her speech.

- Helena focuses on several shortcomings of Hermia. What are these?

- Is Helena's definition of love an accurate one?

- What are the shortcomings or confusions about love that appear in Helena's speech?

What followed was another lively discussion about how the word *love* is defined and how "love" behaves in present-day life.

Then we moved on to "Letters from a Father" by Mona Van Duyn.

"Letters from a Father"
by Mona Van Duyn

I

Ulcerated tooth keeps me awake, there is
such pain, would have to go to the hospital to have
it pulled or would bleed to death from the blood thinners,
but can't leave Mother, she falls and forgets her salve
and her tranquilizers, her ankles swell so and her bowels
are so bad, she almost had a stoppage and sometimes
what she passes is green as grass. There are big holes
in my thigh where my leg brace buckles the size of dimes.
My head pounds from the high pressure. It is awful
not to be able to get out, and I fell in the bathroom
and the girl could hardly get me up at all.
Sure thought my back was broken, it will be next time.
Prostate is bad and heart has given out,
feel bloated after supper. Have made my peace
because am just plain done for and have no doubt
that the Lord will come any day with my release.
You say you enjoy your feeder, I don't see why
you want to spend good money on grain for birds
and you say you have a hundred sparrows, I'd buy
poison and get rid of their diseases and turds.

II

We enjoyed your visit, it was nice of you to bring
the feeder but a terrible waste of your money
for that big bag of feed since we won't be living
more than a few weeks long. We can see
them good from where we sit, big ones and little ones
but you know when I farmed I used to like to hunt
and we had many a good meal from pigeons
and quail and pheasant but these birds won't
be good for nothing and are dirty to have so near
the house. Mother likes the redbirds though.
My bad knee is so sore and I can't hardly hear
and Mother says she is hoarse from yelling but I know
it's too late for a hearing aid. I belch up all the time
and have a sour mouth and of course with my heart
it's no use to go to a doctor. Mother is the same.
Has a scab she thinks is going to turn to a wart.

III

The birds are eating and fighting, Ha! Ha! All shapes
and colors and sizes coming out of our woods
but we don't know what they are. Your Mother hopes
you can send us a kind of book that tells about birds.
There is one the folks called snowbirds, they eat on the ground,
we had the girl sprinkle extra there, but say,
they eat something awful. I sent the girl to town
to buy some more feed, she had to go anyway.

IV

Almost called you on the telephone
but it costs so much to call thought better write.
Say, the funniest thing is happening, one
day we had so many birds and they fight
and get excited at their feed you know
and it's really something to watch and two or three
flew right at us and crashed into our window
and bang, poor little things knocked themselves silly.
They come to after while on the ground and flew away.
And they been doing that. We felt awful
and didn't know what to do but the other day
a lady from our Church drove out to call
and a little bird knocked itself out while she sat

and she bought it in her hands right into the house,
it looked like dead. It had a kind of hat
of feathers sticking up on its head, kind of rose
or pinky color, don't know what it was,
and I petted it and it come to life right there
in her hands and she took it out and it flew. She says
they think the window is the sky on a fair
day, she feeds birds too but hasn't got
so many. She says to hang strips of aluminum foil
in the window so we'll do that. She raved about
our birds. P.S. The book just come in the mail.

V

Say, that book is sure good, I study
in it every day and enjoy our birds.
Some of them I can't identify
for sure, I guess they're females, the Latin words
I just skip over. Bet you'd never guess
the sparrow I've got here, House Sparrow you wrote,
but I have Fox Sparrows, Song Sparrows, Vesper Sparrows,
Pine Woods and Tree and Chipping and White Throat
and White Crowned Sparrows. I have six Cardinals,
three pairs, they come at early morning and night,
the males at the feeder and on the ground the females.
Juncos, maybe 25, they fight
for the ground, that's what they used to call snowbirds. I miss
the Bluebirds since the weather warmed. Their breast
is the color of a good ripe muskmelon. Tufted Titmouse
is sort of blue with a little tiny crest.
And I have Flicker and Red-Bellied and Red-
Headed Woodpeckers, you would die laughing
to see Red-Bellied, he hangs on with his head
flat on the board, his tail braced up under,
wing out. And Dickcissel and Ruby Crowned Kinglet
and Nuthatch stands on his head and Veery on top
the color of a bird dog and Hermit Thrush with spot
on breast, Blue Jay so funny, he will hop
right on the backs of the other birds to get the grain.
We bought some sunflower seeds just for him.
And Purple Finch I bet you never seen,
color of a watermelon, sits on the rim
of the feeder with his streaky wife, and the squirrels,
you know, they are cute too, they sit tall

and eat with their little hands, they eat bucketfuls.
I pulled my own tooth, it didn't bleed at all.

VI

It's sure a surprise how well Mother is doing,
she forgets her laxative but bowels move fine.
Now that windows are open she says our birds sing
all day. The girl took a Book of Knowledge on loan
from the library and I am reading up
on the habits of birds, did you know some males have three
wives, some migrate some don't. I am going to keep
feeding all spring, maybe summer, you can see
they expect it. Will need thistle seed for Goldfinch and Pine
Siskin next winter. Some folks are going to come see us
from Church, some bird watchers, pretty soon.
They have birds in town but nothing to equal this.
So the world woos its children back for an evening kiss.

My students shared wonderful observations comparing and contrasting the two pieces. There were only a few comparisons:

- In both works, true love is blind, and it sees with the heart and mind.

- In both works, love elevates, sees beauty in something unattractive at first and gives dignity to something that seems low (i.e., at first the parents are overwhelmed by all their physical ailments and feel like giving in to feelings of hopelessness, and Helena feels defeated by Hermia's looks). In both cases, feelings of lowliness are overcome by loving actions.

The contrasts, however, were more striking to students:

- In "Letters from a Father," the daughter's love is patient, generous, and kind toward all—people and animals; Demetrius is not patient, generous, or kind to Helena, and most importantly, his love is not enduring.

- In "Letters," the speaker's familial love for her parents is enduring and long lasting.

- Love even transforms the speaker's parents' attitude of despair into spiritual joy, a renewed reverence for life, their own and others; they have a renewed desire to rejoin community.

- Demetrius's love for Helena is hasty and short-lived.

Students made subtle connections between both texts, defining true love and then distinguishing it from infatuation. Perhaps their most surprising connection—to me and to themselves—was literature as the catalyst for their exploration of the nature of love: a fuller exploration and how it behaves in any context—both romantic and familial.

I find that offering my students a chance to dive into two very different texts and explore the connections or lack of connections between them expands both their skills and perceptions—and mine too!

Sources

Douglass, Frederick. *Narrative of the Life of Frederick Douglass: An American Slave.* New York: Penguin Books, 1968. Print. https://docsouth.unc.edu/neh/douglass/douglass.html.

Grennan, Eamon. "Look Out," from *Out of Sight: New and Selected Poems.* Copyright © 2008 by Eamon Grennan. Reprinted with the permission of The Permissions Company, LLC on behalf of Graywolf Press, graywolfpress.org.

Van Duyn, Mona. "Letters from a Father," from *Selected Poems by Mona Van Duyn*, copyright © 2002 by Mona Van Duyn. Used by permission of Alfred A. Knopf, an imprint of the Knopf Doubleday Publishing Group, a division of Penguin Random House LLC. All rights reserved.

PART FOUR

Five More Resources for You

- *Folger Teaching*—folger.edu/teach—The Folger's online universe for teachers! Search lesson plans, podcasts, videos, and other classroom resources. Connect with like-minded colleagues and experts. Access on-demand teacher workshops and participate in a range of live professional development opportunities from hour-long sessions to longer courses, all offering CEU credit. Complete access to *Folger Teaching* is one of many benefits of joining the Folger as a Teacher Member.

- *Folger Shakespeare* online—folger.edu/shakespeares-works—Shakespeare's complete works free and online, and all downloadable in various formats that are particularly useful for teachers and students. The Folger texts are the most up-to-date available online; behind the scenes, they have been encoded to make the plays easy to read, search, and index. Also available here are audio clips of selected lines performed.

- *Folger Shakespeare* in print—Shakespeare's plays and sonnets in single-volume paperbacks and ebooks. The texts are identical to those of *Folger Shakespeare* online; the books, however, are all in the format featuring the text on the right-hand page with glosses and definitions on the left. Used in many, many classrooms, the *Folger Shakespeare* in print is published by Simon & Schuster and available from booksellers everywhere.

- *The Folger Shakespeare Library*—folger.edu—The online home of the wide world of the Folger Shakespeare Library, offering all kinds of experiences and resources from the world's largest Shakespeare collection. Become a Folger researcher, join scholarly seminars, explore the Folger collection, enjoy the magic of theater, music, and poetry, and prepare for a visit to the Folger. We're waiting for you, your class, and your family! An opportunity for deep, lively, and satisfying engagement with the humanities.

- *Shakespeare Documented*—shakespearedocumented.folger.edu—A singular site that brings together digitized versions of hundreds of the known primary source documents pertaining to Shakespeare—the playwright, actor, and stakeholder; the poet; and the man engaged in family and legal matters. A destination for curious students! Convened by the Folger, this collection is a collaboration among the Folger and Shakespeare Birthplace Trust, the National Archives of Great Britain, the Bodleian Library at Oxford, and the British Library.

ACKNOWLEDGMENTS

Seven or eight years ago, Mark Miazga, an exceptional high school teacher from Baltimore—and a Folger teacher—said, "We should make a series of books where we lay out for teachers key specifics about the play, and then how to teach the whole play using the Folger Method."

Ignition.

An important idea with a huge scope: five books, each focused on a single play—*Hamlet*, *Macbeth*, *Romeo and Juliet*, *Othello*, and *A Midsummer Night's Dream.* Each one a pretty revolutionary dive into basic info, scholarship, and the how of teaching each of the plays to *all* students. *Every* student. This demanded assembling an extraordinarily strong array of knowledge, expertise, and experience and moving it into action.

It is finally time to name and celebrate this crowd of people who, with generosity of all kinds, had a hand in creating the book that you are reading right now:

Folger director Michael Witmore, a deep believer in the importance of learning, teaching, and the power of the Folger to support both for all and at all levels, has been a fan and a wise advisor from the start.

The generosity of the Carol and Gene Ludwig Family Foundation—and in particular our fairy godmother, Carol Ludwig—has fueled every part of the creation of this series, including making certain that every English teacher in Washington, DC, has their own set of books *gratis*. I express the gratitude of the Folger as well as that of teachers in DC and beyond.

None of these volumes would exist without Folger Education's extraordinary Katie Dvorak, who, from the first minute to the last, herded not cats but our many authors, contracts, editorial conferences, publisher meetings, the general editor, and a series of deadlines that *never ever* stopped changing. Much of this was accomplished as Covid covered all lives, work, families, everything. Katie's persistence, along with her grace, humor, empathy, and patience kept us moving and was the glue we never did not need.

We appreciate the support and guidance of our team at Simon & Schuster: Irene Kheradi, Johanna Li, and Amanda Mulholland.

All along, the overall project benefited from the wisdom and support of these key players: Skip Nicholson, Heather Lester, Michael LoMonico, Corinne Viglietta, Maryam Trowell, Shanta Bryant, Missy Springsteen-Haupt, and Jessica Frazier . . . and from the creative genius of Mya Gosling.

Major gratitude to colleagues across the Folger who contributed to building these books in terms of content and business support. Our thanks to Erin Blake, Caroline Duroselle-Melish, Beth Emelson, Abbey Fagan, Esther French, Eric Johnson, Adrienne

Jones, Ruth Taylor Kidd, Melanie Leung, Mimi Newcastle, Rebecca Niles, Emma Poltrack, Sara Schliep, Emily Wall, and Heather Wolfe.

We are in debt to the schoolteachers and scholars who generously shared their time and wisdom as we got started, helping us to map our path and put it in motion—all along the intersections where scholarship and teaching practice inform each other. Massive gratitude to Patricia Akhimie, Bernadette Andreas, Ashley Bessicks, David Sterling Brown, Patricia Cahill, Jocelyn Chadwick, Ambereen Dadabhoy, Eric DeBarros, Donna Denizé, Ruben Espinosa, Kyle Grady, Kim Hall, Caleen Sinnette Jennings, Stefanie Jochman, Heather Lester, Catherine Loomis, Ellen McKay, Mark Miazga, Noémie Ndiaye, Gail Kern Paster, Amber Phelps, Katie Santos, Ian Smith, Christina Torres, and Jessica Cakrasenjaya Zeiss.

It's impossible to express our thanks here without a special shout-out to Ayanna Thompson, the scholarly powerhouse who has been nudging Folger Education for the last decade. Know that nudges from Ayanna are more like rockets . . . always carrying love and a challenge. We could not be more grateful for them, or for her.

With endless admiration, I give the close-to-last words and thanks to the working schoolteachers who authored major portions of these books. First here, I honor our colleague Donnaye Moore, teacher at Brookwood High School in Snellville, Georgia, who started on this project teaching and writing about *Othello* but succumbed to cancer far too soon. None of us have stopped missing her or trying to emulate her brilliant practicality.

I asked working teachers to take on this challenge because I know that no one knows the "how" of teaching better than those who do it in classrooms every day. The marvels I am about to name were teaching and living through all the challenges that Covid presented in their own lives *and* thinking about your students too, putting together (and testing and revising) these lessons for you who will use these books. Over a really loud old-fashioned PA system, I am shouting the names of Ashley Bessicks, Noelle Cammon, Donna Denizé, Roni DiGenno, Liz Dixon, David Fulco, Deborah Gascon, Stefanie Jochman, Mark Miazga, Amber Phelps, Vidula Plante, Christina Porter, and Jessica Cakrasenjaya Zeiss! You rock in every way possible. You honor the Folger—and teachers everywhere—with your wisdom, industry, and generosity.

Finally, I wrap up this project with humility, massive gratitude to all, for all, and—perhaps amazingly in the complicated days in which we are publishing—relentless HOPE. Hamza, Nailah, and Shazia O'Brien, Soraya Margaret Banta, and gazillions of children in all parts of the world deserve all we've got. Literature—in school, even!—can get us talking to, and learning from, one another in peace. Let's get busy.

—Peggy O'Brien,
General Editor

ABOUT THE AUTHORS

Catherine Loomis holds a PhD in Renaissance Literature from the University of Rochester, and an MA in Shakespeare and Performance from the Shakespeare Institute. She is the author of *William Shakespeare: A Documentary Volume* (Gale, 2002) and *The Death of Elizabeth I: Remembering and Reconstructing the Virgin Queen* (Palgrave, 2010) and, with Sid Ray, the editor of *Shaping Shakespeare for Performance: The Bear Stage* (Fairleigh Dickinson, 2016). She has taught at the University of New Orleans, the University of North Carolina at Greensboro, and the Rochester Institute of Technology.

Christina Porter is a 2006 alumna of the Folger's Teaching Shakespeare Institute. She began her career as an English teacher and literacy coach for Revere Public Schools in Revere, Massachusetts. Currently, she is Director of Humanities for her school district. She is also a faculty at Salem State University. She resides in Salem, Massachusetts, with her two precocious daughters.

Corinne Viglietta teaches Upper School English at The Bryn Mawr School in Baltimore, Maryland. From 2014 to 2022, Corinne was Associate Director of Education at the Folger Shakespeare Library, where she had the honor of exploring the wonders of language with thousands of amazing teachers, students, and visitors. Corinne played a key role in Folger's national teaching community and school partnerships. She has led workshops on the Folger Method for numerous organizations, including the Smithsonian, National Council of Teachers of English, and American Federation of Teachers. Corinne is a lifelong Folger educator, having first discovered the power of this approach with her multilingual students in DC and France. She has degrees in English from the University of Notre Dame and the University of Maryland.

Of Haitian American descent, **Donna Denizé** holds a BA from Stonehill College and an M.A in Renaissance drama from Howard University, where she was also a student of poet Robert Hayden, while he served as Consultant to the Library of Congress. She has contributed to scholarly books and journals, and she is the author of a chapbook, *The Lover's Voice* (1997) and a book, *Broken Like Job* (2005). She currently Chairs the English Department at St. Albans School for boys, where she teaches Freshman

English; a junior/senior elective in Shakespeare, and Crossroads in American Identity, a course she designed years ago and which affords her the opportunity to do what she most enjoys—exploring not only the cultural and inter-textual crossroads of literary works but also their points of human unity.

Gail Kern Paster was Director of the Folger Shakespeare Library in Washington, DC, from 2002 until 2011. Until January 2018, she also served as editor of *Shakespeare Quarterly,* the leading scholarly journal devoted to Shakespeare. She earned a B.A., magna cum laude, at Smith College and a Ph.D. in English Renaissance Literature at Yale University. From 1974 to 2002, she was a Professor of English at George Washington University. She has won many national fellowships and awards, including fellowships from the National Endowment for the Humanities, the John Simon Guggenheim Memorial Foundation, and the Mellon Foundation. She was named to the Queen's Honours List as a Commander of the British Empire in May 2011. The author of numerous scholarly articles and three books on Shakespeare and the drama of his time, she also lectures nationally and internationally. Dr. Paster has been a trustee of the Shakespeare Association of America and served as its president in 2003. She is a member of the governing boards of the Folger and the Newberry Library in Chicago.

Jessica Cakrasenjaya Zeiss has been teaching English Language Arts in central Iowa since 2011. She received her undergraduate degree from Iowa State University and fell in love with Ames, where she is currently teaching ELA 9–12. Jess received her master's degree in Teaching English in Secondary Schools from the University of Northern Iowa, where she was introduced to the Shakespeare Folger Library. She had the opportunity to participate in the 2014 Folger Teaching Shakespeare Institute, which was a life-changing experience. Jess loves spending time with her family, cuddling up with a good book, walking her dog, laughing, and embracing all that life has to offer.

Dr. Jocelyn A. Chadwick is a lifelong English teacher and international scholar. She was a full-time professor at Harvard Graduate School of Education and now occasionally lectures and conducts seminars there. In addition to teaching and writing, Chadwick also consults and works with teachers and with elementary, middle, and high school students around the country. Chadwick has worked with PBS, BBC Radio, and NBC News Learn and is a past president of the National Council of Teachers of English. She has written many articles and books, including *The Jim Dilemma: Reading Race in Adventures of Huckleberry Finn* and *Teaching Literature in the Context of Literacy Instruction.* Chadwick is currently working on her next book, *Writing for Life: Using Literature to Teach Writing.*

Michael LoMonico has taught Shakespeare courses and workshops for teachers and students in 40 states as well as in Canada, England, and the Bahamas. He was an assistant to the editor for the curriculum section of all three volumes of the Folger's Shakespeare Set Free series. Until 2019, he was the Senior Consultant on National Education for the Folger. He is the author of *The Shakespeare Book of Lists, Shakespeare 101,* and a novel, *That Shakespeare Kid.* He was the co-founder and editor of *Shakespeare*, a magazine published by Cambridge University Press and Georgetown University.

Michael Witmore is the seventh director of the Folger Shakespeare Library, the world's largest Shakespeare collection and the ultimate resource for exploring Shakespeare and his world. He was appointed to this position in July 2011; prior to leading the Folger, he was a professor of English at the University of Wisconsin–Madison and at Carnegie Mellon University. Under his leadership and across a range of programs and policies, the Folger has begun the process of opening up to and connecting with greater and more diverse audiences nationally, internationally, and here at home in Washington, DC. He believes deeply in the importance of teachers; also under his leadership, the Library's work in service of schoolteachers continues to grow in breadth, depth, and accessibility.

Mya Lixian Gosling (she/her) is the artist and author of *Good Tickle Brain*, the world's foremost (and possibly only) stick-figure Shakespeare comic, which has been entertaining Shakespeare geeks around the world since 2013. Mya also draws *Keep Calm and Muslim On*, which she co-authors with Muslim-American friends, and *Sketchy Beta*, an autobiographical comic documenting her misadventures as an amateur rock climber. In her so-called spare time, Mya likes to read books on random Plantagenets, play the ukulele badly, and pretend to be one of those outdoorsy people who is in touch with nature but actually isn't. You can find her work at goodticklebrain.com.

Peggy O'Brien founded the Folger Shakespeare Library's Education Department in 1981. She set the Library's mission for K–12 students and teachers then and began to put it in motion; among a range of other programs, she founded and directed the Library's intensive Teaching Shakespeare Institute, was instigator and general editor of the popular *Shakespeare Set Free* series, and expanded the Library's education work across the country. In 1994, she took a short break from the Folger—20 years—but returned to further expand the education work and to engage in the Folger's transformation under the leadership of Library director Michael Witmore. She is the instigator and general editor of the *Folger Guides to Teaching Shakespeare* series.

Roni DiGenno is a special education teacher at Calvin Coolidge Senior High School in Washington, DC. She earned her BA in Literature from Stockton University in Pomona, NJ and her MA in English from Rutgers University in Camden, NJ. Her background in English and passion for special education lead her to the educational mission of the Folger Shakespeare Library, participating in the Teaching Shakespeare Institute in 2016. She currently lives in Maryland with her husband, daughter, and two dogs.

Vidula Plante is a National Board Certified Teacher with 25 years of experience teaching and learning from her middle school students. She is proud to be a Teacher Fellow for Folger Shakespeare Education since 2016. A Shakespeare lover since she was in eighth grade, and a strong believer in student-centered learning, Vidula taught several Shakespeare plays to her middle school ELA students. For the past six years, she has brought the Folger Method and Shakespeare to sixth-grade students in her project-based learning class. Vidula has an M.A. in English from Jadavpur University and an M.Ed. in Curriculum and Instruction from Lesley University. She received the Veterans of Foreign Wars Massachusetts Teacher of the Year award in 2015, the Sontag Prize in Education in 2020, and the American Legion's John Mulkern Massachusetts Educator of the Year award in 2022. When she's not teaching, Vidula enjoys travel, books, and theater.